FALLING SKIES

Television series created by
ROBERT RODAT

Mike Richardson President and Publisher • Neil Hankerson Executive Vice President • Tom Weddle
Chief Financial Officer • Randy Stradley Vice President of Publishing • Michael Martens Vice President
of Book Trade Sales • Anita Nelson Vice President of Business Affairs • David Scroggy Vice President
of Product Development • Dale LaFountain Vice President of Information Technology • Darlene Vogel
Senior Director of Print, Design, and Production • Ken Lizzi General Counsel • Matt Parkinson Senior
Director of Marketing • Davey Estrada Editorial Director • Scott Allie Senior Managing Editor • Chris
Warner Senior Books Editor • Diana Schutz Executive Editor • Cary Grazzini Director of Print and
Development • Lia Ribacchi Art Director • Cara Niece Director of Scheduling

Special thanks to Whitney Melancon and Jennifer Giddens

This volume collects the webcomic *Falling Skies: The Battle of Fitchburg*; "Falling Skies: The Fall"; "A
Boy without Toys"; and "Falling Skies: Luck," originally published in *Dark Horse Presents* #14 in 2012.

Published by Dark Horse Books
A division of Dark Horse Comics, Inc.
10956 SE Main Street
Milwaukie, OR 97222

DarkHorse.com   FallingSkies.com

To find a comics shop in your area, call the Comic Shop Locator Service toll-free at (888) 266-4226.

First edition: October 2012
ISBN 978-1-61655-014-1

10 9 8 7 6 5 4 3 2 1
Printed by Midas Printing International, Ltd., Huizhou, China.

THE BATTLE OF FITCHBURG

PAUL TOBIN JUAN FERREYRA

PATRIC REYNOLDS DANILO BEYRUTH MARK NELSON

MARK VERHEIDEN REMI AUBUCHON KATIE ALTMAN BRYAN OH

Cover **STEVE MORRIS**

Editors **SCOTT ALLIE** and **DANIEL CHABON**   Assistant Editor **SHANTEL LAROCQUE**

Designer **DAVID NESTELLE**   Publisher **MIKE RICHARDSON**

DARK HORSE BOOKS

...mused by the humans' war efforts, and they battle back with increased resolve.

Tom's sons Hal, Ben, and Matt must learn to cope with the loss of their father, each one affected in a very different way. Hal becomes a consummate warrior, trying to fill his father's shoes; Ben finds himself still changing even after the alien-installed harness was removed; and young Matt finds himself yearning to join the battle but ignored by pretty much everyone.

Dr. Anne Glass, having lost her husband and son in the initial attack of the invasion, had cautiously given her heart to Tom but now finds herself alone once again. She has been trying to fulfill her promise to take care of Tom's three sons. But that is no easy task, especially since Weaver's aggressive strategy of attacking the alien forces has produced an overwhelming number of wounded, leaving precious little time to mourn Tom's absence.

And finally there's John Pope. Arguably, there was never any love lost between him and the professor; Pope counts Tom's disappearance as a good thing. He's taken the opportunity to cobble his own group of warriors out of Second Mass rejects and degenerates, calling themselves the "Berserkers." An uneasy alliance is formed with the Second Mass, but distrust of Pope and his gang of miscreants is high.

And now, as we continue the saga in volume 2 of Dark Horse Comics' *Falling Skies* graphic novel, the Second Mass is faced with being

When asked to head up the creation of the second season, I was, to say the least, overwhelmed. But this daunting task was greatly aided by Paul Tobin and Juan Ferreyra's amazing first volume of the *Falling Skies* graphic novel. The writers and I constantly referred to it almost as a "bible," and many of the ideas and concepts in that book directly influenced our storytelling in the television series. I can't begin to tell you how excited we were to be able to collaborate with Mike Richardson and the DH team, and doubly excited to have Paul and Juan at the helm once again. They have created a tense, action-packed saga of survival in a post–alien invasion world. I have no doubt we will be referencing this book for the third season as well!

Special thanks to my right-hand person Katie Altman, writer Heather Regnier, and my comrade in arms, the indomitable Mark Verheiden for their careful supervision, input, and contributions to the story.

Also, many thanks to TNT's creative team of Whitney Melancon and Jennifer Giddens, who patiently nudged the process along, providing great feedback and solid encouragement.

And now, as you turn the page, allow yourself to enter the world of skitters and mechs, freedom fighters and outlaws—the world of *Falling Skies*!

REMI AUBUCHON
executive producer of *Falling Skies*

THE FALL

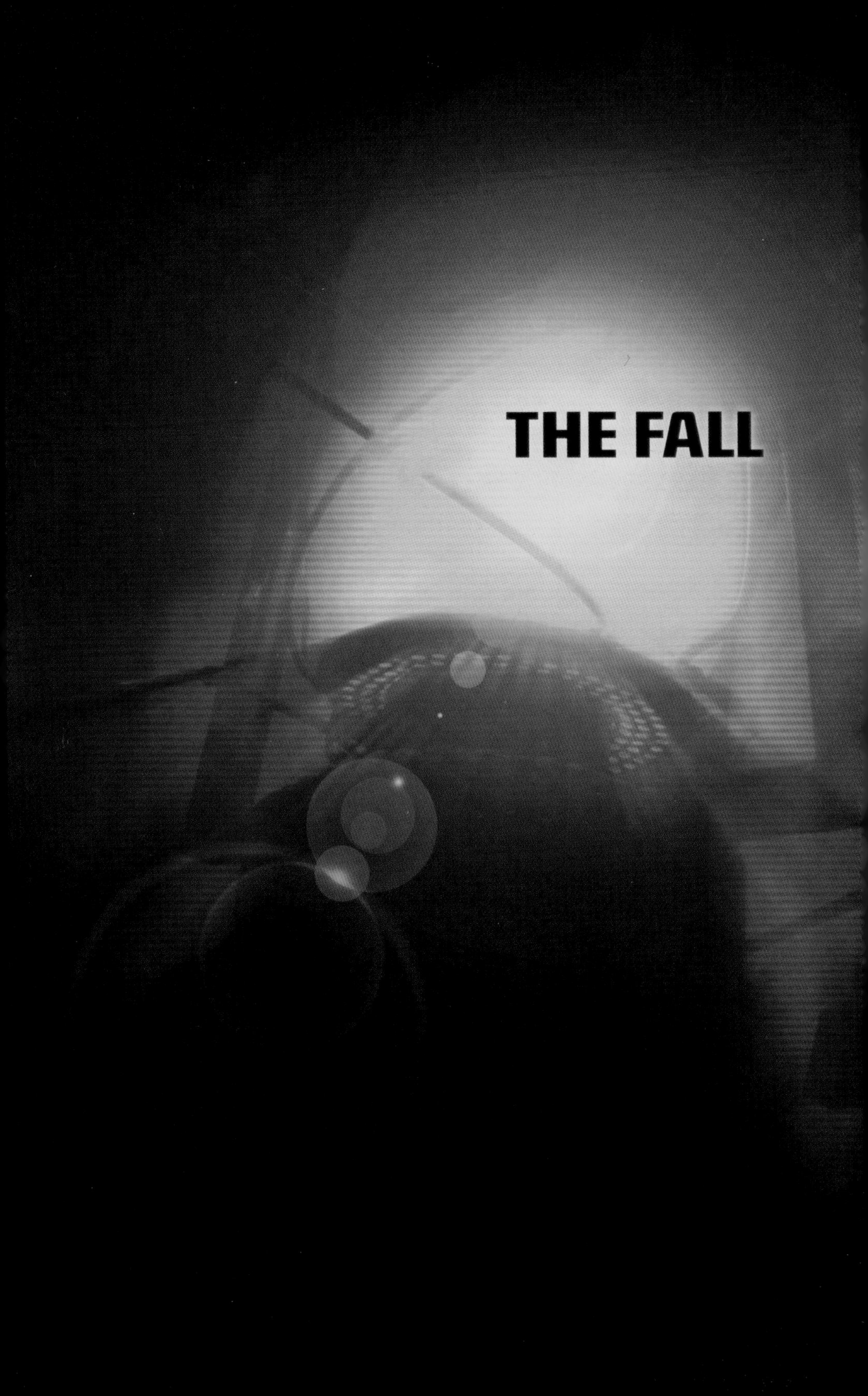

Script by **PAUL TOBIN** with **REMI AUBUCHON** and **KATIE ALTMAN**

Art by **PATRIC REYNOLDS**

Colors by **ANDREW DALHOUSE**

Lettering by **NATE PIEKOS OF BLAMBOT®**

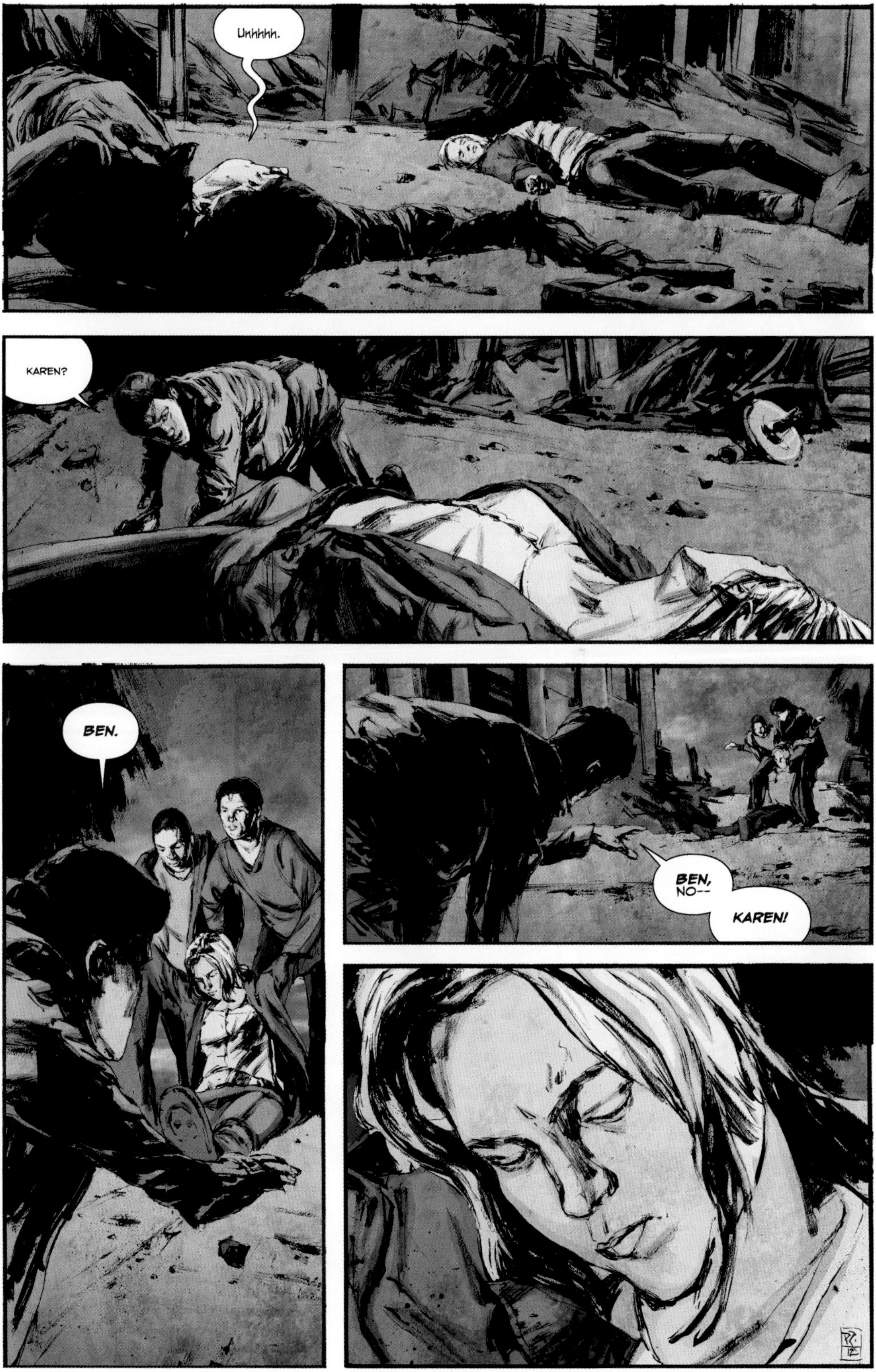
Unhhhh.
KAREN?
BEN.
BEN, NO--
KAREN!

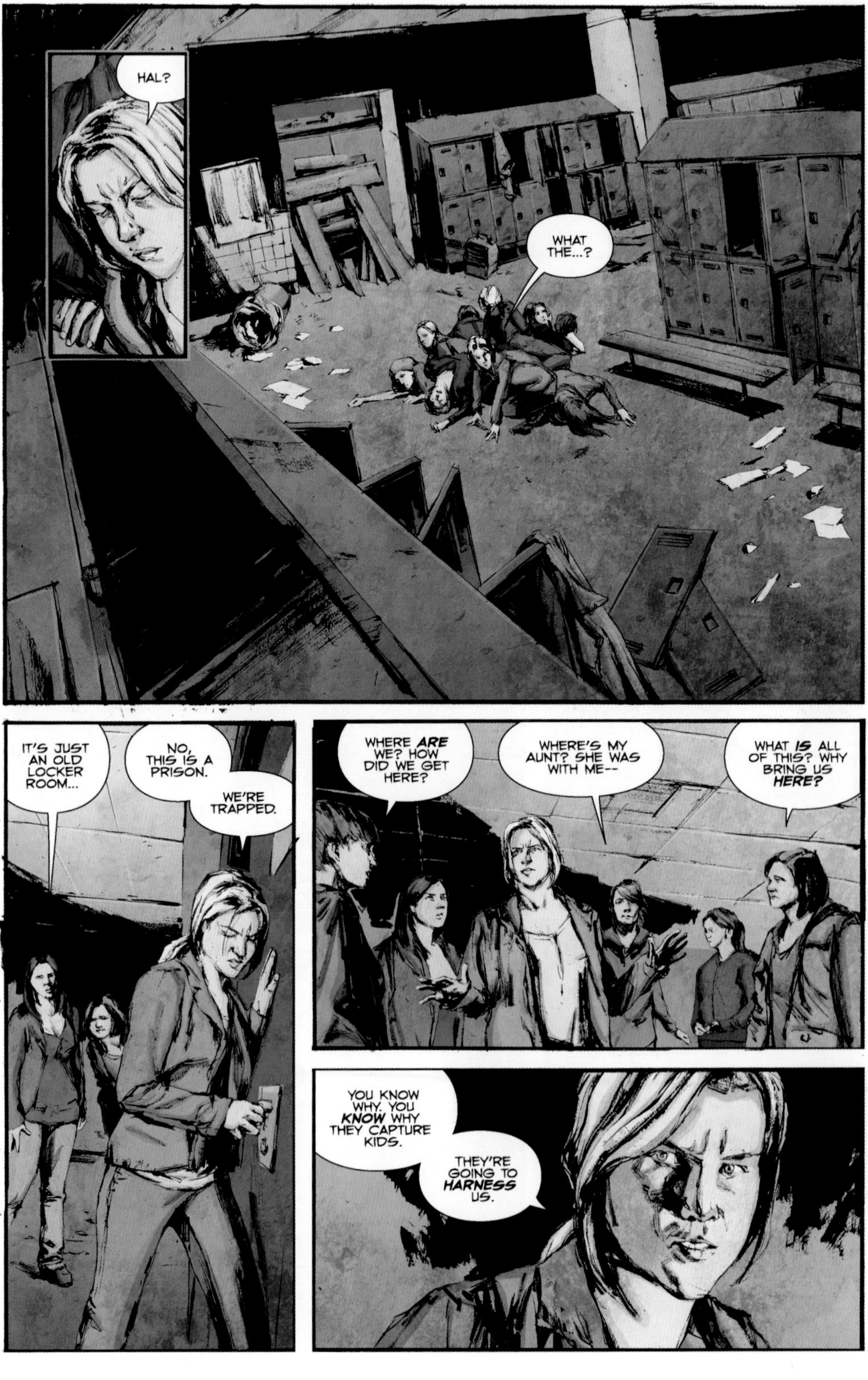
HAL?
WHAT THE...?
IT'S JUST AN OLD LOCKER ROOM...
NO, THIS IS A PRISON.
WE'RE TRAPPED.
WHERE ARE WE? HOW DID WE GET HERE?
WHERE'S MY AUNT? SHE WAS WITH ME--
WHAT IS ALL OF THIS? WHY BRING US HERE?
YOU KNOW WHY. YOU KNOW WHY THEY CAPTURE KIDS.
THEY'RE GOING TO HARNESS US.

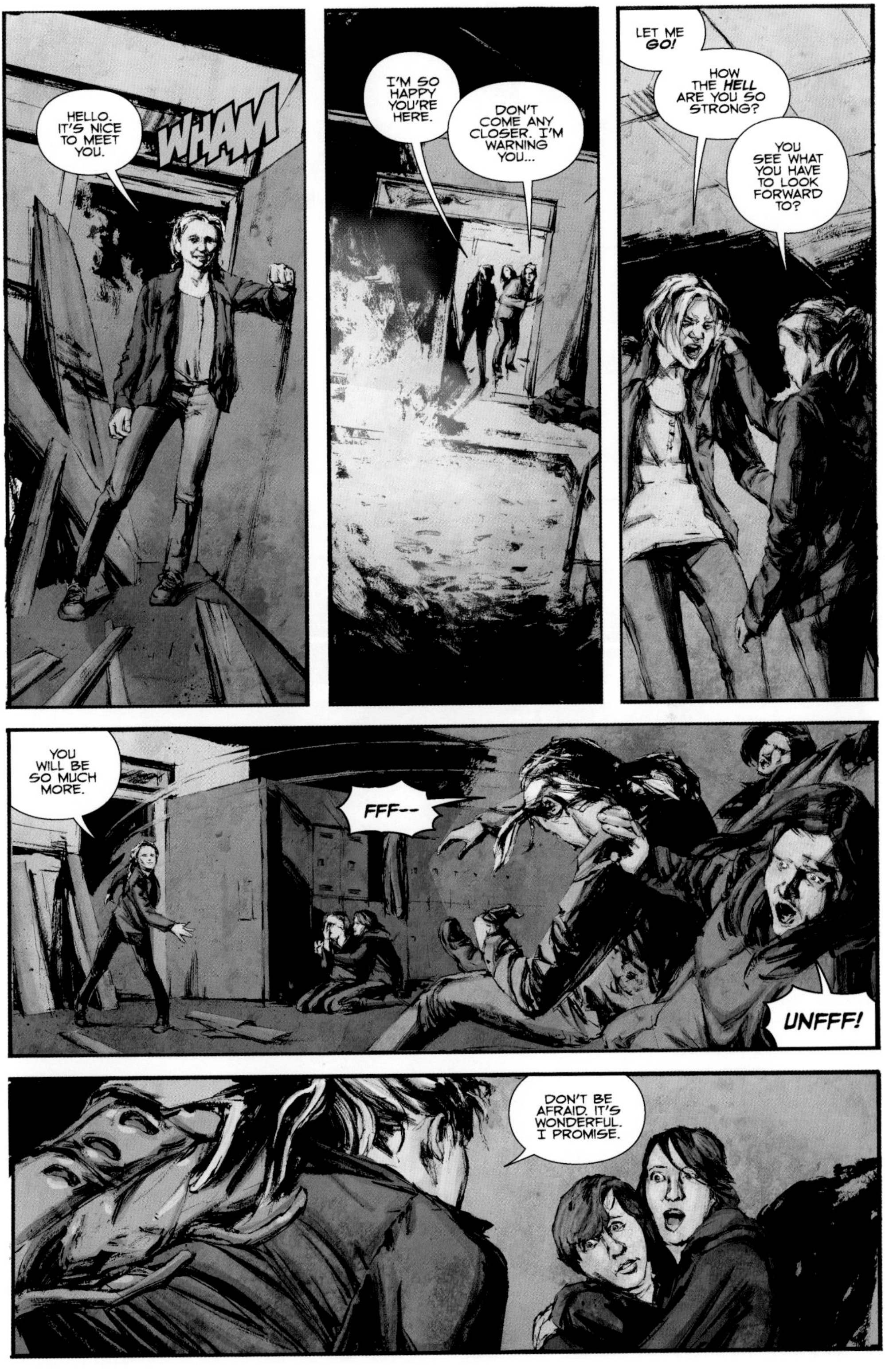
HELLO. IT'S NICE TO MEET YOU.
WHAM
I'M SO HAPPY YOU'RE HERE.
DON'T COME ANY CLOSER. I'M WARNING YOU...
LET ME GO!
HOW THE HELL ARE YOU SO STRONG?
YOU SEE WHAT YOU HAVE TO LOOK FORWARD TO?
YOU WILL BE SO MUCH MORE.
FFF--
UNFFF!
DON'T BE AFRAID. IT'S WONDERFUL. I PROMISE.

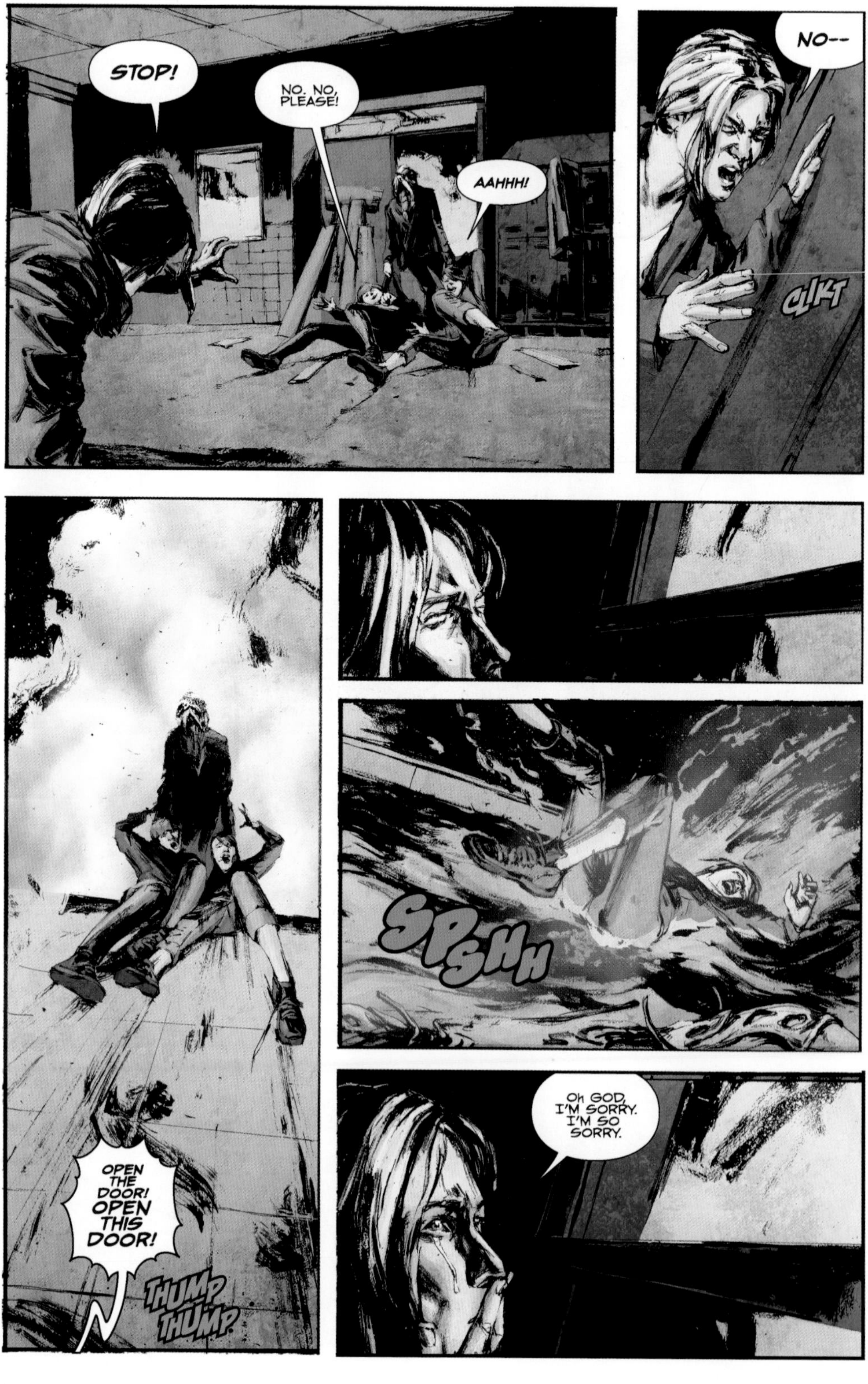
STOP!
NO. NO, PLEASE!
AAHHH!
NO--
CLIKT
OPEN THE DOOR! OPEN THIS DOOR!
THUMP THUMP
SPSHH
OH GOD, I'M SORRY. I'M SO SORRY.

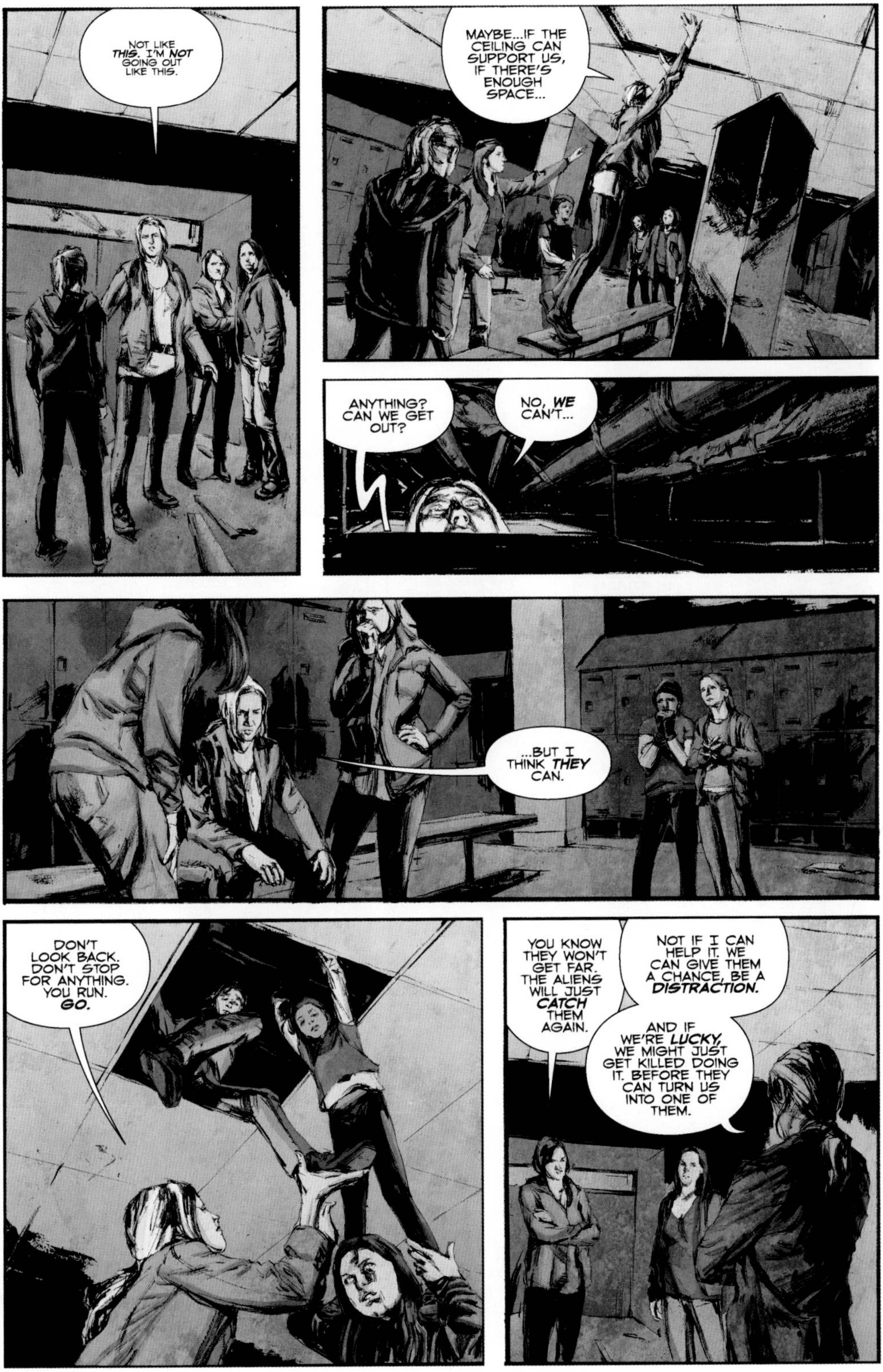
NOT LIKE THIS. I'M NOT GOING OUT LIKE THIS.
MAYBE...IF THE CEILING CAN SUPPORT US, IF THERE'S ENOUGH SPACE...
ANYTHING? CAN WE GET OUT?
NO, WE CAN'T...
...BUT I THINK THEY CAN.
DON'T LOOK BACK. DON'T STOP FOR ANYTHING. YOU RUN. GO.
YOU KNOW THEY WON'T GET FAR. THE ALIENS WILL JUST CATCH THEM AGAIN.
NOT IF I CAN HELP IT. WE CAN GIVE THEM A CHANCE, BE A DISTRACTION.
AND IF WE'RE LUCKY, WE MIGHT JUST GET KILLED DOING IT. BEFORE THEY CAN TURN US INTO ONE OF THEM.

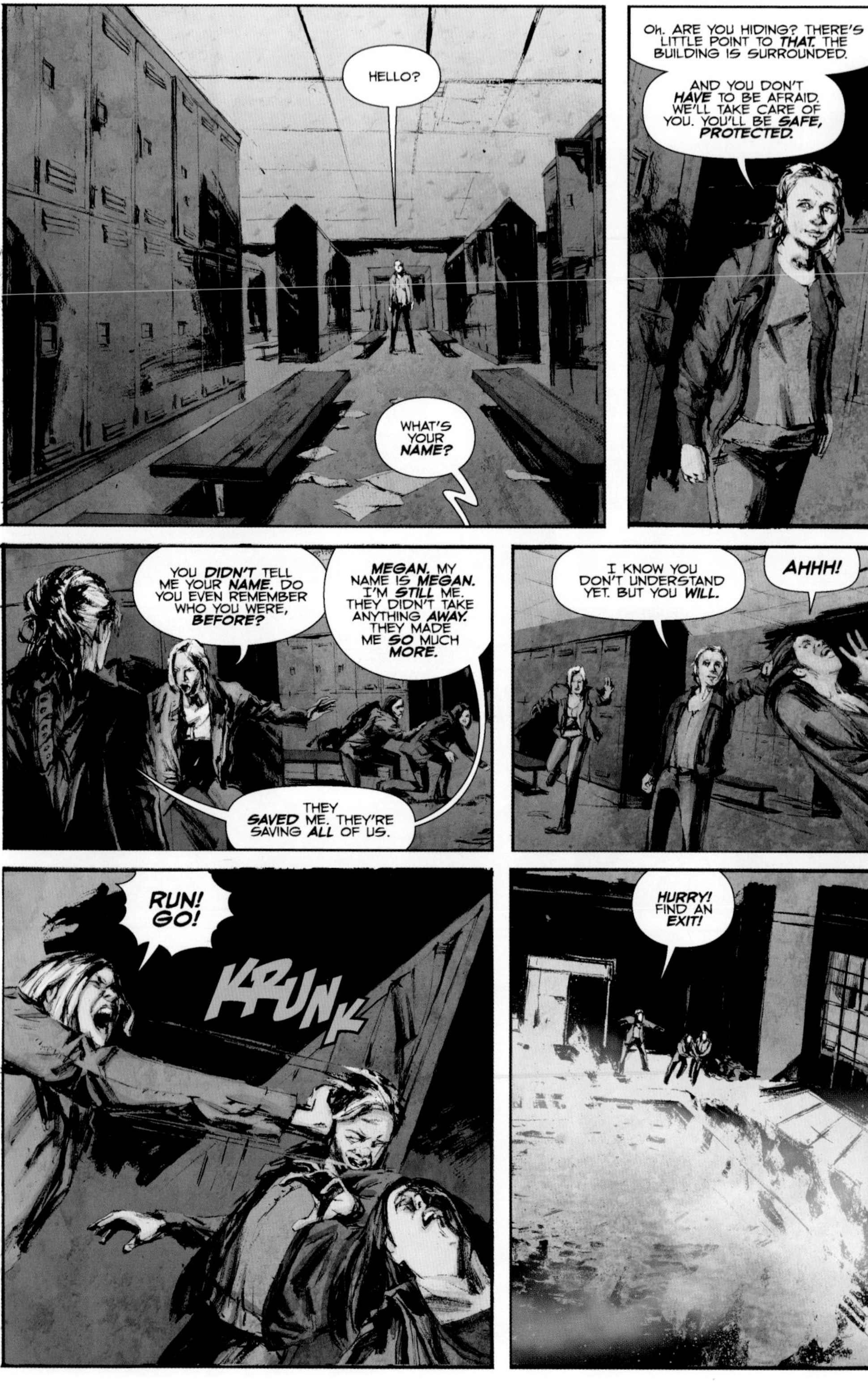
HELLO?
WHAT'S YOUR NAME?
Oh. ARE YOU HIDING? THERE'S LITTLE POINT TO THAT. THE BUILDING IS SURROUNDED.
AND YOU DON'T HAVE TO BE AFRAID. WE'LL TAKE CARE OF YOU. YOU'LL BE SAFE, PROTECTED.
YOU DIDN'T TELL ME YOUR NAME. DO YOU EVEN REMEMBER WHO YOU WERE, BEFORE?
MEGAN. MY NAME IS MEGAN. I'M STILL ME. THEY DIDN'T TAKE ANYTHING AWAY. THEY MADE ME SO MUCH MORE.
THEY SAVED ME. THEY'RE SAVING ALL OF US.
I KNOW YOU DON'T UNDERSTAND YET. BUT YOU WILL.
AHHH!
RUN! GO!
KRUNK
HURRY! FIND AN EXIT!

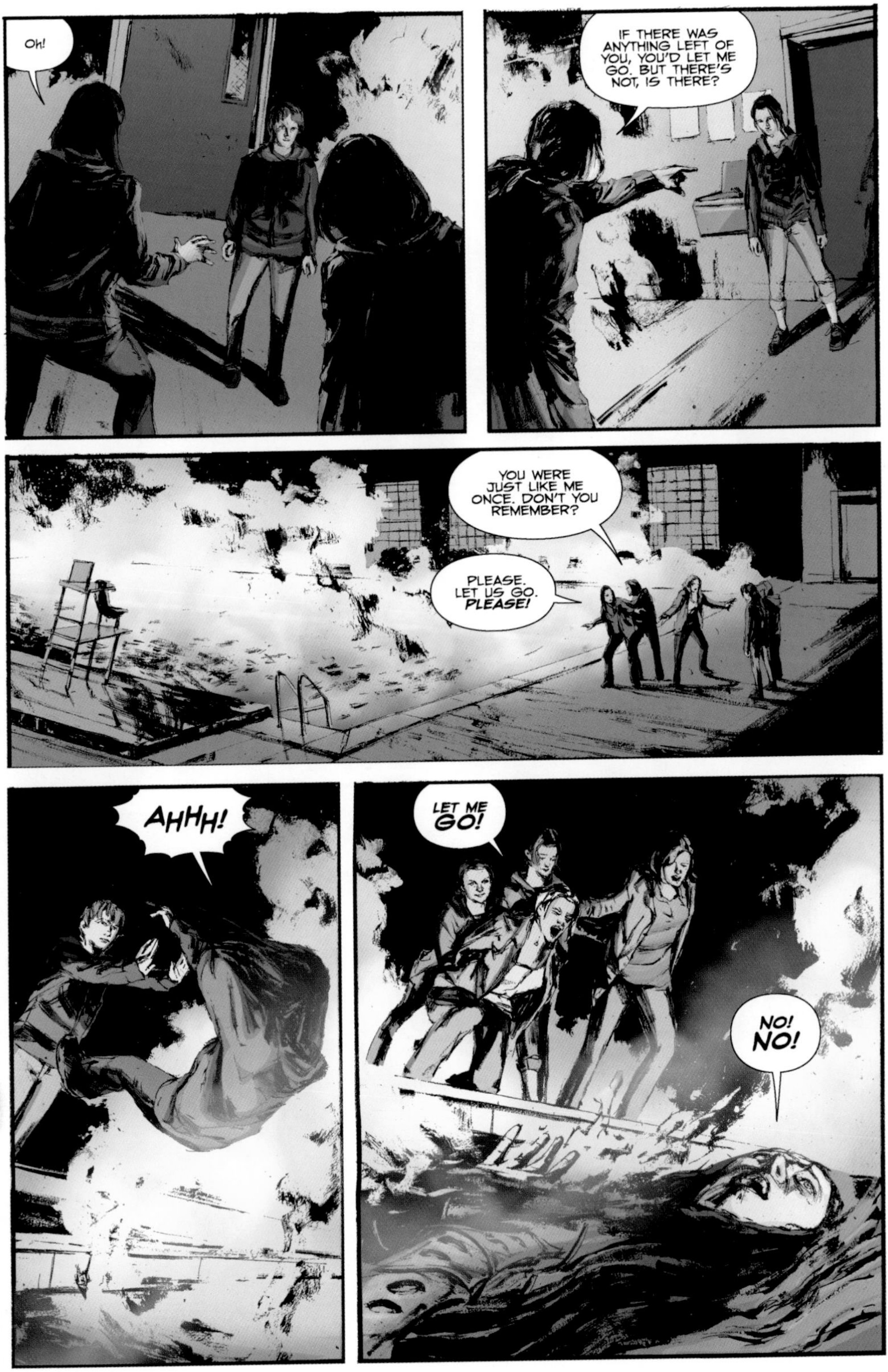
Oh!
IF THERE WAS ANYTHING LEFT OF YOU, YOU'D LET ME GO. BUT THERE'S NOT, IS THERE?
YOU WERE JUST LIKE ME ONCE. DON'T YOU REMEMBER?
PLEASE. LET US GO. PLEASE!
AHHH!
LET ME GO!
NO! NO!

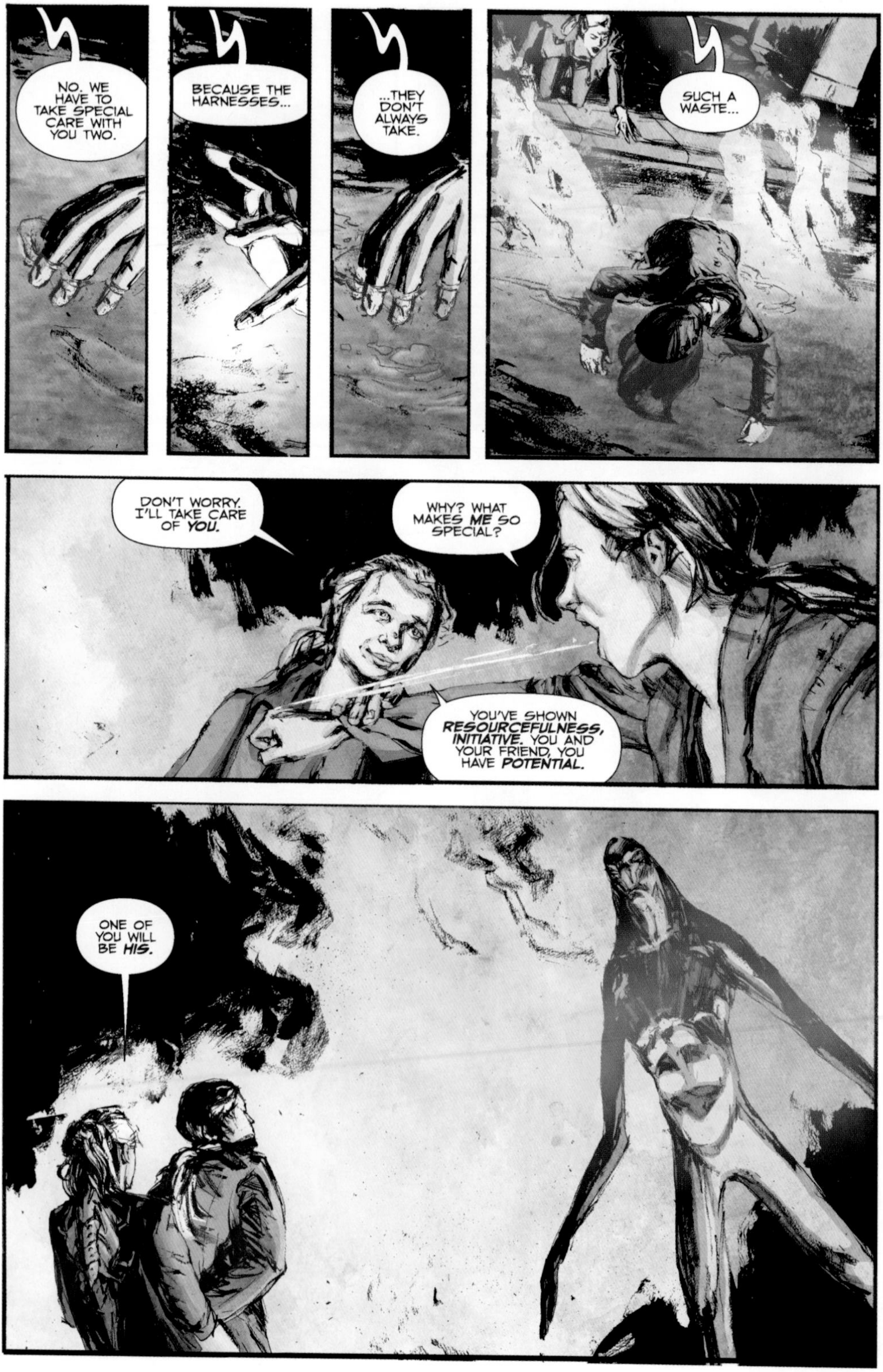
NO. WE HAVE TO TAKE SPECIAL CARE WITH YOU TWO.
BECAUSE THE HARNESSES...
...THEY DON'T ALWAYS TAKE.
SUCH A WASTE...
DON'T WORRY. I'LL TAKE CARE OF YOU.
WHY? WHAT MAKES ME SO SPECIAL?
YOU'VE SHOWN RESOURCEFULNESS, INITIATIVE. YOU AND YOUR FRIEND, YOU HAVE POTENTIAL.
ONE OF YOU WILL BE HIS.

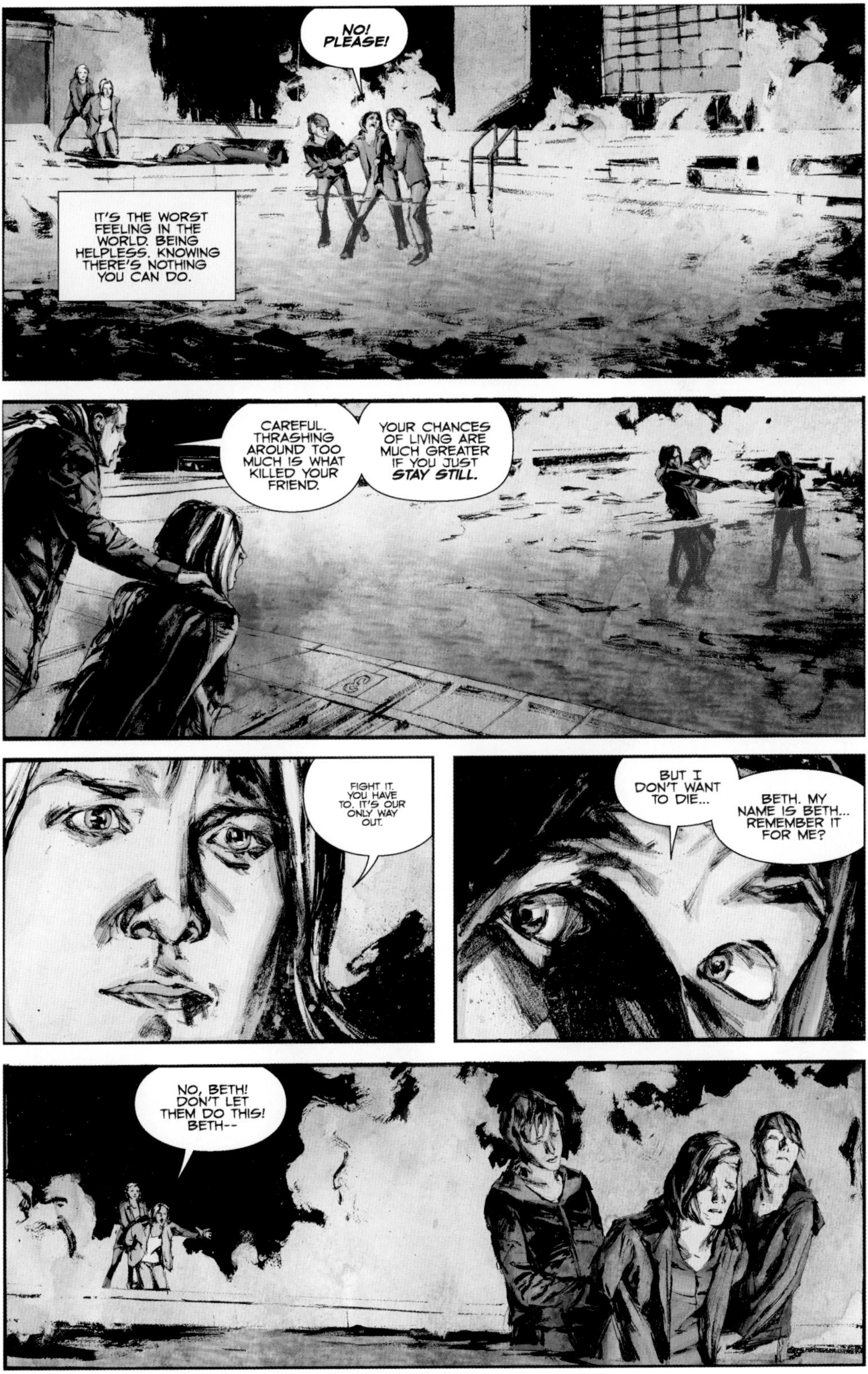
NO! PLEASE!
IT'S THE WORST FEELING IN THE WORLD. BEING HELPLESS. KNOWING THERE'S NOTHING YOU CAN DO.
CAREFUL. THRASHING AROUND TOO MUCH IS WHAT KILLED YOUR FRIEND.
YOUR CHANCES OF LIVING ARE MUCH GREATER IF YOU JUST *STAY STILL.*
FIGHT IT. YOU HAVE TO. IT'S OUR ONLY WAY OUT.
BUT I DON'T WANT TO DIE...
BETH. MY NAME IS BETH... REMEMBER IT FOR ME?
NO, BETH! DON'T LET THEM DO THIS! BETH--

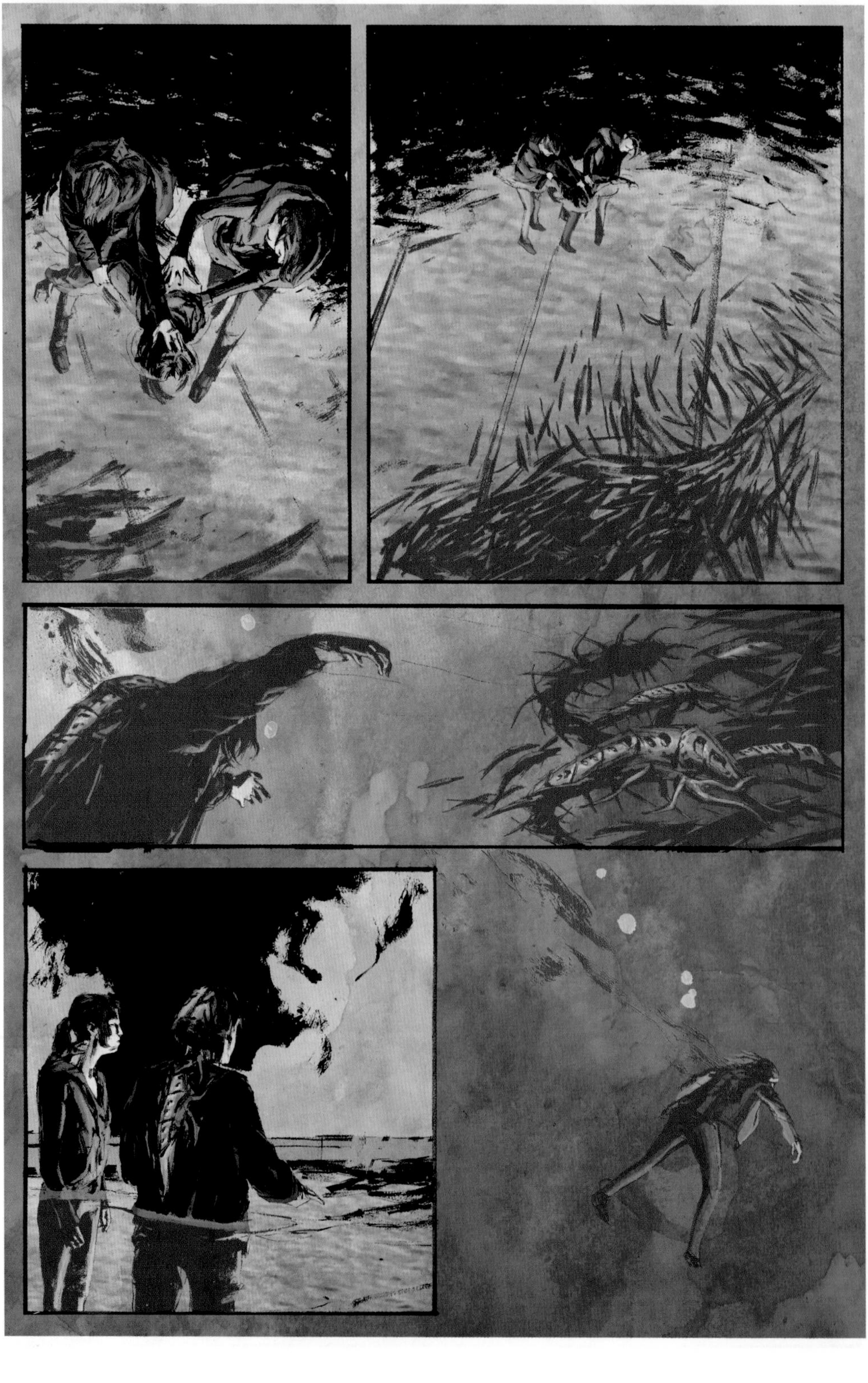

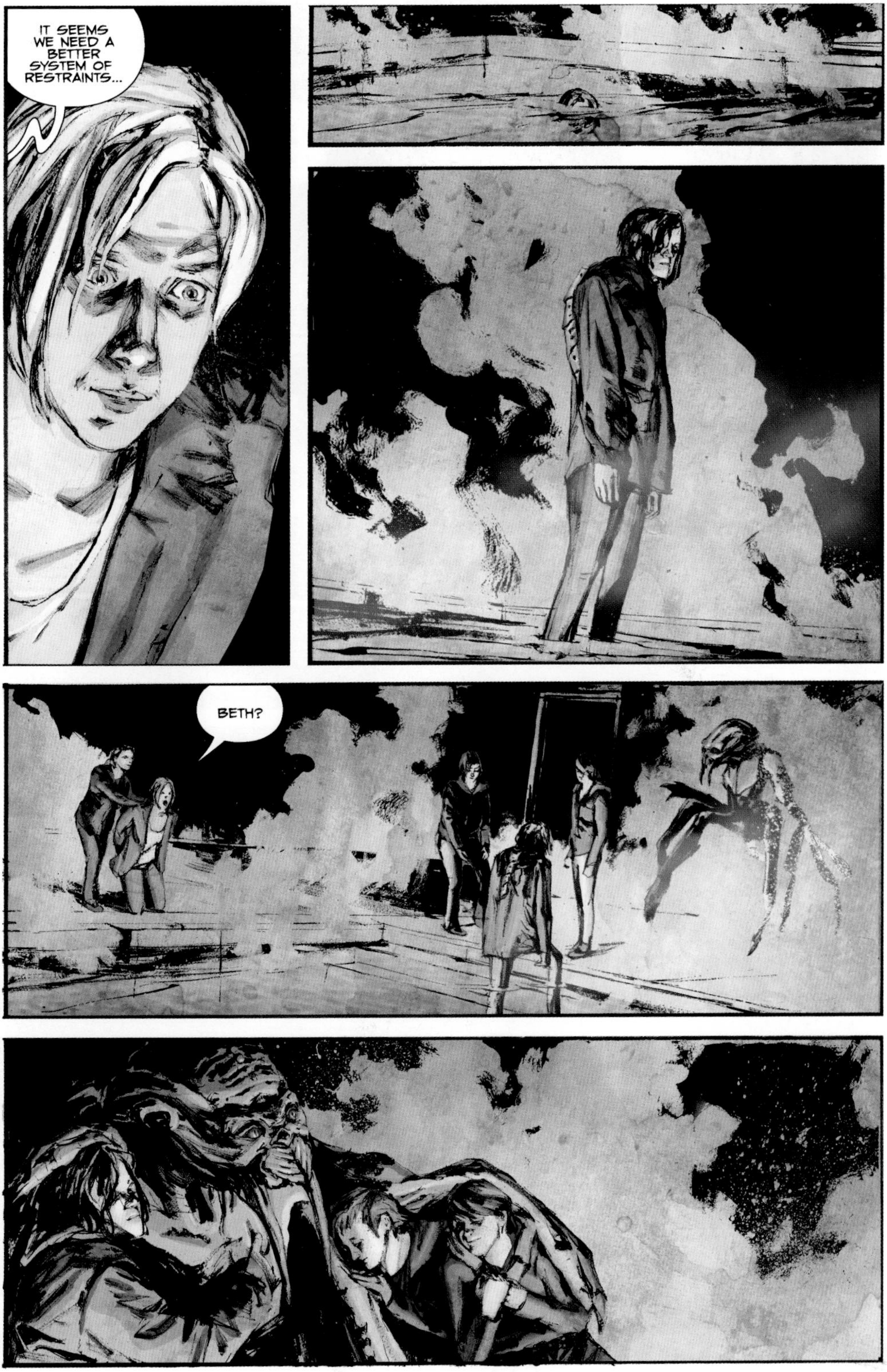
IT SEEMS WE NEED A BETTER SYSTEM OF RESTRAINTS...
BETH?

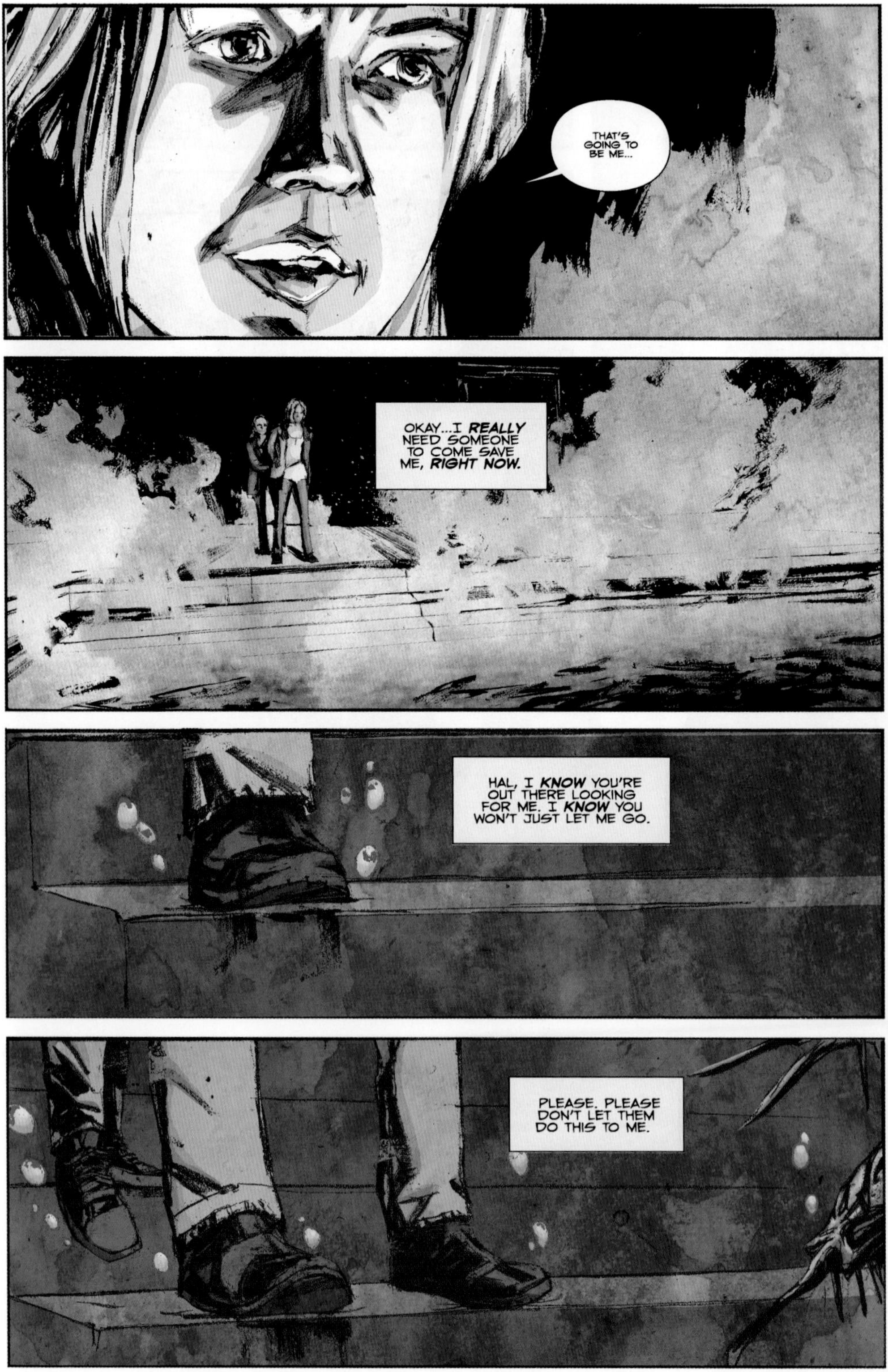
THAT'S GOING TO BE ME...
OKAY...I **REALLY** NEED SOMEONE TO COME SAVE ME, **RIGHT NOW.**
HAL, I **KNOW** YOU'RE OUT THERE LOOKING FOR ME. I **KNOW** YOU WON'T JUST LET ME GO.
PLEASE. PLEASE DON'T LET THEM DO THIS TO ME.

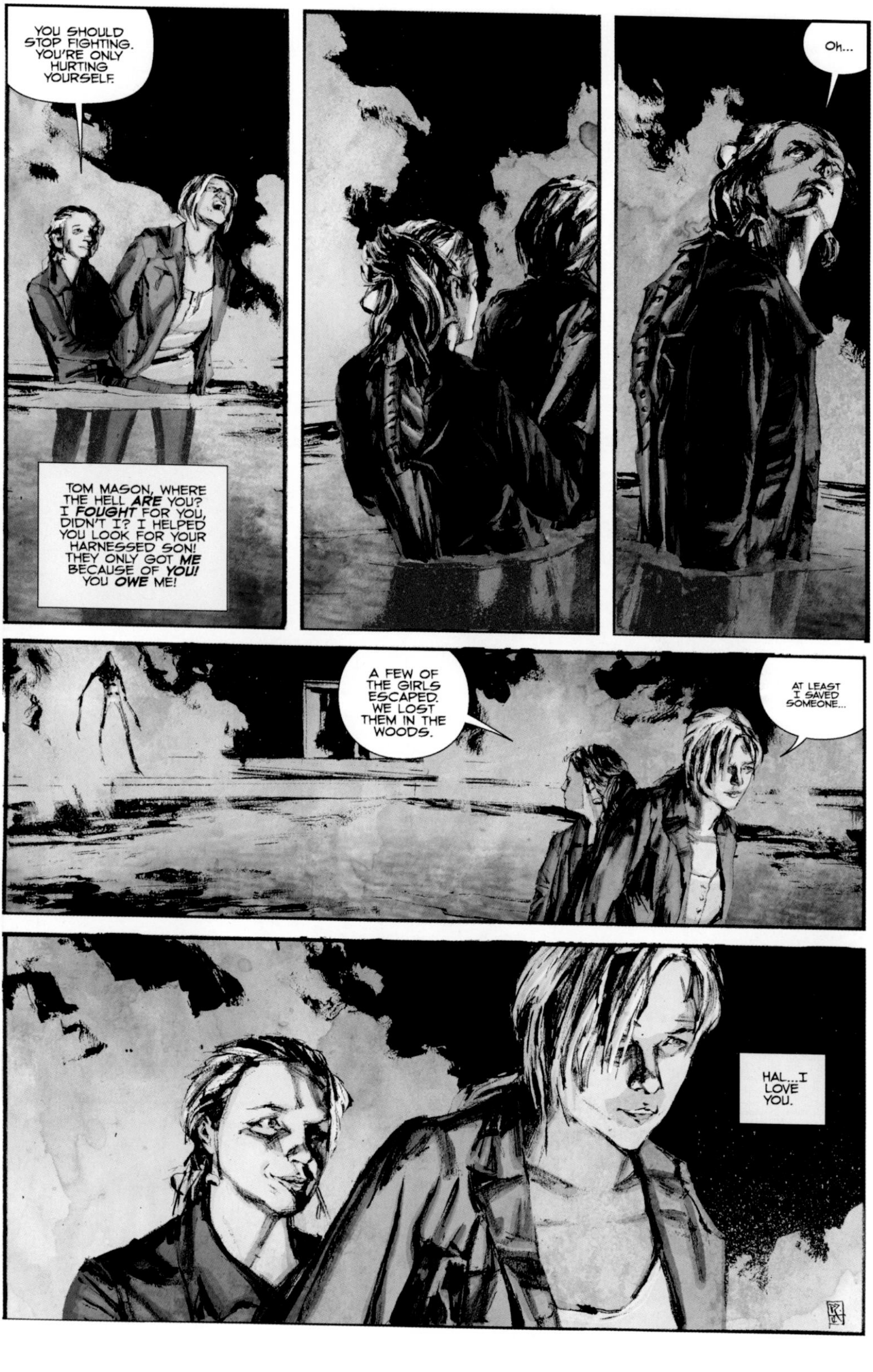
YOU SHOULD STOP FIGHTING. YOU'RE ONLY HURTING YOURSELF.
TOM MASON, WHERE THE HELL ARE YOU? I FOUGHT FOR YOU, DIDN'T I? I HELPED YOU LOOK FOR YOUR HARNESSED SON! THEY ONLY GOT ME BECAUSE OF YOU! YOU OWE ME!
Oh...
A FEW OF THE GIRLS ESCAPED. WE LOST THEM IN THE WOODS.
AT LEAST I SAVED SOMEONE...
HAL...I LOVE YOU.

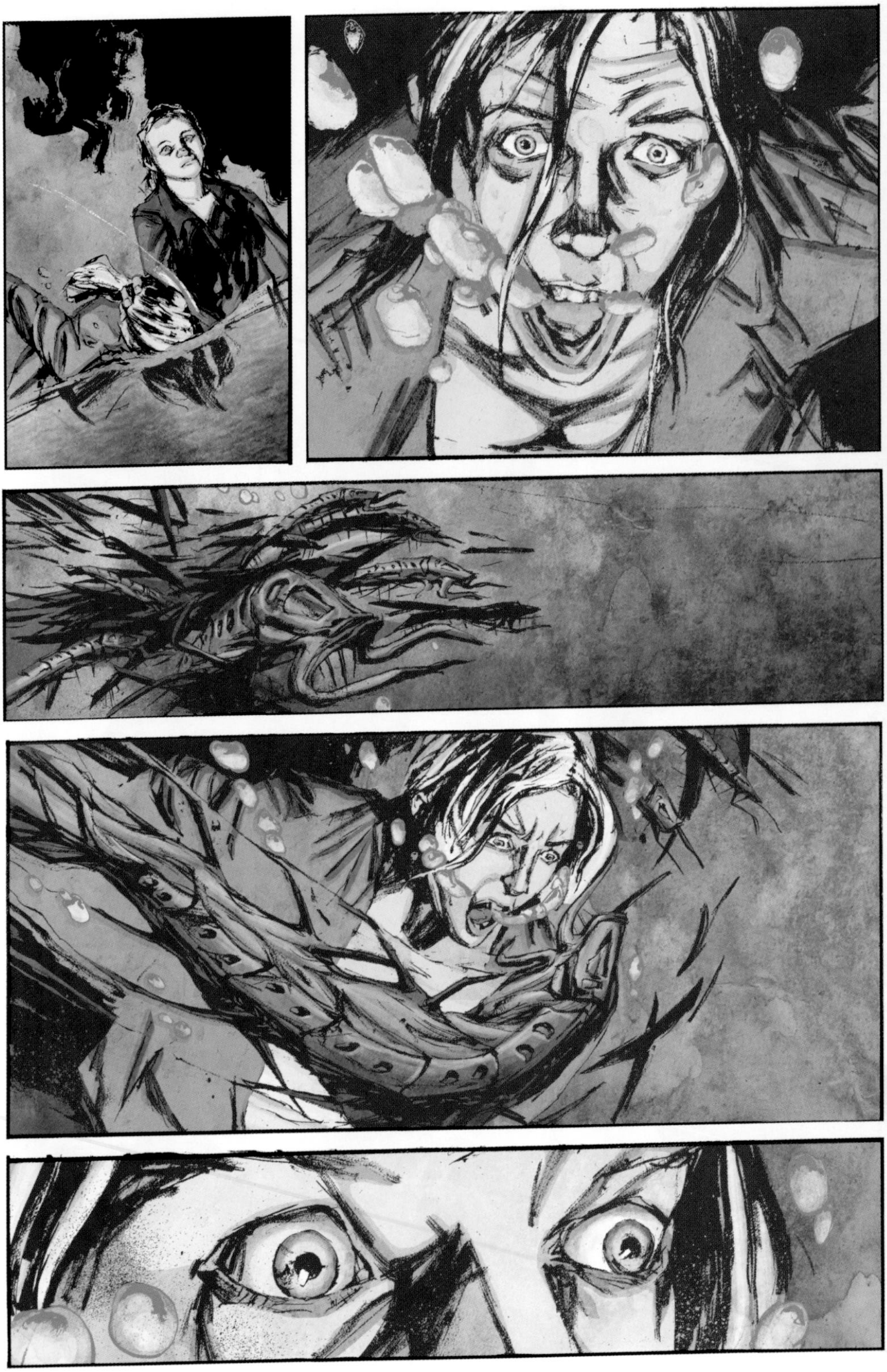

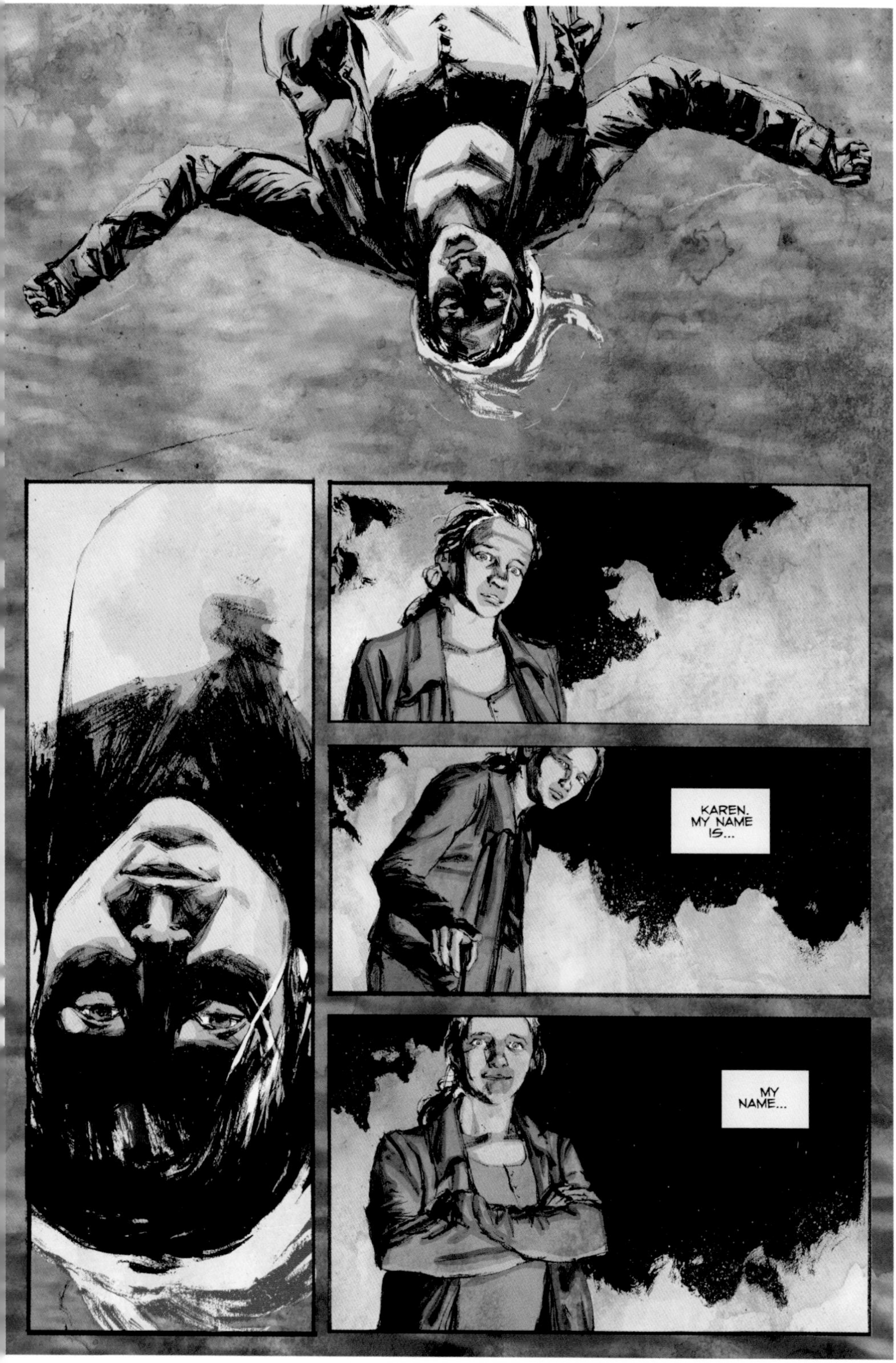
KAREN. MY NAME IS...
MY NAME...

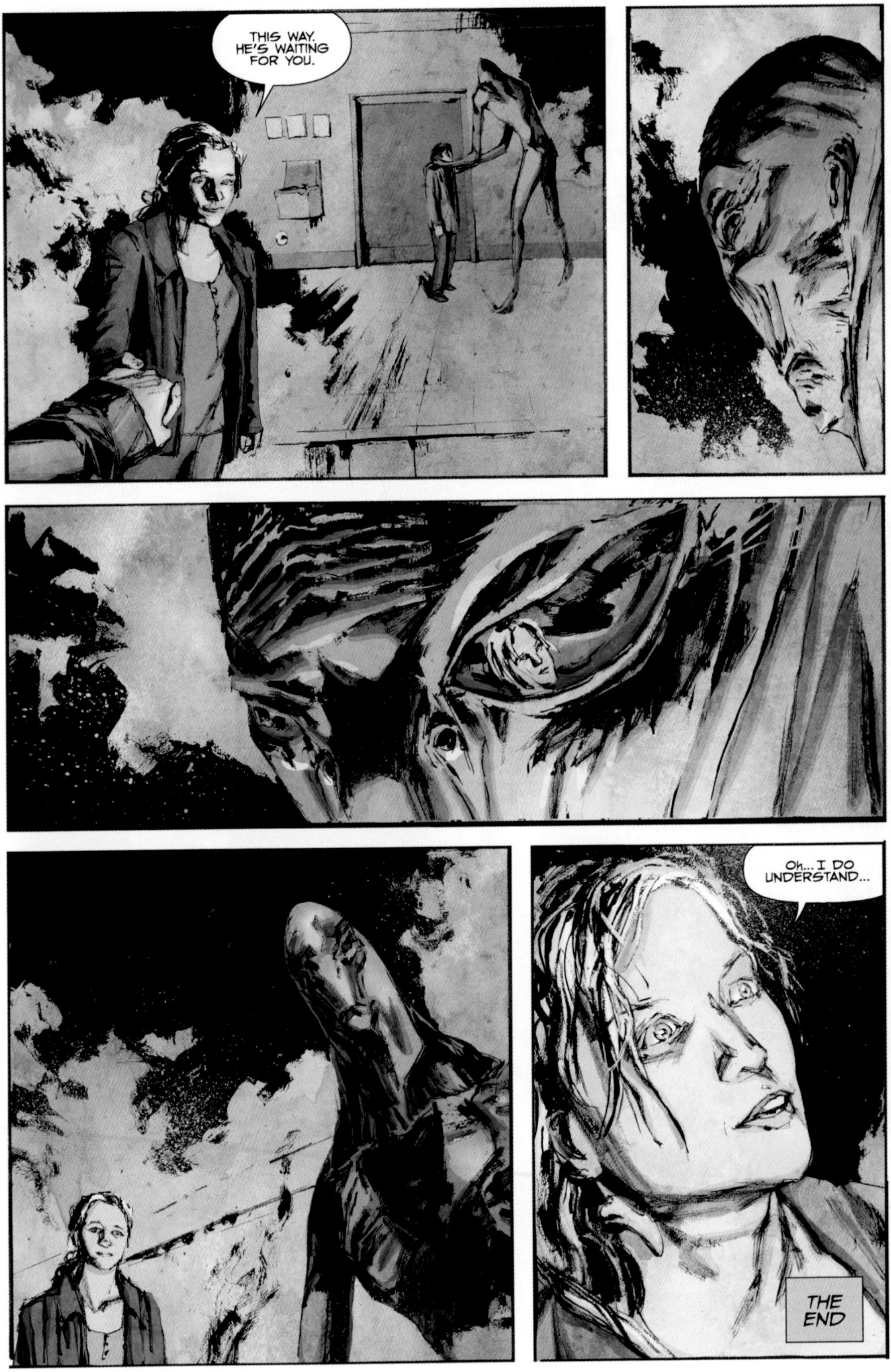
THIS WAY. HE'S WAITING FOR YOU.
Oh... I DO UNDERSTAND...
THE END

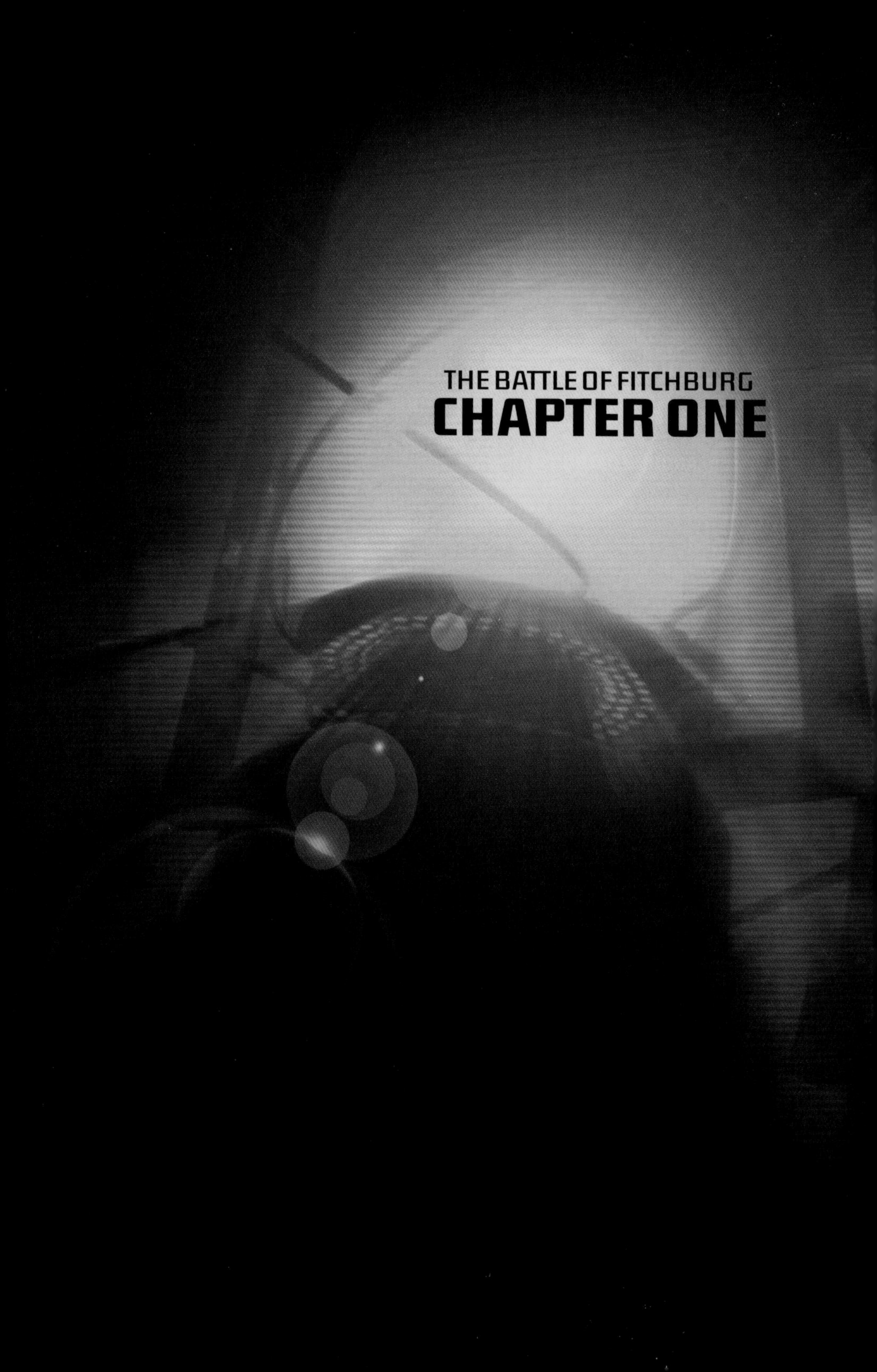

THE BATTLE OF FITCHBURG
CHAPTER ONE

Script by **PAUL TOBIN** with **REMI AUBUCHON** and **KATIE ALTMAN**

Art by **JUAN FERREYRA**

Colors by **ANDREW DALHOUSE**

Lettering by **NATE PIEKOS OF BLAMBOT**®

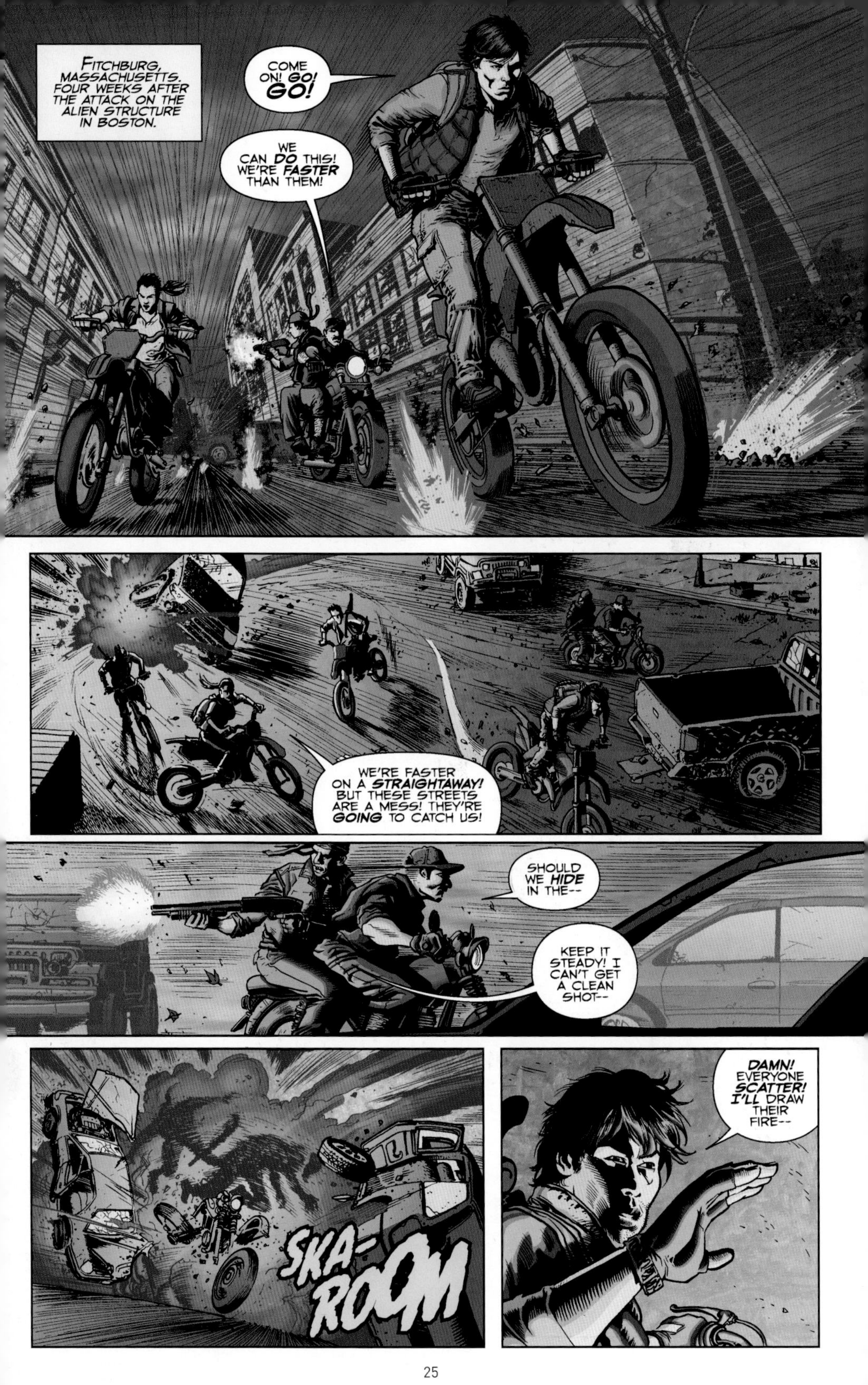
FITCHBURG, MASSACHUSETTS. FOUR WEEKS AFTER THE ATTACK ON THE ALIEN STRUCTURE IN BOSTON.
COME ON! GO! GO!
WE CAN DO THIS! WE'RE FASTER THAN THEM!
WE'RE FASTER ON A STRAIGHTAWAY! BUT THESE STREETS ARE A MESS! THEY'RE GOING TO CATCH US!
SHOULD WE HIDE IN THE--
KEEP IT STEADY! I CAN'T GET A CLEAN SHOT--
SKA-ROOM
DAMN! EVERYONE SCATTER! I'LL DRAW THEIR FIRE--

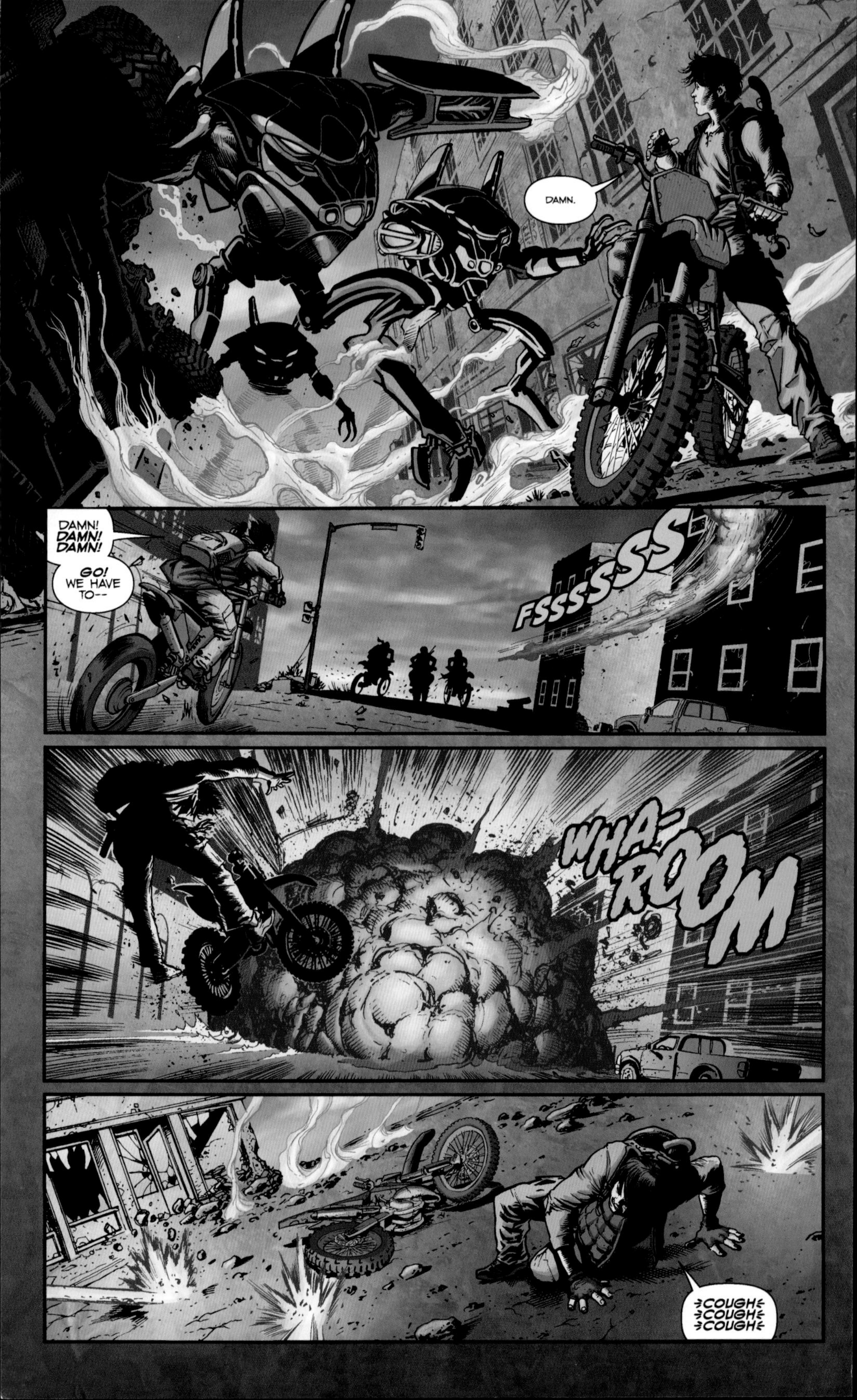
DAMN.
DAMN! DAMN! DAMN!
GO! WE HAVE TO--
FSSSSSSS
WHA-ROOM
COUGH COUGH COUGH

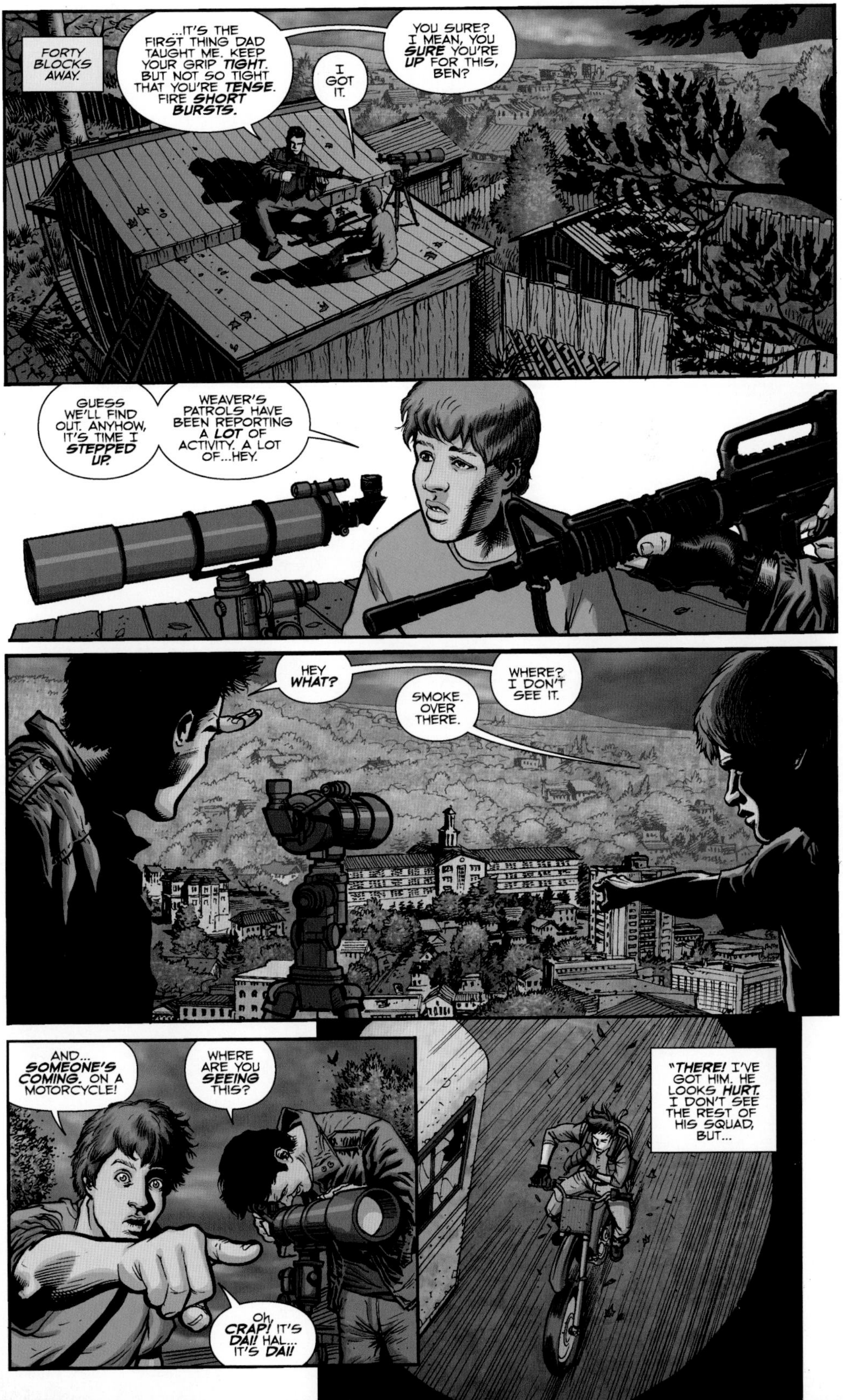
FORTY BLOCKS AWAY.
...IT'S THE FIRST THING DAD TAUGHT ME. KEEP YOUR GRIP TIGHT. BUT NOT SO TIGHT THAT YOU'RE TENSE. FIRE SHORT BURSTS.
I GOT IT.
YOU SURE? I MEAN, YOU SURE YOU'RE UP FOR THIS, BEN?
GUESS WE'LL FIND OUT. ANYHOW, IT'S TIME I STEPPED UP.
WEAVER'S PATROLS HAVE BEEN REPORTING A LOT OF ACTIVITY. A LOT OF...HEY.
HEY WHAT?
WHERE? I DON'T SEE IT.
SMOKE. OVER THERE.
AND... SOMEONE'S COMING. ON A MOTORCYCLE!
WHERE ARE YOU SEEING THIS?
"THERE! I'VE GOT HIM. HE LOOKS HURT. I DON'T SEE THE REST OF HIS SQUAD, BUT...
OH, CRAP! IT'S DAI! HAL... IT'S DAI!

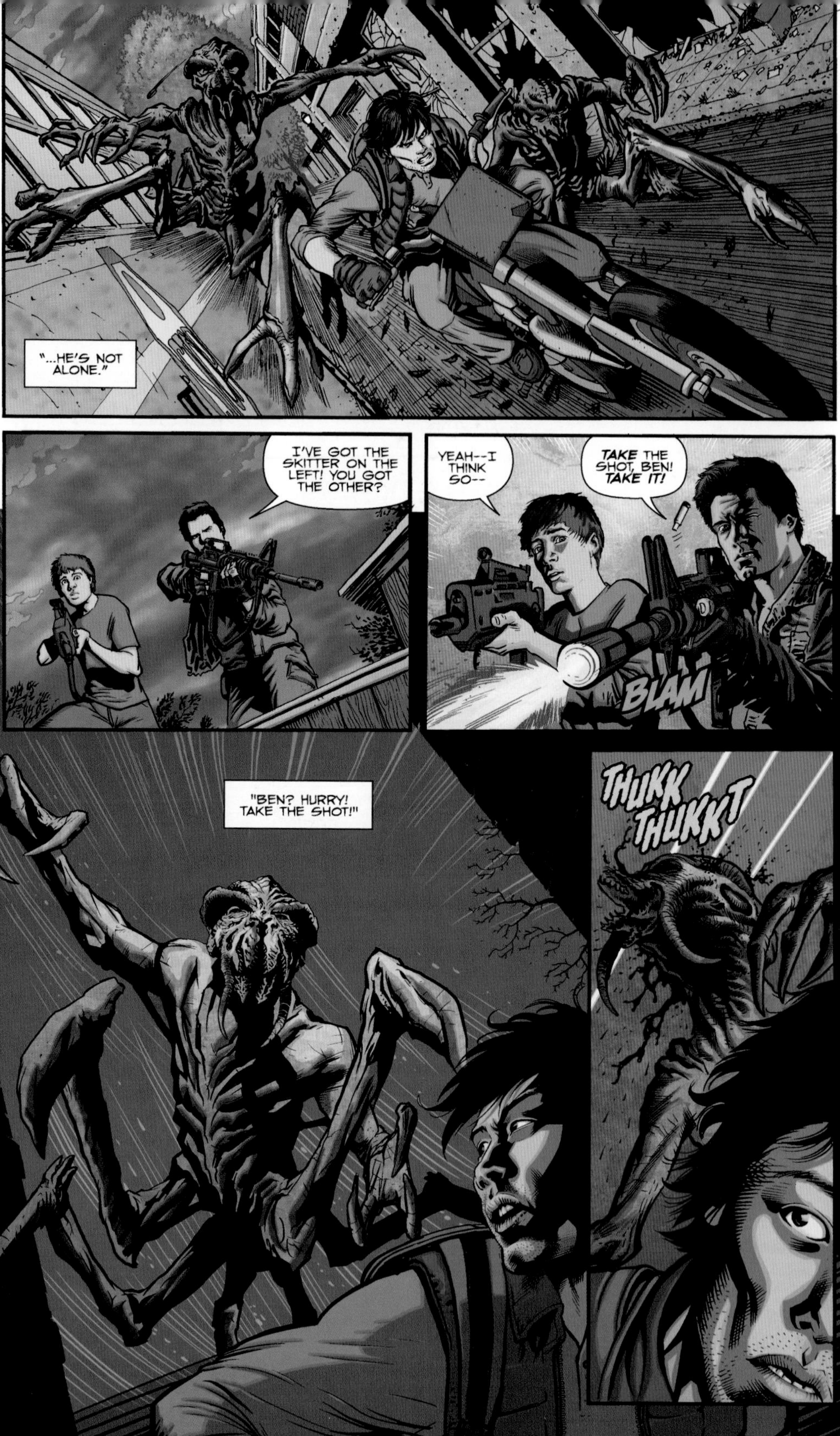
"...HE'S NOT ALONE."
I'VE GOT THE SKITTER ON THE LEFT! YOU GOT THE OTHER?
YEAH--I THINK SO--
TAKE THE SHOT, BEN! TAKE IT!
BLAM
"BEN? HURRY! TAKE THE SHOT!"
THUKK THUKKT

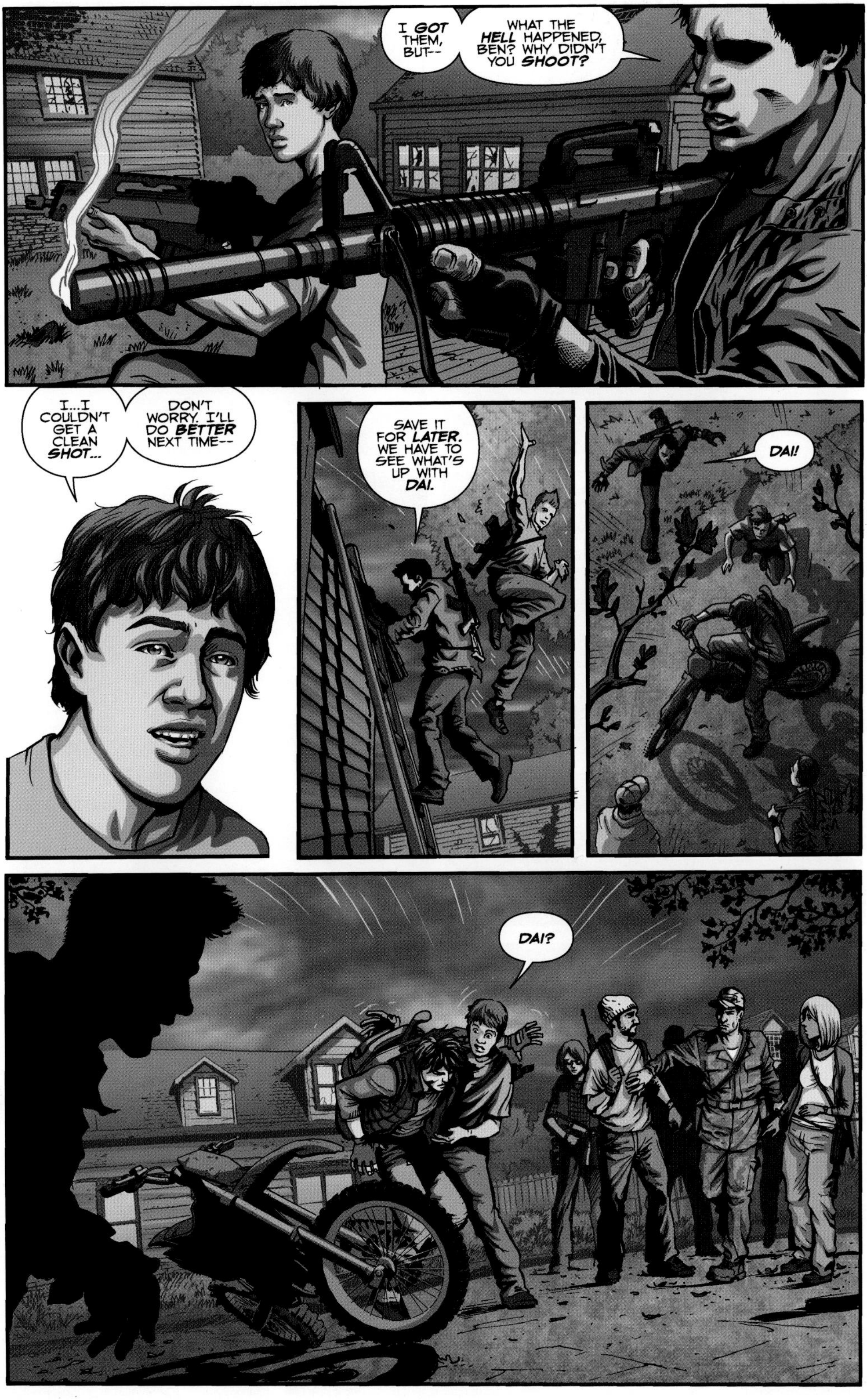
I GOT THEM, BUT--
WHAT THE HELL HAPPENED, BEN? WHY DIDN'T YOU SHOOT?
I...I COULDN'T GET A CLEAN SHOT...
DON'T WORRY. I'LL DO BETTER NEXT TIME--
SAVE IT FOR LATER. WE HAVE TO SEE WHAT'S UP WITH DAI.
DAI!
DAI?

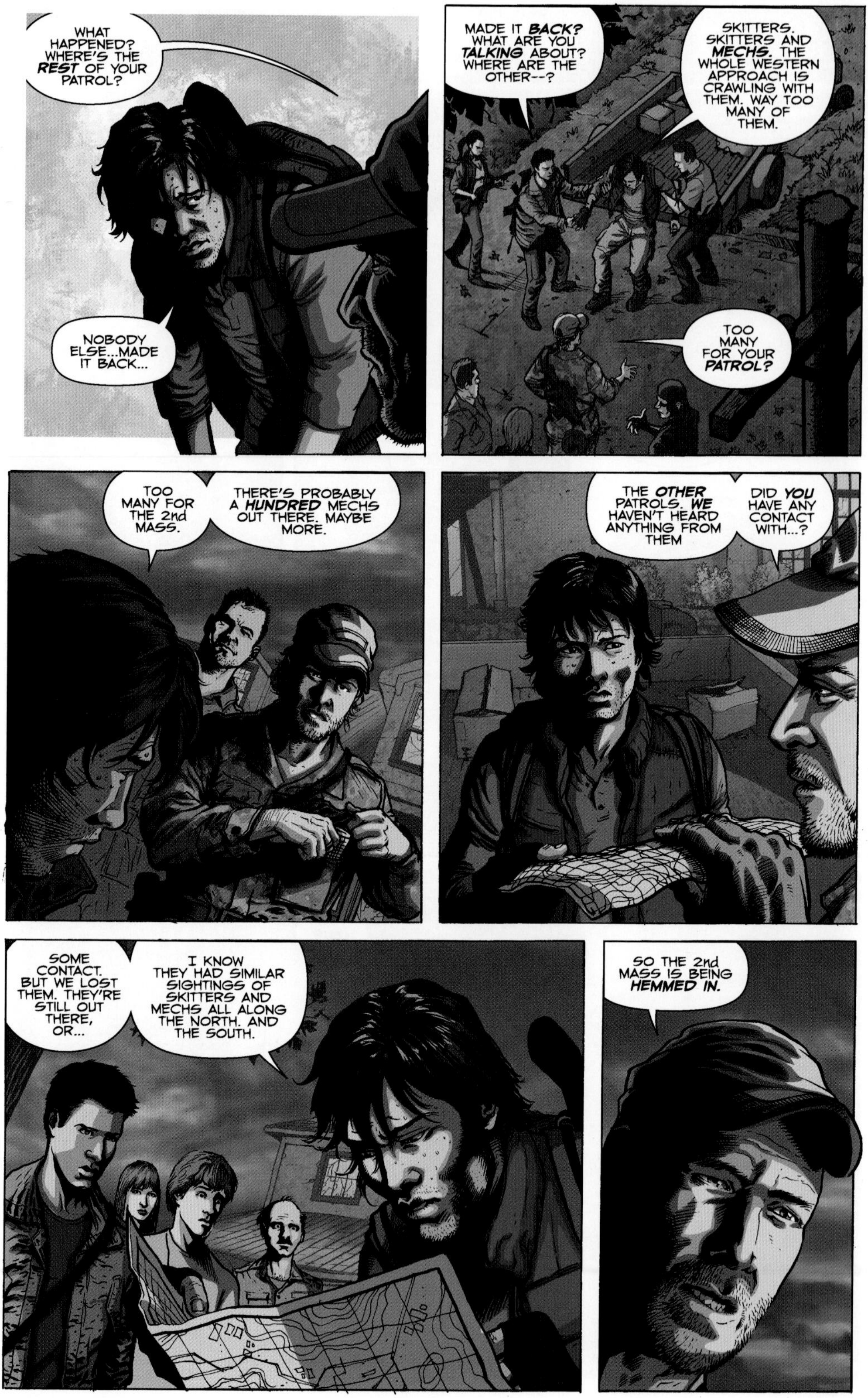
WHAT HAPPENED? WHERE'S THE REST OF YOUR PATROL?
NOBODY ELSE...MADE IT BACK...
MADE IT BACK? WHAT ARE YOU TALKING ABOUT? WHERE ARE THE OTHER--?
SKITTERS. SKITTERS AND MECHS. THE WHOLE WESTERN APPROACH IS CRAWLING WITH THEM. WAY TOO MANY OF THEM.
TOO MANY FOR YOUR PATROL?
TOO MANY FOR THE 2nd MASS.
THERE'S PROBABLY A HUNDRED MECHS OUT THERE. MAYBE MORE.
THE OTHER PATROLS. WE HAVEN'T HEARD ANYTHING FROM THEM
DID YOU HAVE ANY CONTACT WITH...?
SOME CONTACT. BUT WE LOST THEM. THEY'RE STILL OUT THERE, OR...
I KNOW THEY HAD SIMILAR SIGHTINGS OF SKITTERS AND MECHS ALL ALONG THE NORTH. AND THE SOUTH.
SO THE 2nd MASS IS BEING HEMMED IN.

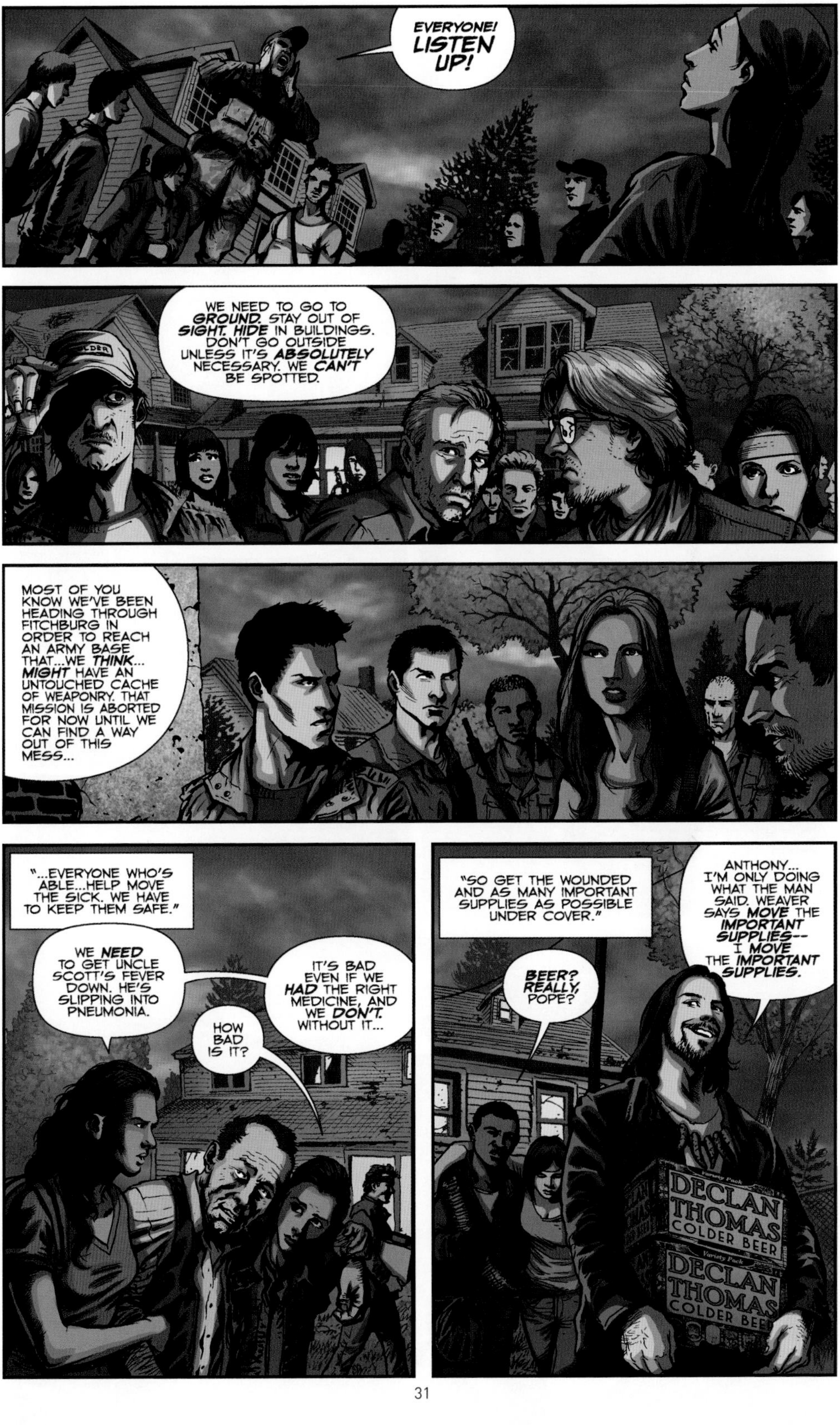

EVERYONE! LISTEN UP!
WE NEED TO GO TO GROUND. STAY OUT OF SIGHT. HIDE IN BUILDINGS. DON'T GO OUTSIDE UNLESS IT'S ABSOLUTELY NECESSARY. WE CAN'T BE SPOTTED.
MOST OF YOU KNOW WE'VE BEEN HEADING THROUGH FITCHBURG IN ORDER TO REACH AN ARMY BASE THAT...WE THINK... MIGHT HAVE AN UNTOUCHED CACHE OF WEAPONRY. THAT MISSION IS ABORTED FOR NOW UNTIL WE CAN FIND A WAY OUT OF THIS MESS...
"...EVERYONE WHO'S ABLE...HELP MOVE THE SICK. WE HAVE TO KEEP THEM SAFE."
WE NEED TO GET UNCLE SCOTT'S FEVER DOWN. HE'S SLIPPING INTO PNEUMONIA.
HOW BAD IS IT?
IT'S BAD EVEN IF WE HAD THE RIGHT MEDICINE, AND WE DON'T. WITHOUT IT...
"SO GET THE WOUNDED AND AS MANY IMPORTANT SUPPLIES AS POSSIBLE UNDER COVER."
BEER? REALLY, POPE?
ANTHONY... I'M ONLY DOING WHAT THE MAN SAID. WEAVER SAYS MOVE THE IMPORTANT SUPPLIES-- I MOVE THE IMPORTANT SUPPLIES.
DECLAN THOMAS COLDER BEER
DECLAN THOMAS COLDER BEER

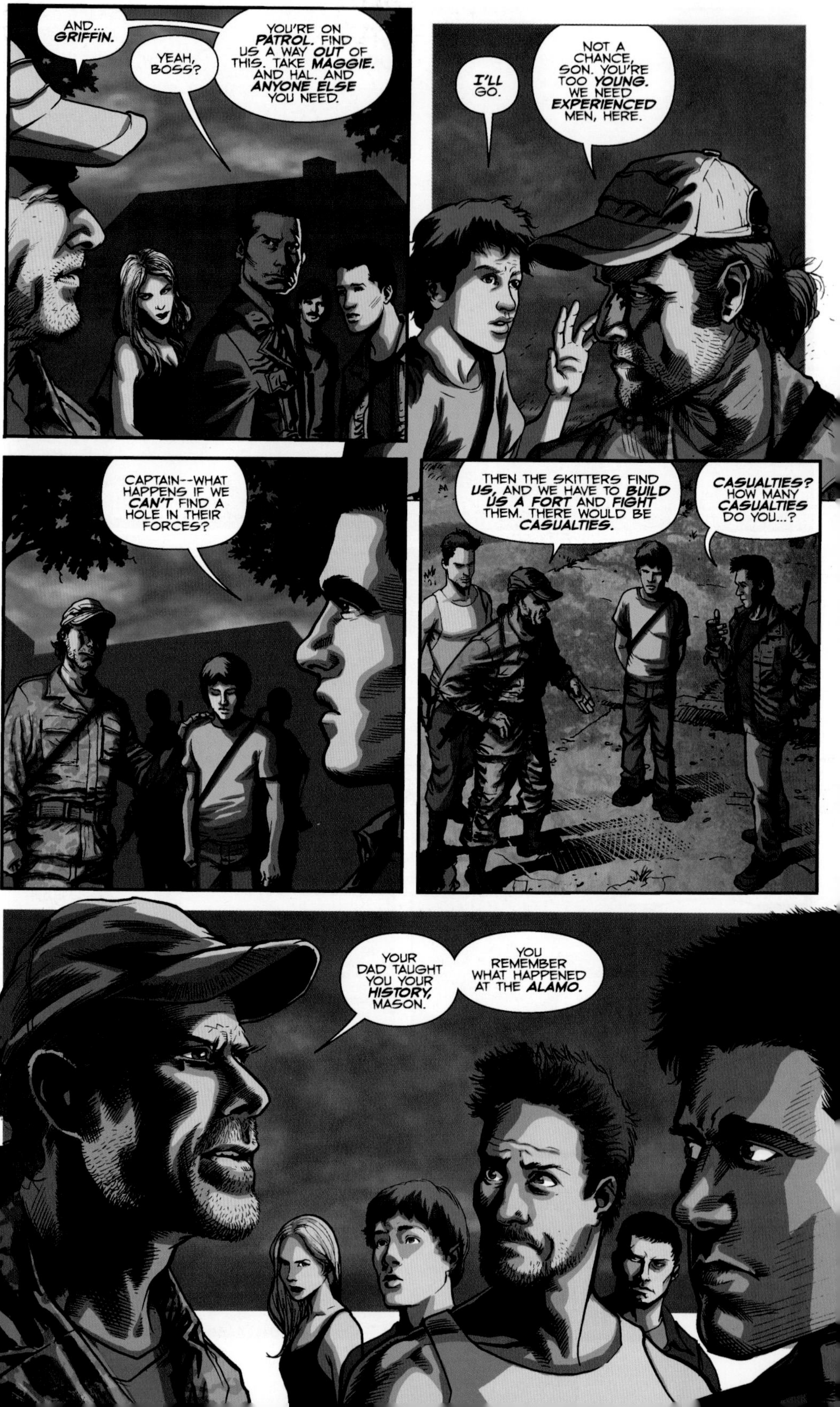
AND... GRIFFIN.
YEAH, BOSS?
YOU'RE ON PATROL. FIND US A WAY OUT OF THIS. TAKE MAGGIE. AND HAL. AND ANYONE ELSE YOU NEED.
I'LL GO.
NOT A CHANCE, SON. YOU'RE TOO YOUNG. WE NEED EXPERIENCED MEN, HERE.
CAPTAIN--WHAT HAPPENS IF WE CAN'T FIND A HOLE IN THEIR FORCES?
THEN THE SKITTERS FIND US, AND WE HAVE TO BUILD US A FORT AND FIGHT THEM. THERE WOULD BE CASUALTIES.
CASUALTIES? HOW MANY CASUALTIES DO YOU...?
YOUR DAD TAUGHT YOU YOUR HISTORY, MASON.
YOU REMEMBER WHAT HAPPENED AT THE ALAMO.

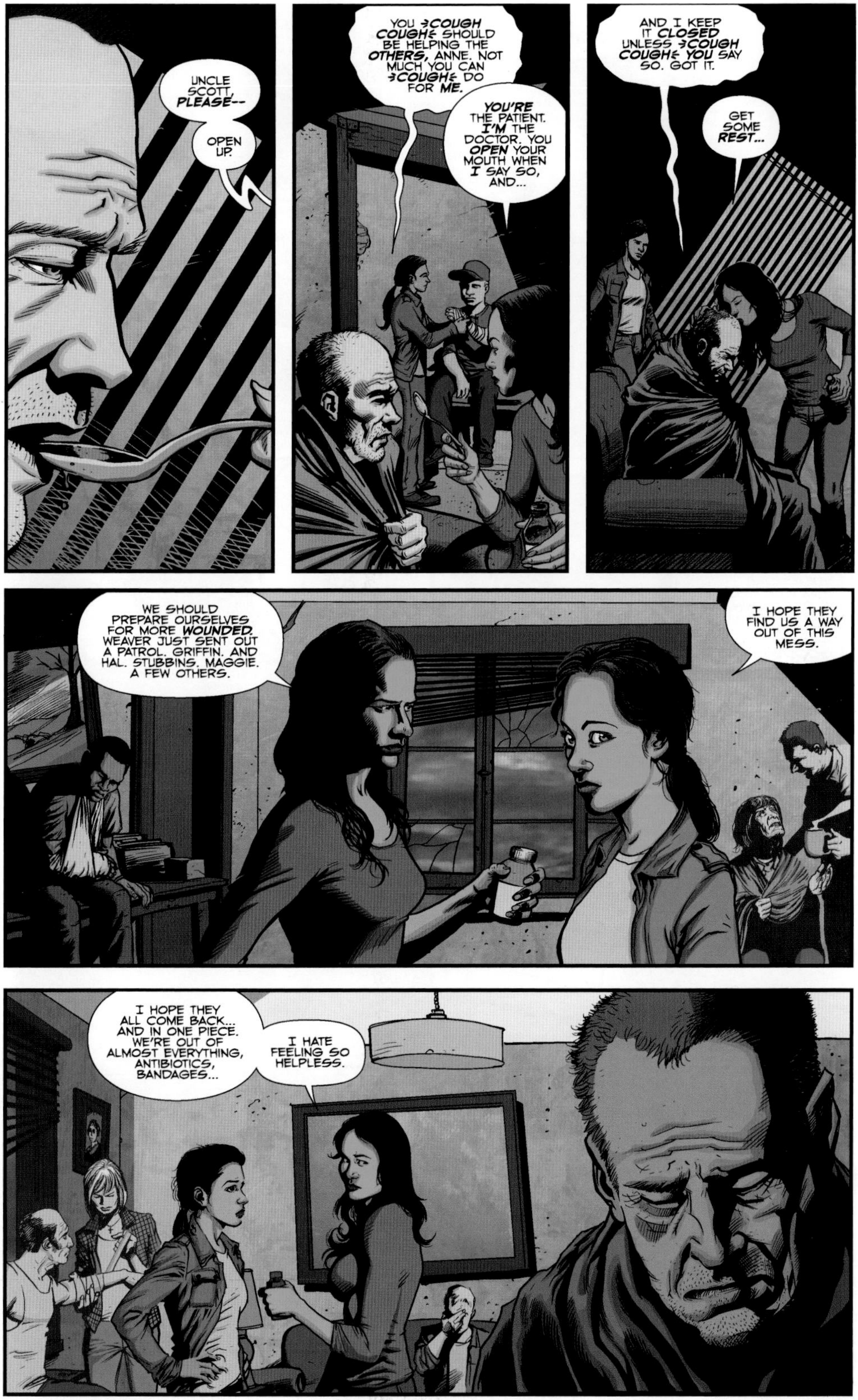
UNCLE SCOTT, PLEASE--
OPEN UP.
YOU ≥COUGH COUGH≤ SHOULD BE HELPING THE OTHERS, ANNE. NOT MUCH YOU CAN ≥COUGH≤ DO FOR ME.
YOU'RE THE PATIENT. I'M THE DOCTOR. YOU OPEN YOUR MOUTH WHEN I SAY SO, AND...
AND I KEEP IT CLOSED UNLESS ≥COUGH COUGH≤ YOU SAY SO. GOT IT.
GET SOME REST...
WE SHOULD PREPARE OURSELVES FOR MORE WOUNDED. WEAVER JUST SENT OUT A PATROL. GRIFFIN. AND HAL. STUBBINS. MAGGIE. A FEW OTHERS.
I HOPE THEY FIND US A WAY OUT OF THIS MESS.
I HOPE THEY ALL COME BACK... AND IN ONE PIECE. WE'RE OUT OF ALMOST EVERYTHING, ANTIBIOTICS, BANDAGES...
I HATE FEELING SO HELPLESS.

WE'RE *SCREWED.*

WHEN I WANT YOUR *TACTICAL* ADVICE, POPE, I'LL ASK FOR IT.

BUT DON'T HOLD YOUR *BREATH.*

YOU KNOW WELL AS I THAT IF WE DON'T GET THAT *WEAPON CACHE* FROM THE *ARMY DEPOT,* WE WON'T BE ABLE TO DO MUCH MORE THAN *KICK* MECHS IN THEIR *SHINS* AND GENERALLY *KISS OUR ASSES* GOODBYE.

I'M *NOT* RISKING ANOTHER SQUAD RIGHT NOW. WE CAN'T *RISK* THE LOSS OF--

RISK *ME.* THAT'S ALL I'M SAYING.

HELL... ALL THE TIMES YOU'VE WANTED ME *DEAD,* DON'T SEE WHY YOU'D CRY ALL THAT MUCH *NOW.*

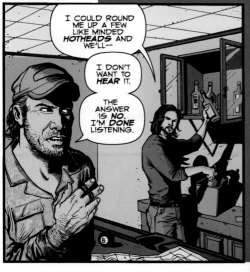

I COULD ROUND ME UP A FEW LIKE MINDED *HOTHEADS* AND WE'LL--

I DON'T WANT TO *HEAR* IT.

THE ANSWER IS *NO.* I'M *DONE* LISTENING.

FAIR ENOUGH, CHIEF COURSE, A MAN DOESN'T ALWAYS HAVE TO *HEAR* ABOUT SOMETHING IN ORDER TO HAVE IT *HAPPEN.*

HEY, COP. JUST 'CAUSE I SAVED YOUR *NECK*, DON'T THINK YOU GOTTA *WATCH OUT* FOR ME.

DON'T *FLATTER* YOURSELF, CONVICT.

I *KNOW* YOU. YOU'RE WORKING WEAVER FOR A *REASON*.

WELL, IT SEEMS THERE'S THIS ARMY DEPOT, AND...

WHY COULDN'T YOU *SHOOT?* WHEN THE SKITTER ALMOST HAD *DAI?*

...I'VE NEVER KILLED ANYTHING BEFORE. IT'S HARDER THAN IT LOOKS.

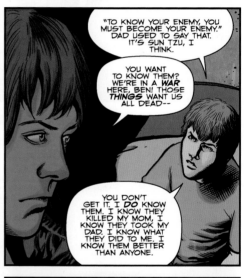

"TO KNOW YOUR ENEMY, YOU MUST BECOME YOUR ENEMY." DAD USED TO SAY THAT. IT'S SUN TZU, I THINK.

YOU WANT TO KNOW THEM? WE'RE IN A *WAR* HERE, BEN! THOSE *THINGS* WANT US ALL DEAD--

YOU DON'T GET IT. I *DO* KNOW THEM. I KNOW THEY KILLED MY MOM, I KNOW THEY TOOK MY DAD. I KNOW WHAT THEY DID TO ME. I KNOW THEM BETTER THAN ANYONE.

I *HATE* THEM. I HATE THEM MORE THAN YOU CAN POSSIBLY KNOW.

AND I'M GOING TO KILL THEM ALL.

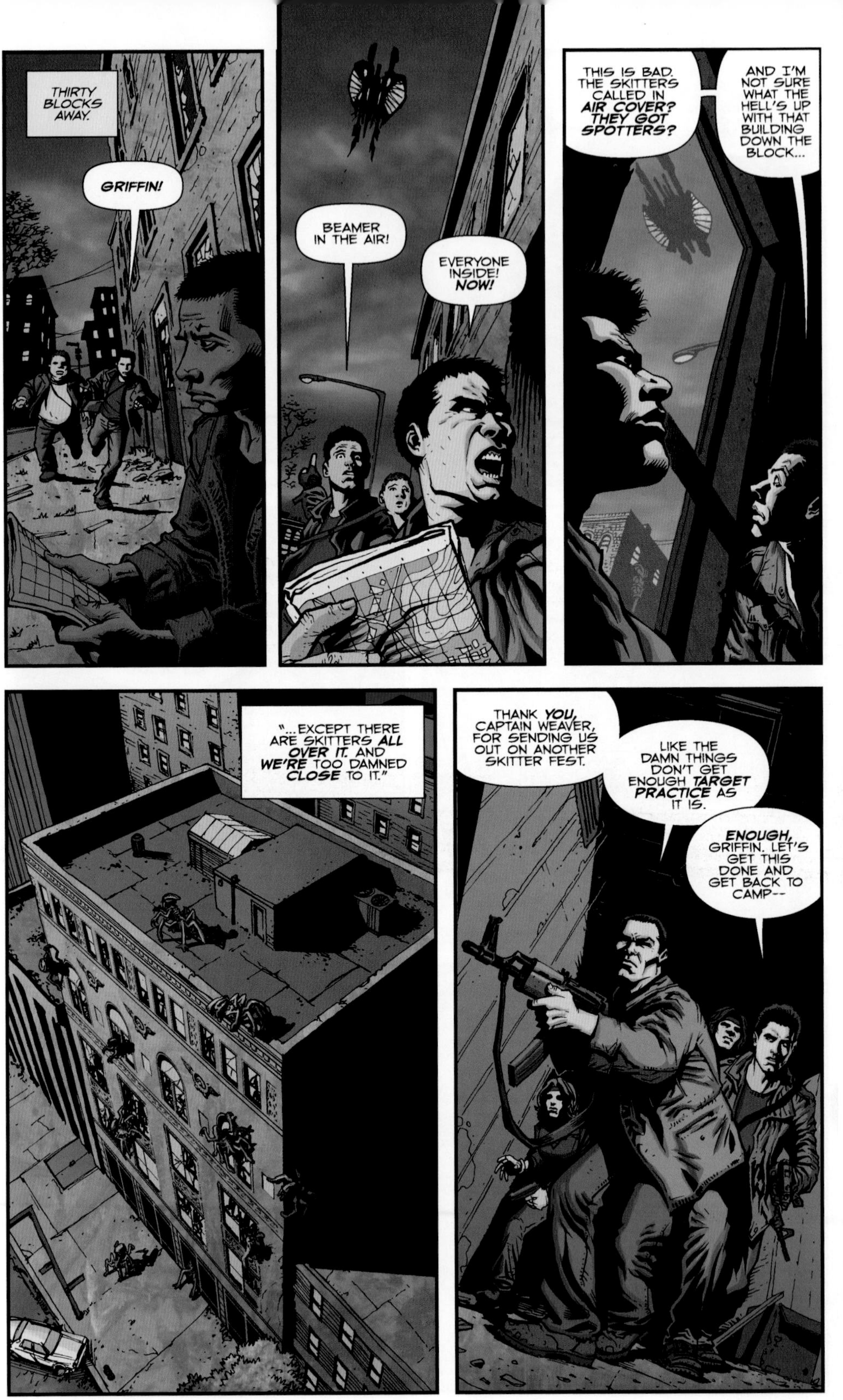
THIRTY BLOCKS AWAY.
GRIFFIN!
BEAMER IN THE AIR!
EVERYONE INSIDE! NOW!
THIS IS BAD. THE SKITTERS CALLED IN AIR COVER? THEY GOT SPOTTERS?
AND I'M NOT SURE WHAT THE HELL'S UP WITH THAT BUILDING DOWN THE BLOCK...
"...EXCEPT THERE ARE SKITTERS ALL OVER IT. AND WE'RE TOO DAMNED CLOSE TO IT."
THANK YOU, CAPTAIN WEAVER, FOR SENDING US OUT ON ANOTHER SKITTER FEST.
LIKE THE DAMN THINGS DON'T GET ENOUGH TARGET PRACTICE AS IT IS.
ENOUGH, GRIFFIN. LET'S GET THIS DONE AND GET BACK TO CAMP--

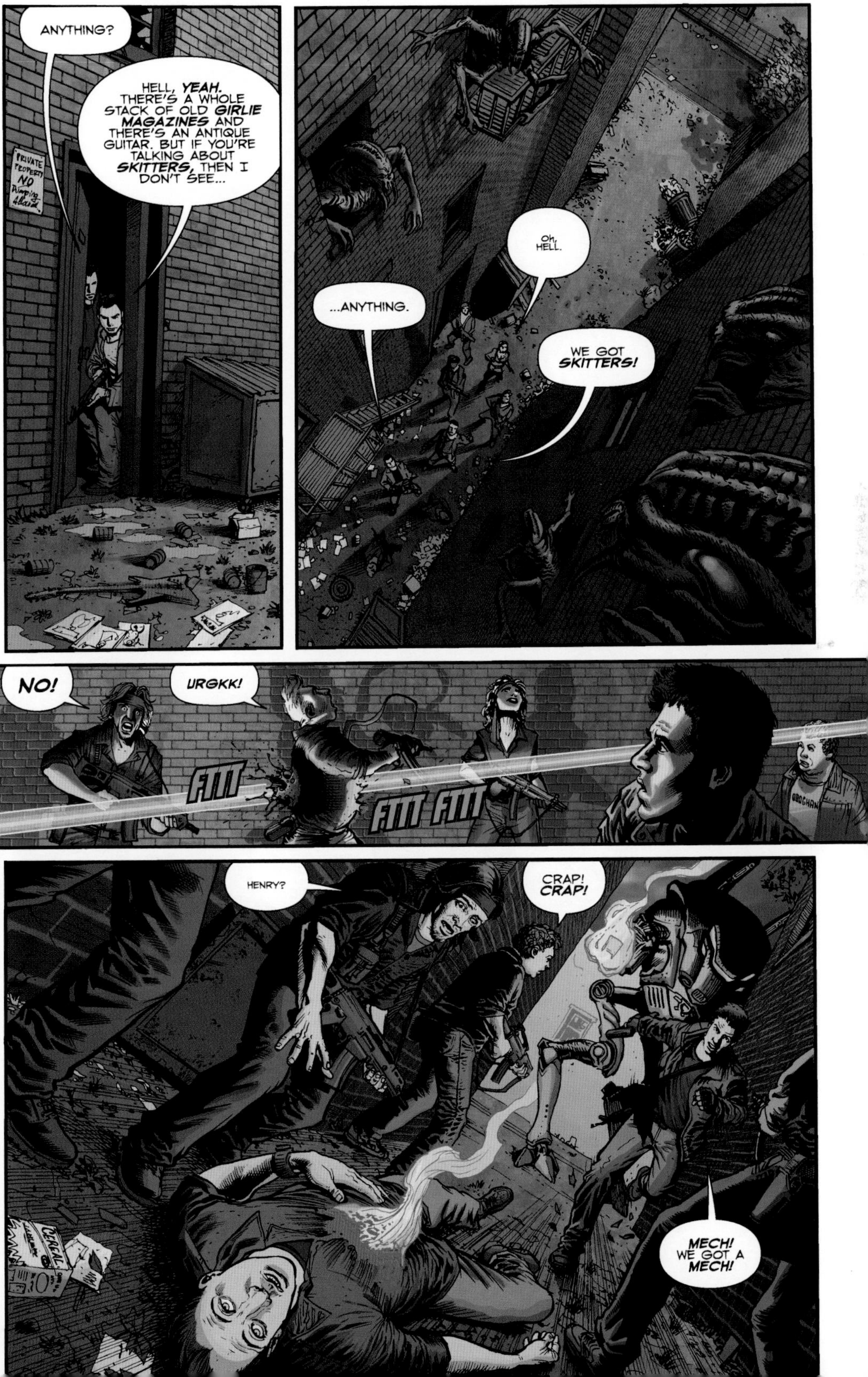
ANYTHING?
HELL, YEAH. THERE'S A WHOLE STACK OF OLD GIRLIE MAGAZINES AND THERE'S AN ANTIQUE GUITAR. BUT IF YOU'RE TALKING ABOUT SKITTERS, THEN I DON'T SEE...
...ANYTHING.
Oh, HELL.
WE GOT SKITTERS!
NO!
URGKK!
FTTT
FTTT FTTT
HENRY?
CRAP! CRAP!
MECH! WE GOT A MECH!

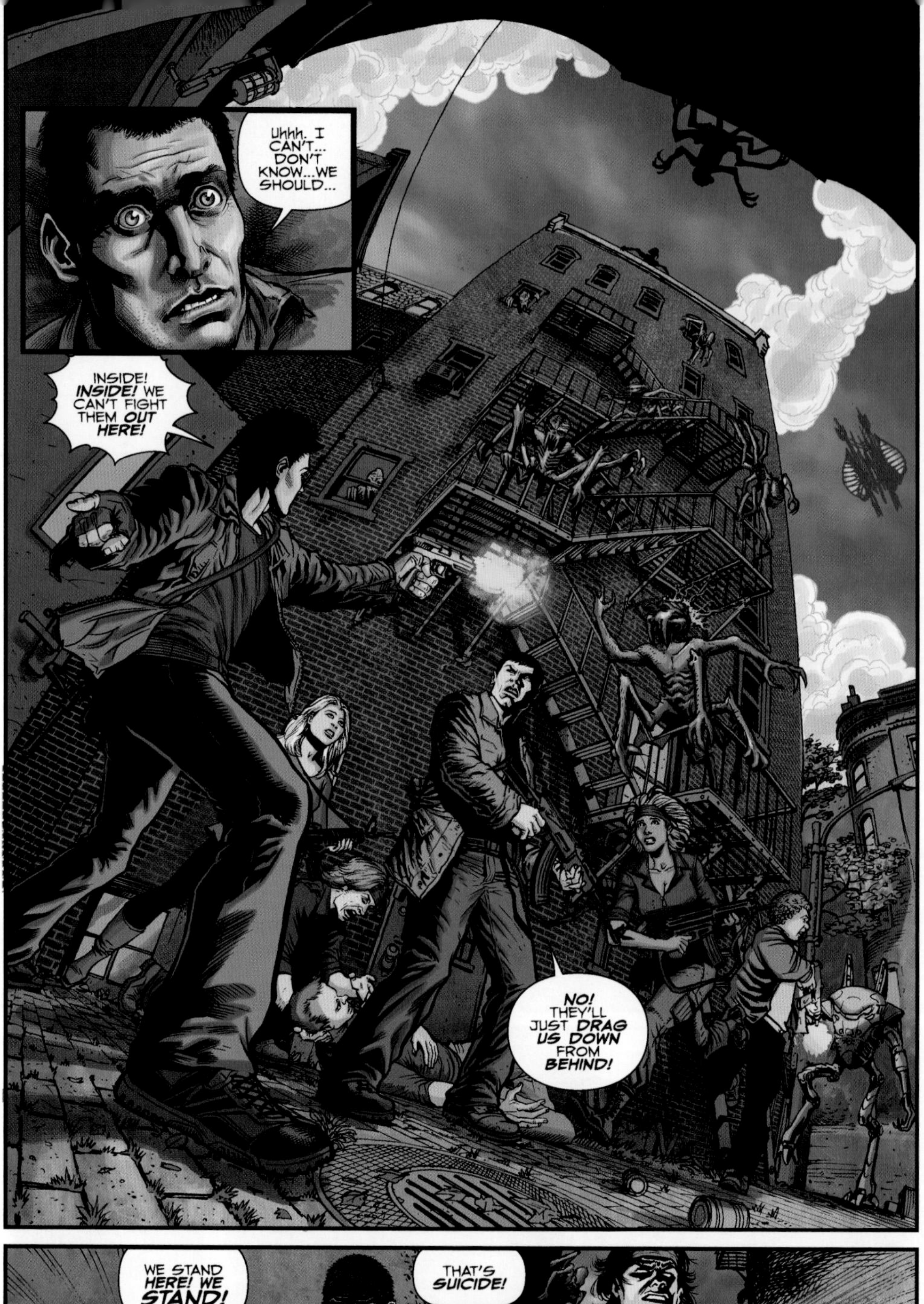
UHHH. I CAN'T... DON'T KNOW...WE SHOULD...
INSIDE! INSIDE! WE CAN'T FIGHT THEM OUT HERE!
NO! THEY'LL JUST DRAG US DOWN FROM BEHIND!

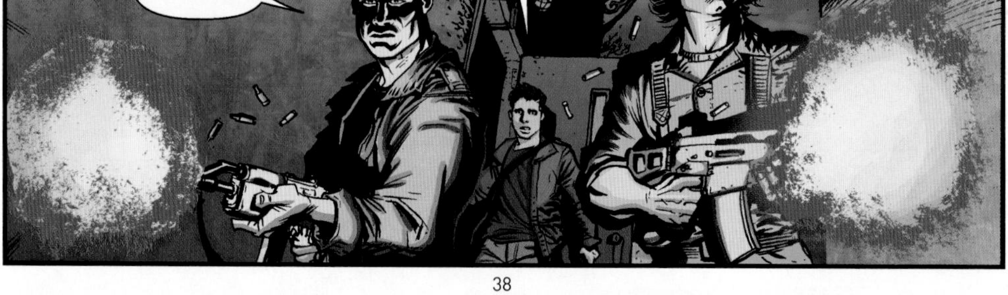
WE STAND HERE! WE STAND!
THAT'S SUICIDE!

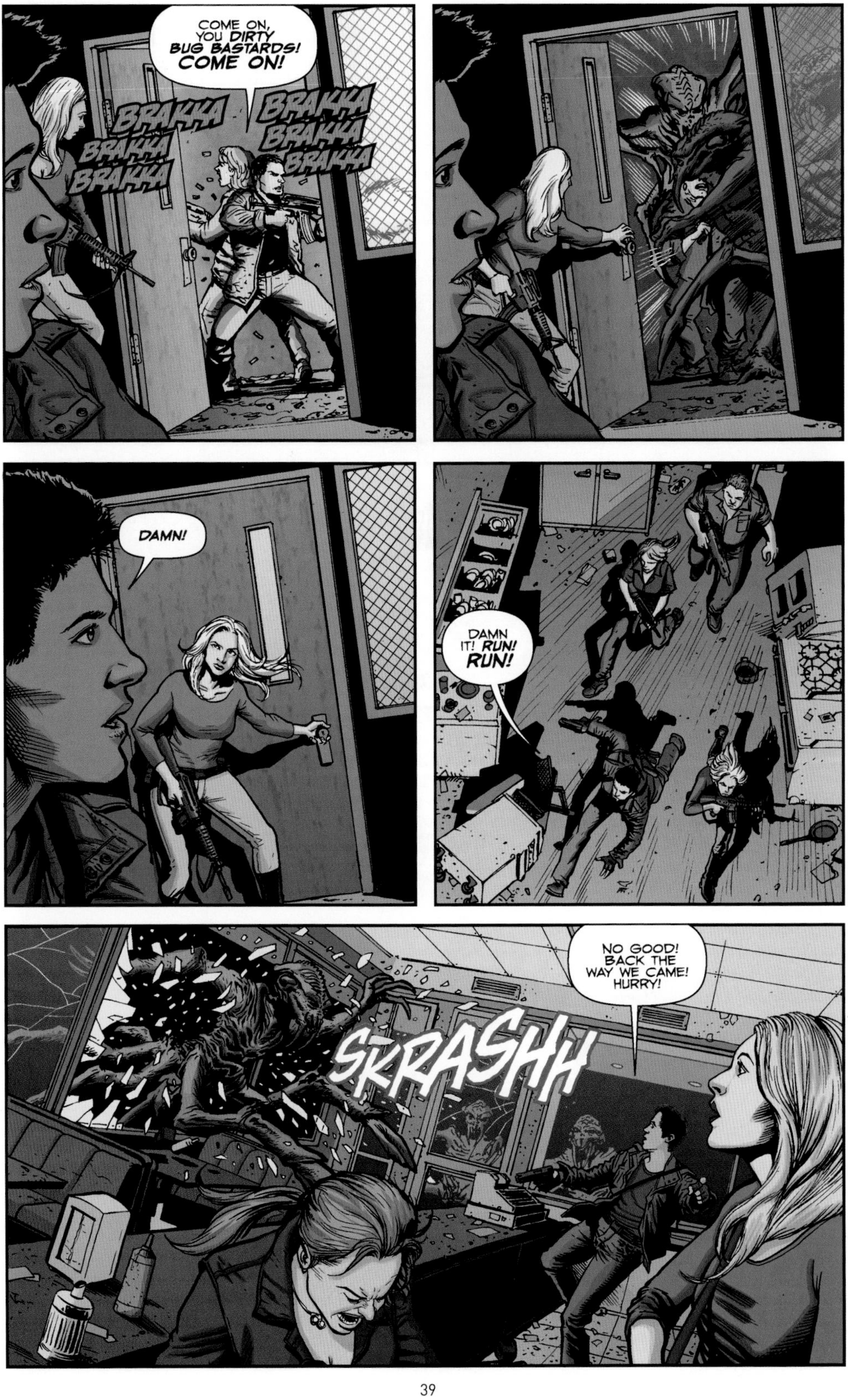
COME ON, YOU DIRTY BUG BASTARDS! COME ON!
BRAKKA BRAKKA BRAKKA
BRAKKA BRAKKA BRAKKA
DAMN!
DAMN IT! RUN! RUN!
NO GOOD! BACK THE WAY WE CAME! HURRY!
SKRASHH

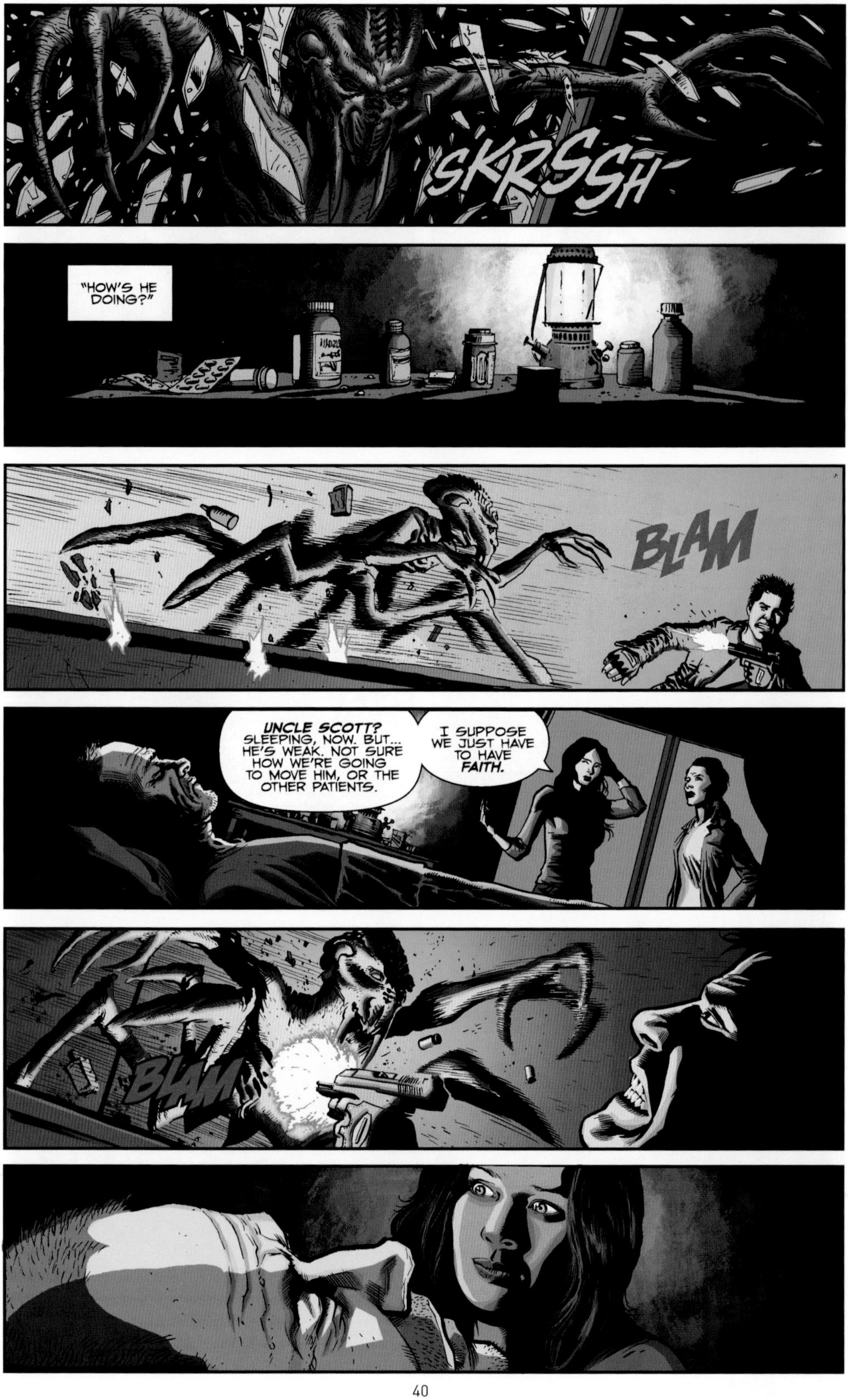
SKRSSH
"HOW'S HE DOING?"
BLAM
UNCLE SCOTT? SLEEPING, NOW. BUT... HE'S WEAK. NOT SURE HOW WE'RE GOING TO MOVE HIM, OR THE OTHER PATIENTS.
I SUPPOSE WE JUST HAVE TO HAVE FAITH.
BLAM

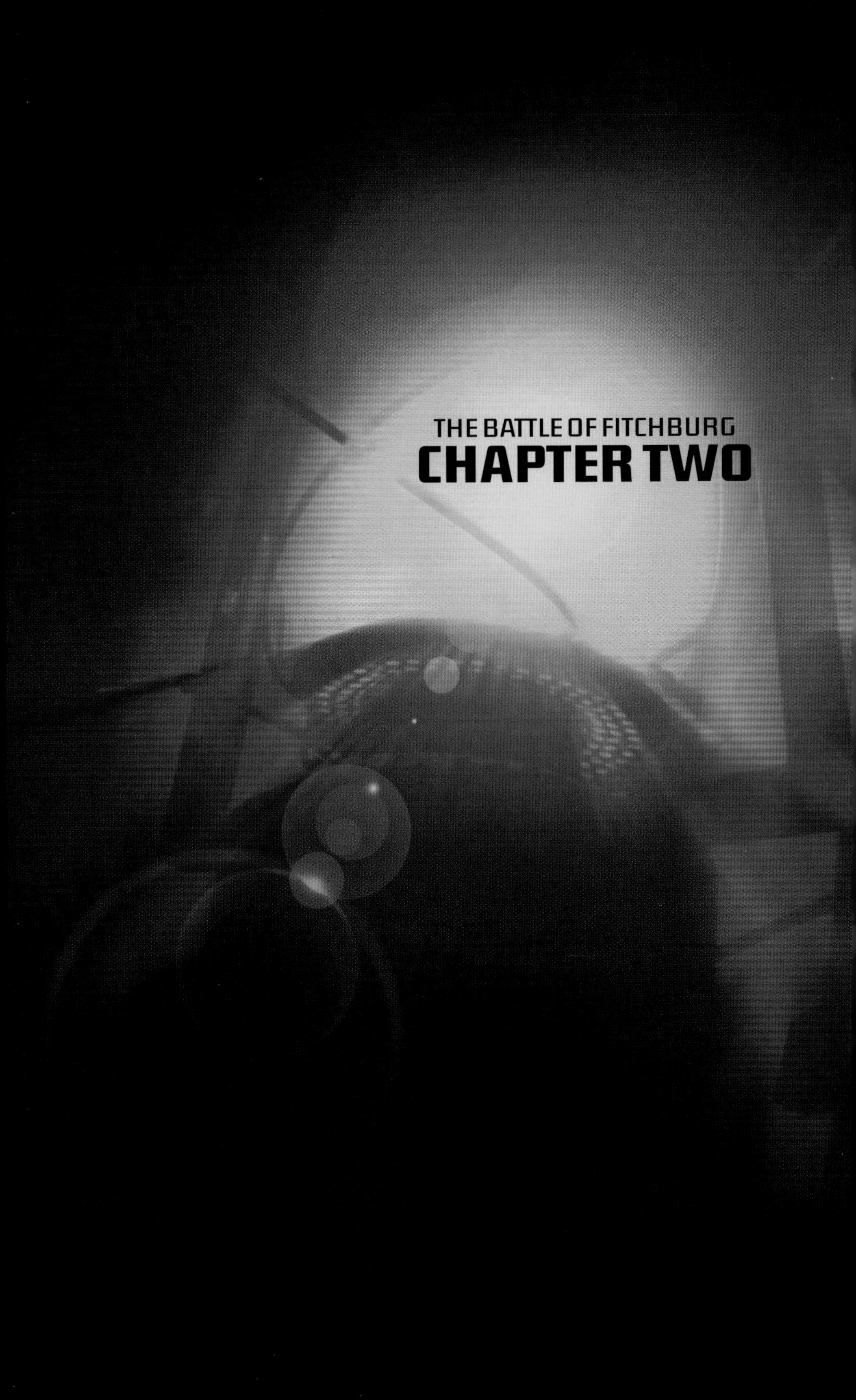

THE BATTLE OF FITCHBURG

CHAPTER TWO

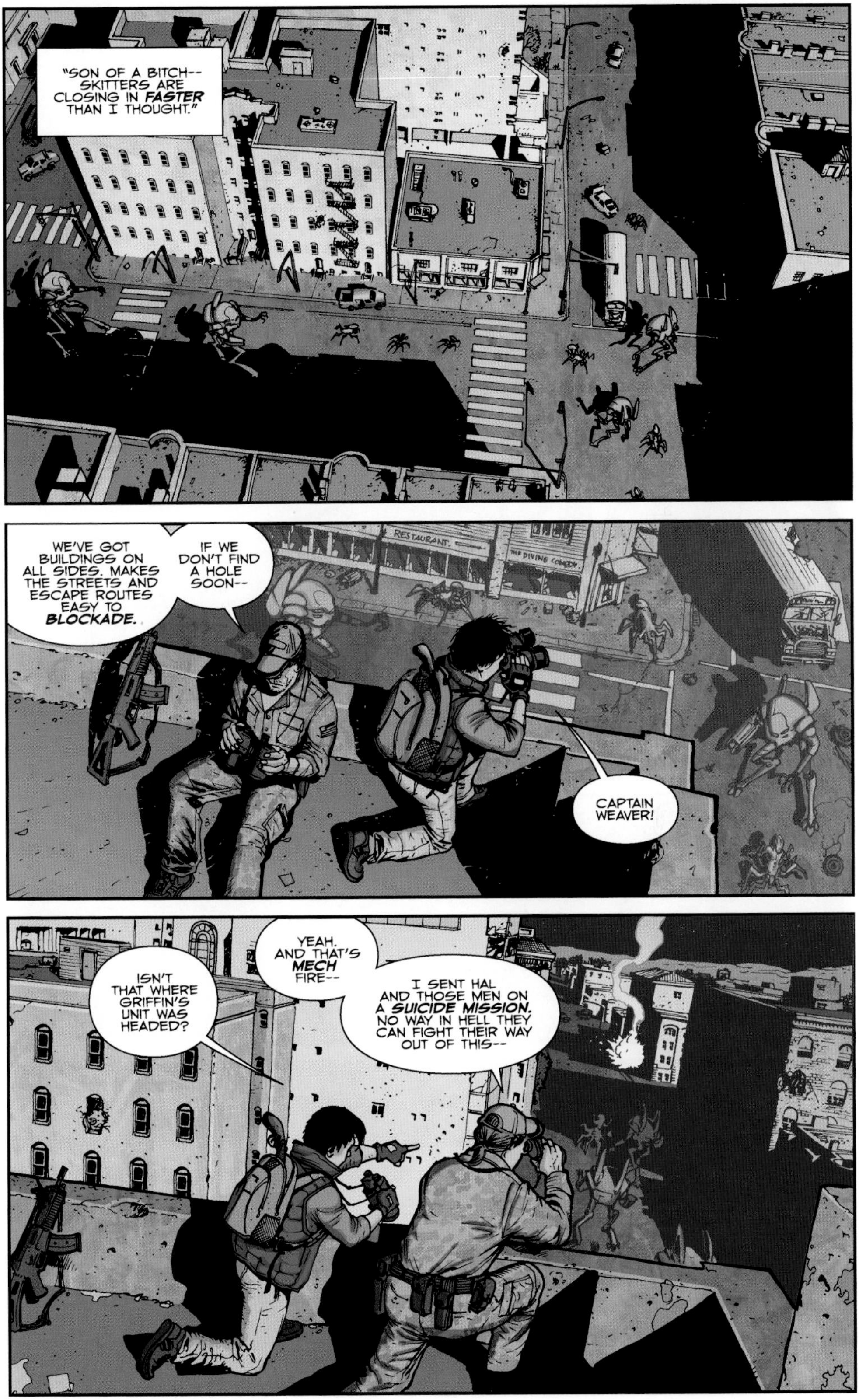
"SON OF A BITCH-- SKITTERS ARE CLOSING IN FASTER THAN I THOUGHT."
WE'VE GOT BUILDINGS ON ALL SIDES. MAKES THE STREETS AND ESCAPE ROUTES EASY TO BLOCKADE.
IF WE DON'T FIND A HOLE SOON--
RESTAURANT
THE DIVINE COMEDY
CAPTAIN WEAVER!
ISN'T THAT WHERE GRIFFIN'S UNIT WAS HEADED?
YEAH. AND THAT'S MECH FIRE--
I SENT HAL AND THOSE MEN ON A SUICIDE MISSION. NO WAY IN HELL THEY CAN FIGHT THEIR WAY OUT OF THIS--

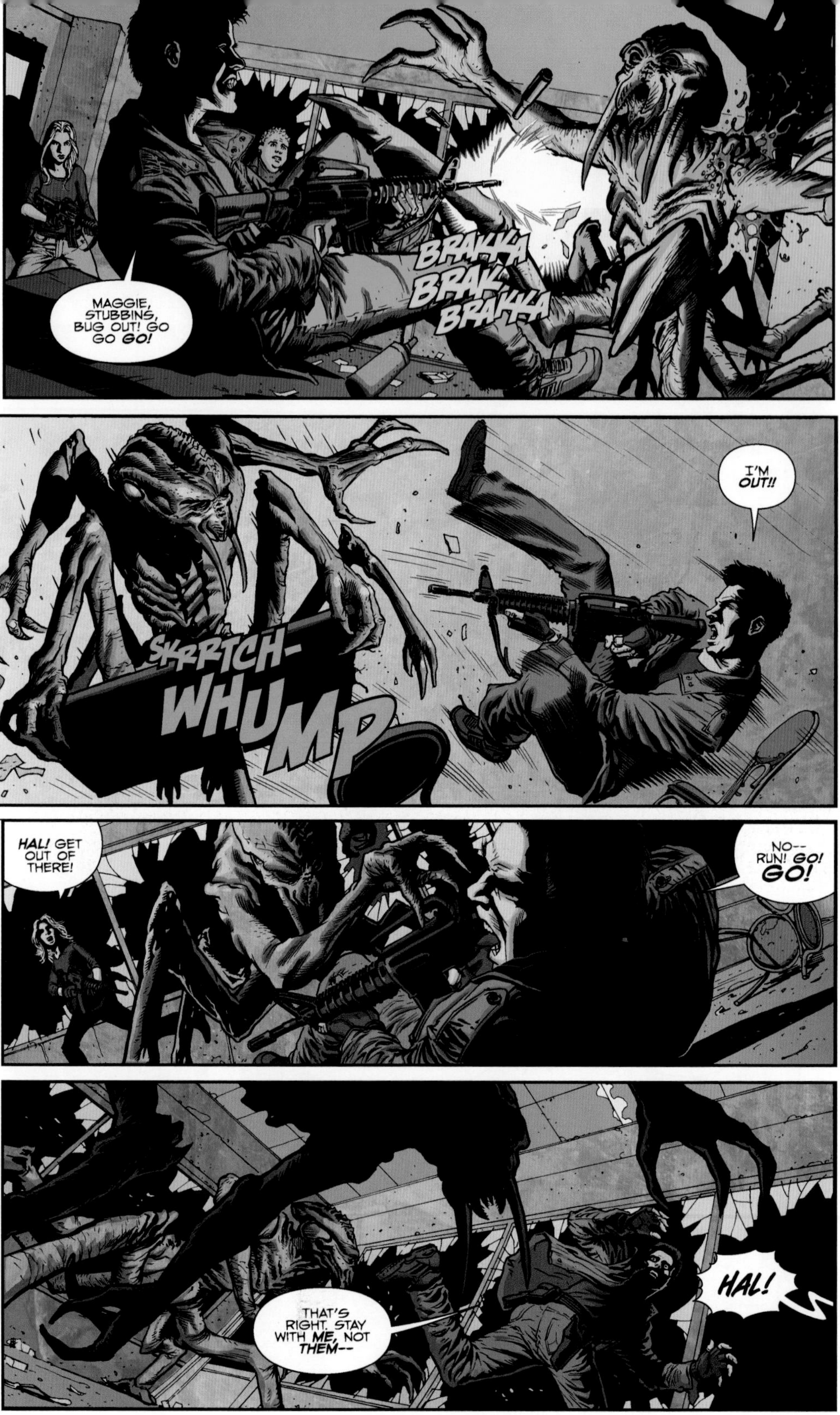
MAGGIE, STUBBINS, BUG OUT! GO GO GO!
BRAKKA BRAK BRAKKA
I'M OUT!!
SKRRTCH-WHUMP
HAL! GET OUT OF THERE!
NO-- RUN! GO! GO!
HAL!
THAT'S RIGHT. STAY WITH ME, NOT THEM--

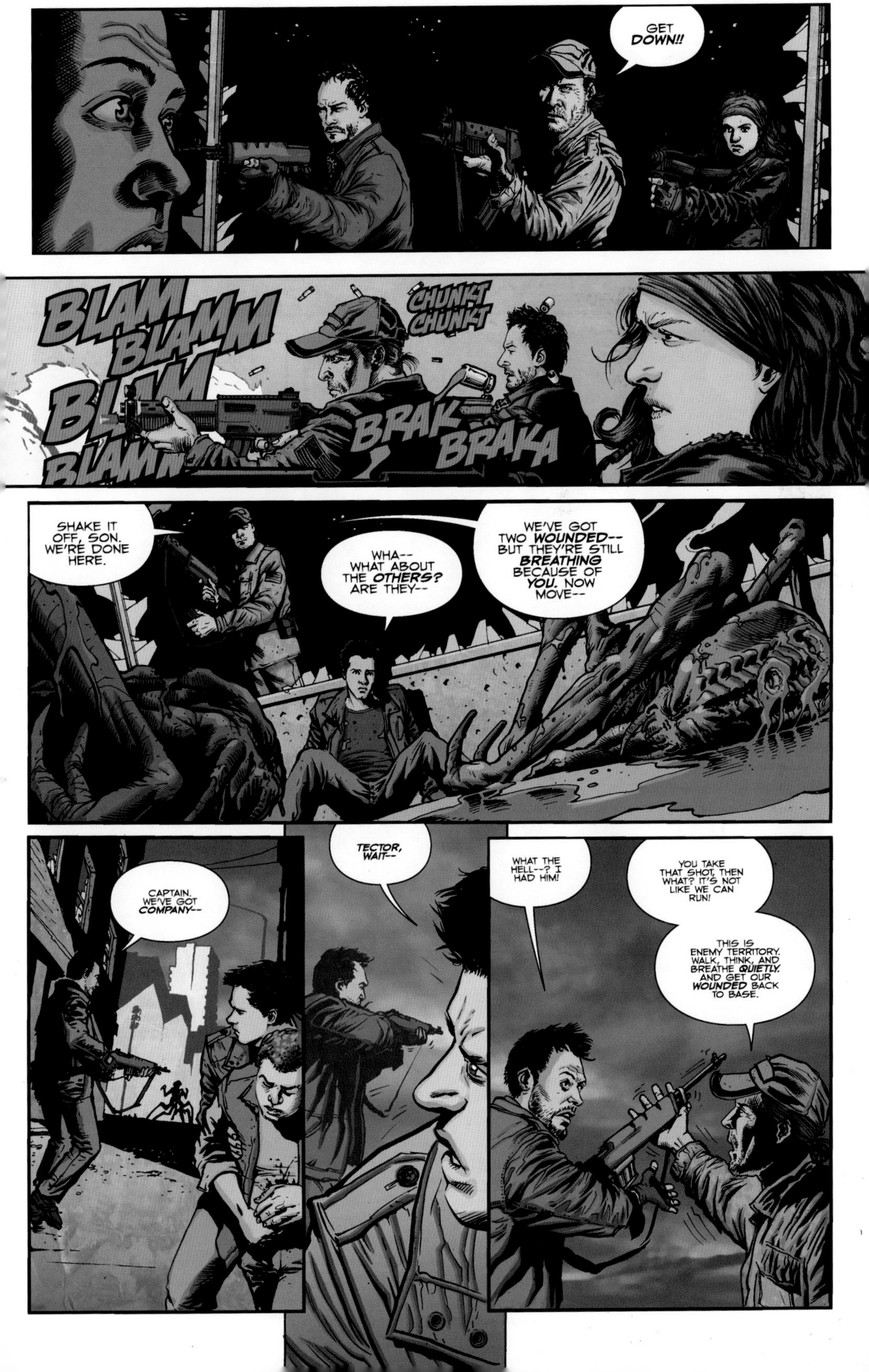
GET DOWN!!
BLAM BLAMM BLAM BLAMM
CHUNKT CHUNKT
BRAK BRAKA
SHAKE IT OFF, SON. WE'RE DONE HERE.
WHA-- WHAT ABOUT THE OTHERS? ARE THEY--
WE'VE GOT TWO WOUNDED-- BUT THEY'RE STILL BREATHING BECAUSE OF YOU. NOW MOVE--
CAPTAIN. WE'VE GOT COMPANY--
TECTOR, WAIT--
WHAT THE HELL--? I HAD HIM!
YOU TAKE THAT SHOT, THEN WHAT? IT'S NOT LIKE WE CAN RUN!
THIS IS ENEMY TERRITORY. WALK, THINK, AND BREATHE QUIETLY. AND GET OUR WOUNDED BACK TO BASE.

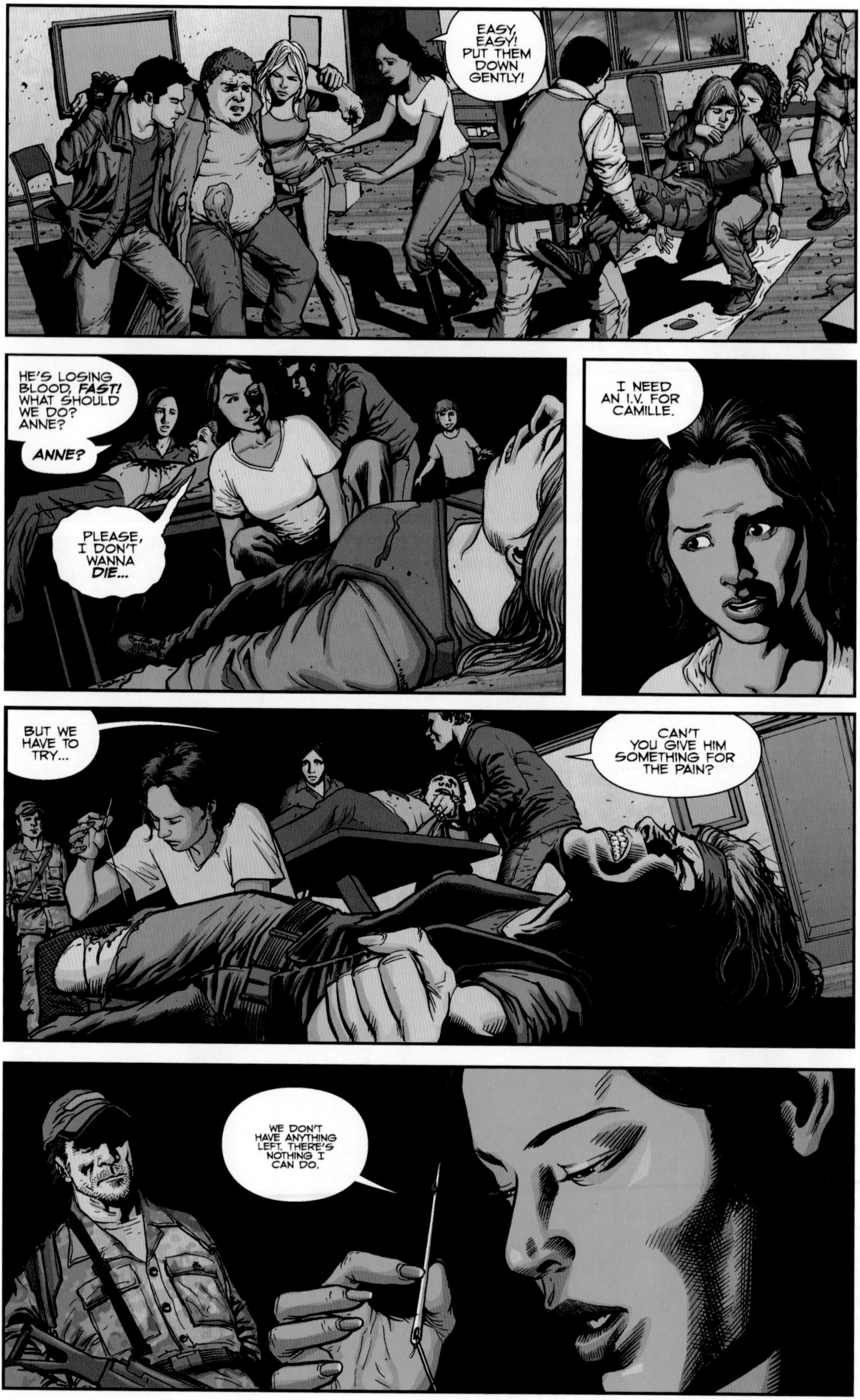
EASY, EASY! PUT THEM DOWN GENTLY!
HE'S LOSING BLOOD, FAST! WHAT SHOULD WE DO? ANNE?
ANNE?
PLEASE, I DON'T WANNA DIE...
I NEED AN I.V. FOR CAMILLE.
BUT WE HAVE TO TRY...
CAN'T YOU GIVE HIM SOMETHING FOR THE PAIN?
WE DON'T HAVE ANYTHING LEFT. THERE'S NOTHING I CAN DO.

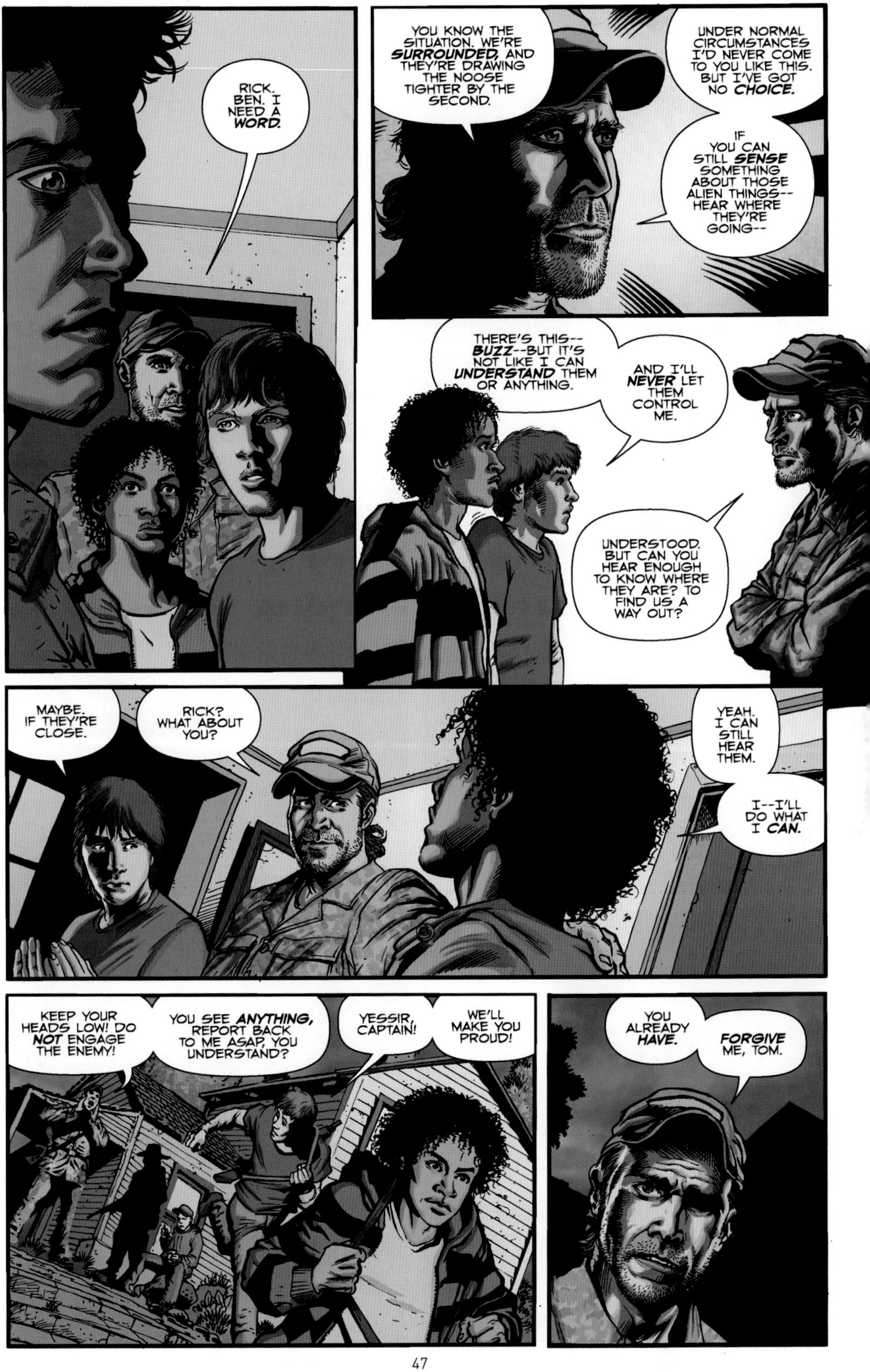
RICK. BEN. I NEED A WORD.
YOU KNOW THE SITUATION. WE'RE SURROUNDED, AND THEY'RE DRAWING THE NOOSE TIGHTER BY THE SECOND.
UNDER NORMAL CIRCUMSTANCES I'D NEVER COME TO YOU LIKE THIS. BUT I'VE GOT NO CHOICE.
IF YOU CAN STILL SENSE SOMETHING ABOUT THOSE ALIEN THINGS-- HEAR WHERE THEY'RE GOING--
THERE'S THIS-- BUZZ--BUT IT'S NOT LIKE I CAN UNDERSTAND THEM OR ANYTHING.
AND I'LL NEVER LET THEM CONTROL ME.
UNDERSTOOD. BUT CAN YOU HEAR ENOUGH TO KNOW WHERE THEY ARE? TO FIND US A WAY OUT?
MAYBE. IF THEY'RE CLOSE.
RICK? WHAT ABOUT YOU?
YEAH. I CAN STILL HEAR THEM.
I--I'LL DO WHAT I CAN.
KEEP YOUR HEADS LOW! DO NOT ENGAGE THE ENEMY!
YOU SEE ANYTHING, REPORT BACK TO ME ASAP, YOU UNDERSTAND?
YESSIR, CAPTAIN!
WE'LL MAKE YOU PROUD!
YOU ALREADY HAVE.
FORGIVE ME, TOM.

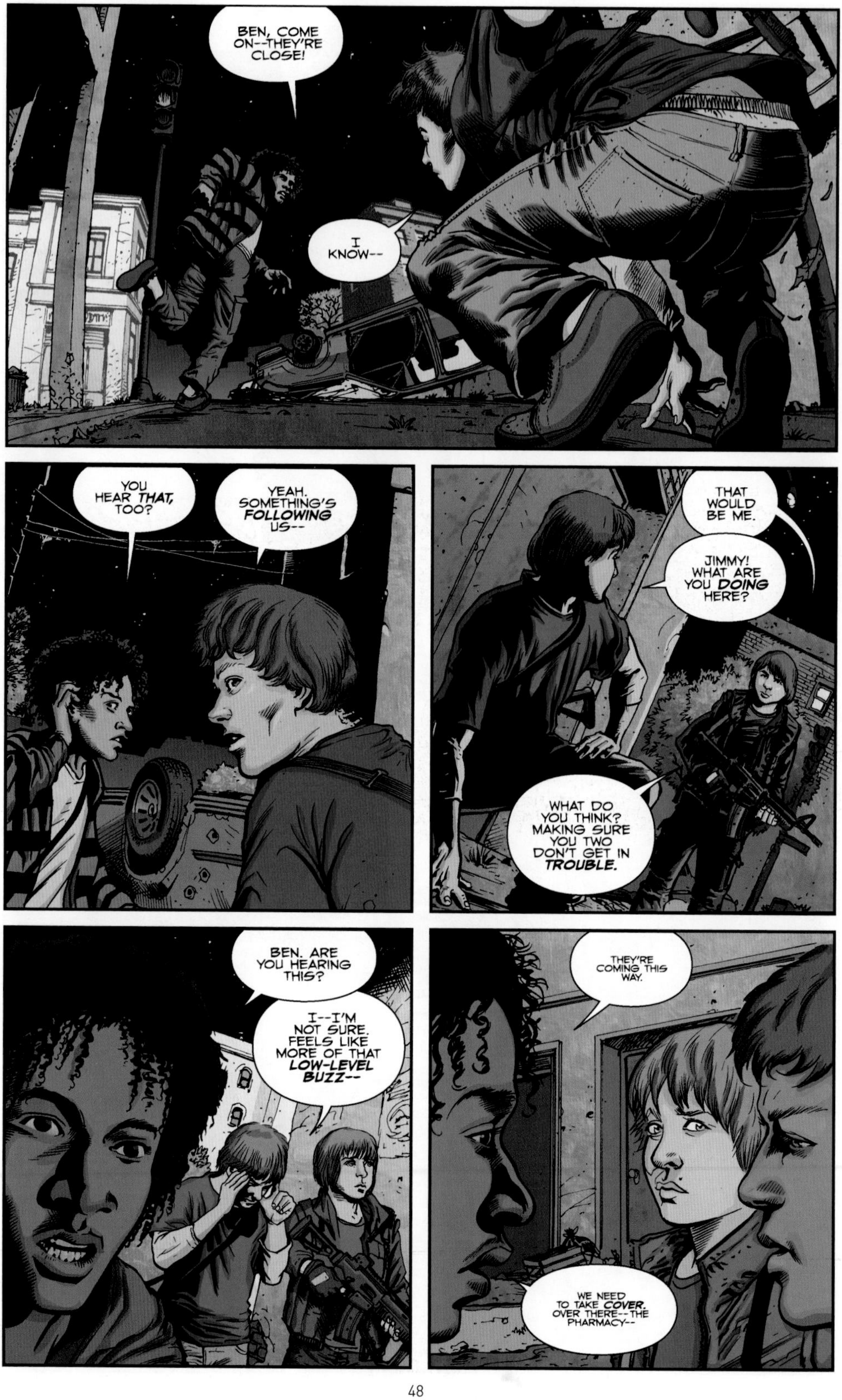
BEN, COME ON--THEY'RE CLOSE!
I KNOW--
YOU HEAR THAT, TOO?
YEAH. SOMETHING'S FOLLOWING US--
THAT WOULD BE ME.
JIMMY! WHAT ARE YOU DOING HERE?
WHAT DO YOU THINK? MAKING SURE YOU TWO DON'T GET IN TROUBLE.
BEN. ARE YOU HEARING THIS?
I--I'M NOT SURE. FEELS LIKE MORE OF THAT LOW-LEVEL BUZZ--
THEY'RE COMING THIS WAY.
WE NEED TO TAKE COVER. OVER THERE--THE PHARMACY--

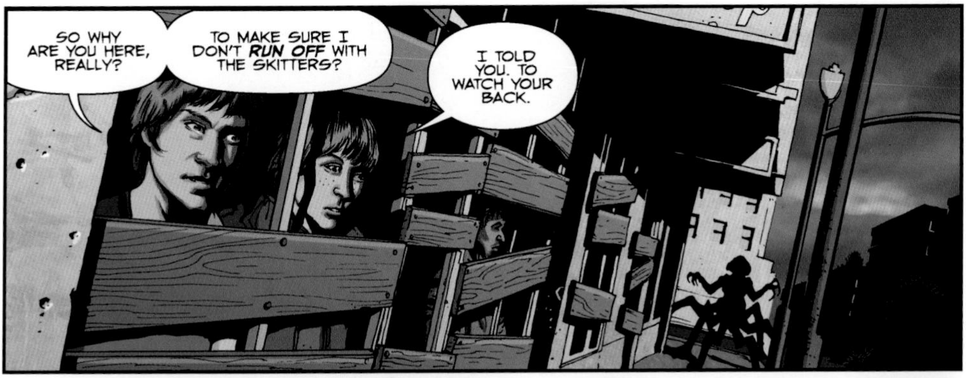
SO WHY ARE YOU HERE, REALLY?
TO MAKE SURE I DON'T **RUN OFF** WITH THE SKITTERS?
I TOLD YOU. TO WATCH YOUR BACK.

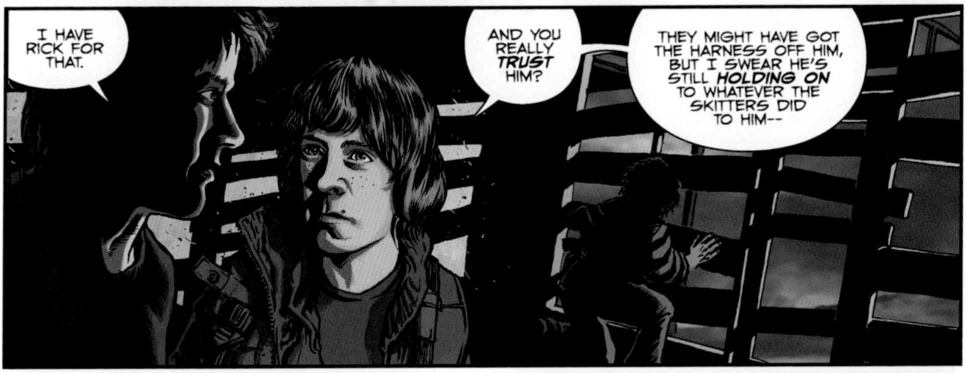
I HAVE RICK FOR THAT.
AND YOU REALLY **TRUST** HIM?
THEY MIGHT HAVE GOT THE HARNESS OFF HIM, BUT I SWEAR HE'S STILL **HOLDING ON** TO WHATEVER THE SKITTERS DID TO HIM--

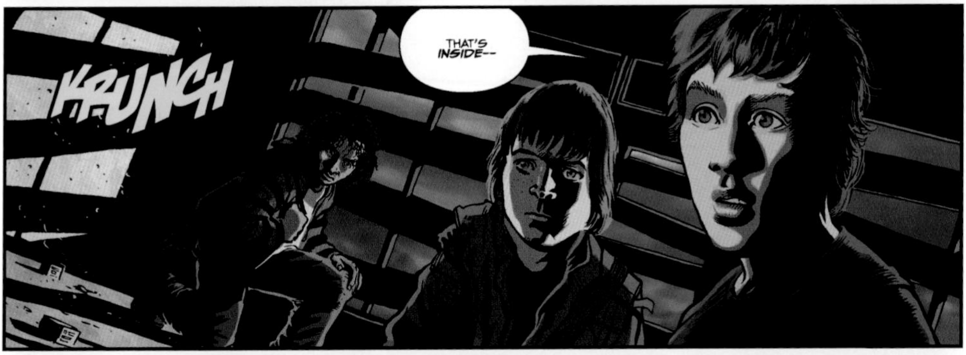
KRUNCH
THAT'S *INSIDE*--

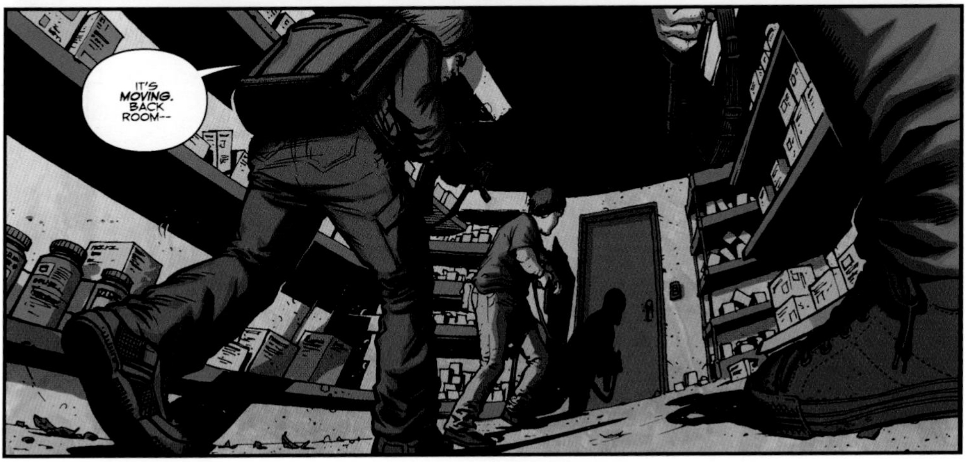
IT'S **MOVING.** BACK ROOM--

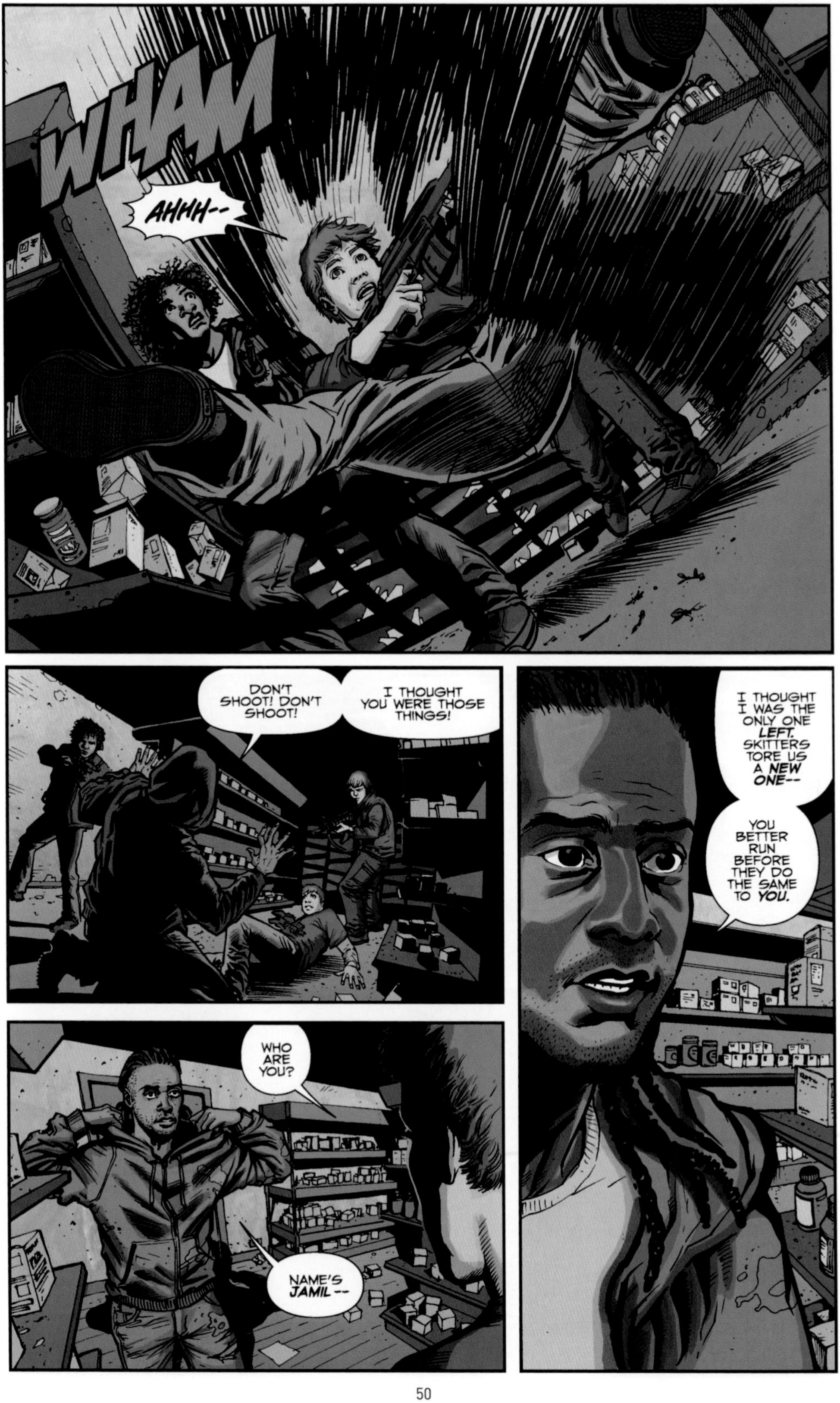
WHAM
AHHH--
DON'T SHOOT! DON'T SHOOT!
I THOUGHT YOU WERE THOSE THINGS!
WHO ARE YOU?
NAME'S JAMIL--
I THOUGHT I WAS THE ONLY ONE LEFT. SKITTERS TORE US A NEW ONE--
YOU BETTER RUN BEFORE THEY DO THE SAME TO YOU.

HOPE TO HELL BEN AND RICK FIND US A **HOLE** IN THE PERIMETER--

ALIEN THINGS ARE **CRAWLIN'** ALL OVER US!

STOMP STOMP STOMP

-COUGH-

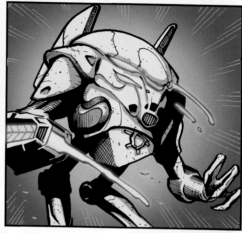

Ssshhhhh.

WEAVER GOT US **INTO** THIS MESS--

THEY'RE NOT GONNA **STOP** UNTIL WE'RE ALL **DEAD!**

WEAVER WILL FIND US A WAY OUT, **YOU KNOW** HE WILL--

WE CAN'T RUN FAST ENOUGH, CAN'T FIGHT **HARD** ENOUGH--

ONLY A MATTER OF TIME BEFORE WE'RE **FOUND.**

TOO BAD ALL THOSE **GUNS** ARE STILL SITTING IN THAT ARMY DEPOT.

IF **SOMEONE** HAD SENT ME TO **GET** THEM, WE'D HAVE A **FIGHTING CHANCE.**

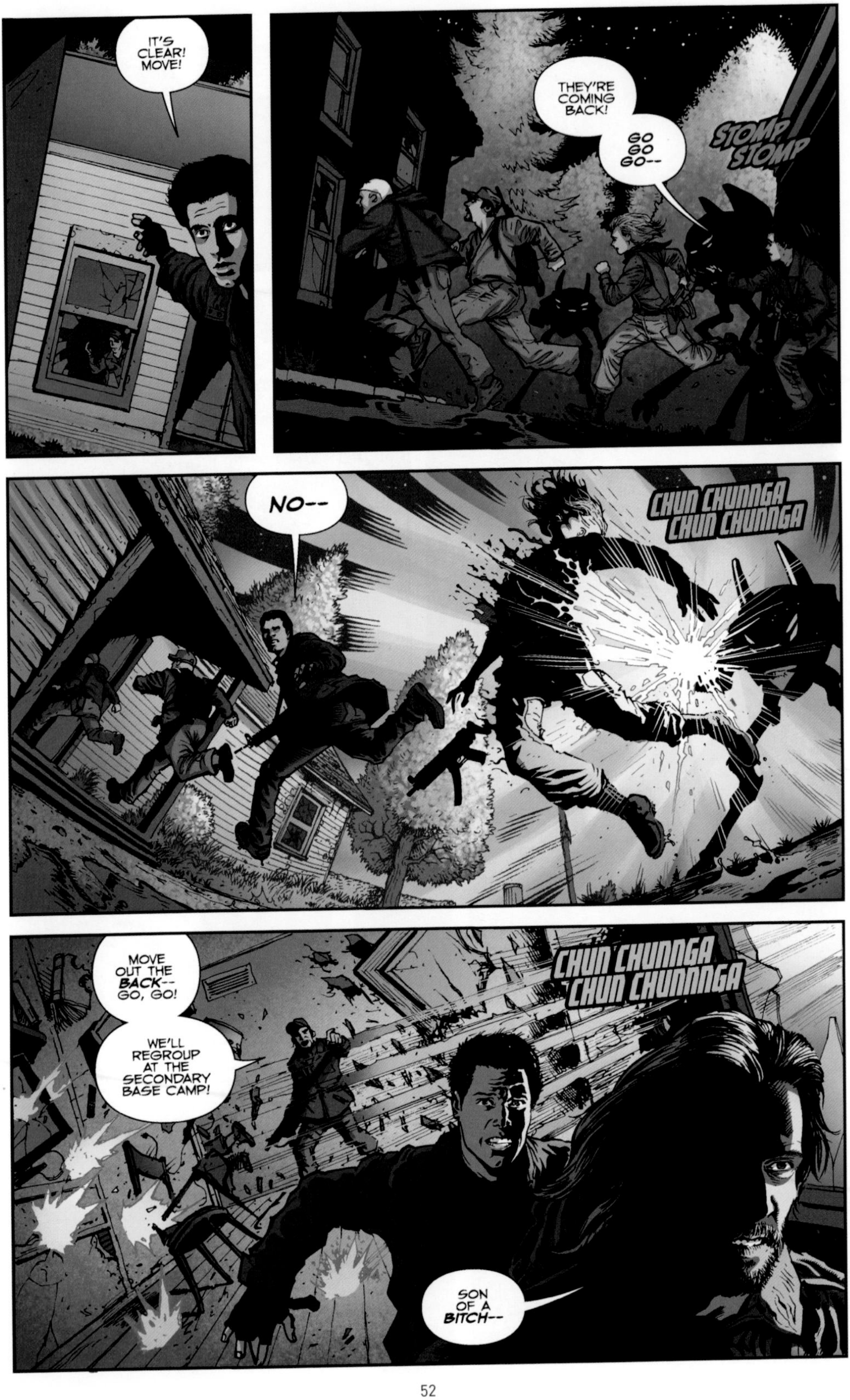
IT'S CLEAR! MOVE!
THEY'RE COMING BACK!
GO GO GO--
STOMP STOMP
NO--
CHUN CHUNNGA CHUN CHUNNGA
MOVE OUT THE BACK-- GO, GO!
WE'LL REGROUP AT THE SECONDARY BASE CAMP!
CHUN CHUNNGA CHUN CHUNNNGA
SON OF A BITCH--

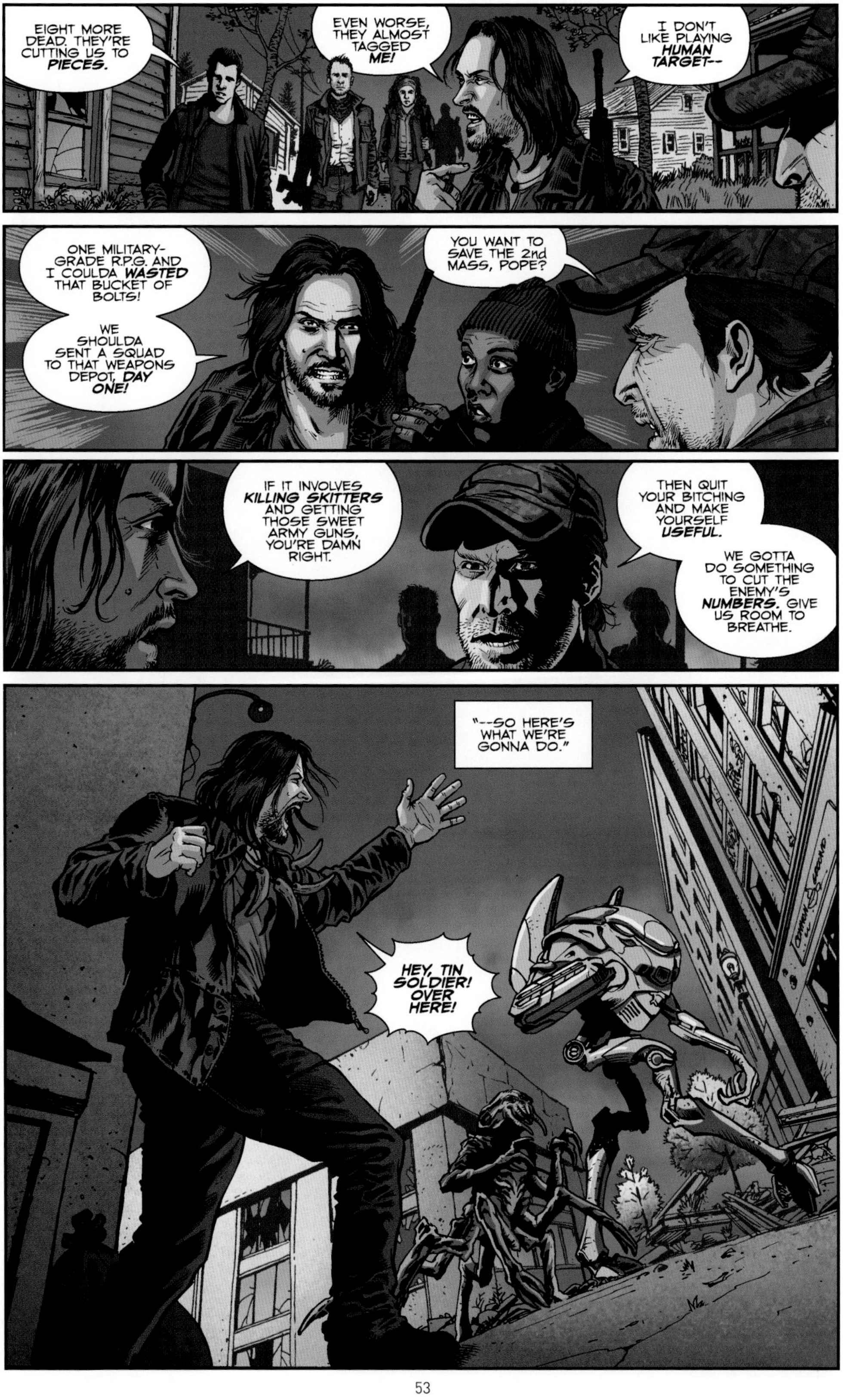
EIGHT MORE DEAD. THEY'RE CUTTING US TO PIECES.
EVEN WORSE, THEY ALMOST TAGGED ME!
I DON'T LIKE PLAYING HUMAN TARGET--
ONE MILITARY-GRADE R.P.G. AND I COULDA WASTED THAT BUCKET OF BOLTS!
WE SHOULDA SENT A SQUAD TO THAT WEAPONS DEPOT, DAY ONE!
YOU WANT TO SAVE THE 2nd MASS, POPE?
IF IT INVOLVES KILLING SKITTERS AND GETTING THOSE SWEET ARMY GUNS, YOU'RE DAMN RIGHT.
THEN QUIT YOUR BITCHING AND MAKE YOURSELF USEFUL.
WE GOTTA DO SOMETHING TO CUT THE ENEMY'S NUMBERS. GIVE US ROOM TO BREATHE.
"--SO HERE'S WHAT WE'RE GONNA DO."
HEY, TIN SOLDIER! OVER HERE!

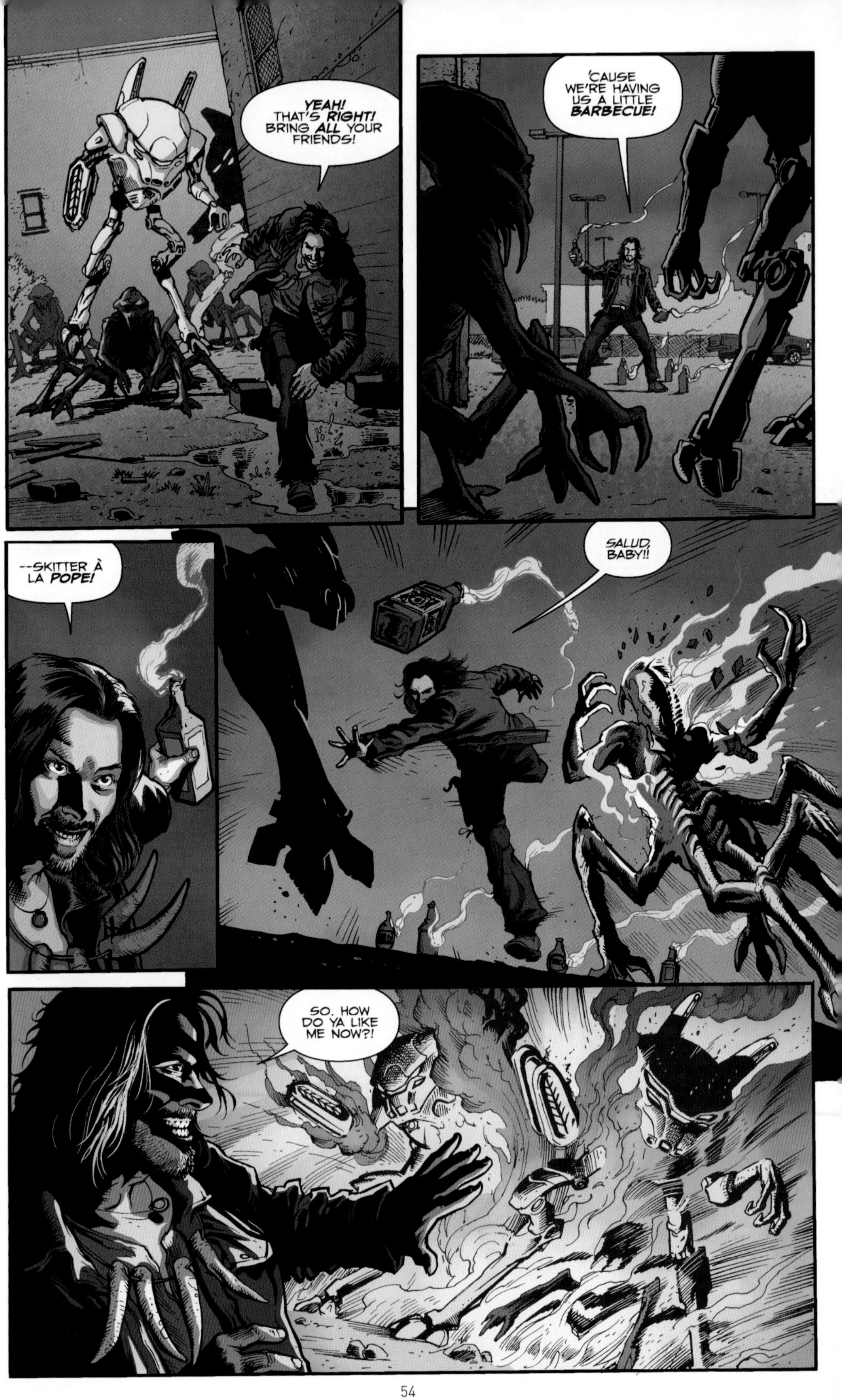
YEAH! THAT'S RIGHT! BRING ALL YOUR FRIENDS!
'CAUSE WE'RE HAVING US A LITTLE BARBECUE!
--SKITTER À LA POPE!
SALUD, BABY!!
SO. HOW DO YA LIKE ME NOW?!

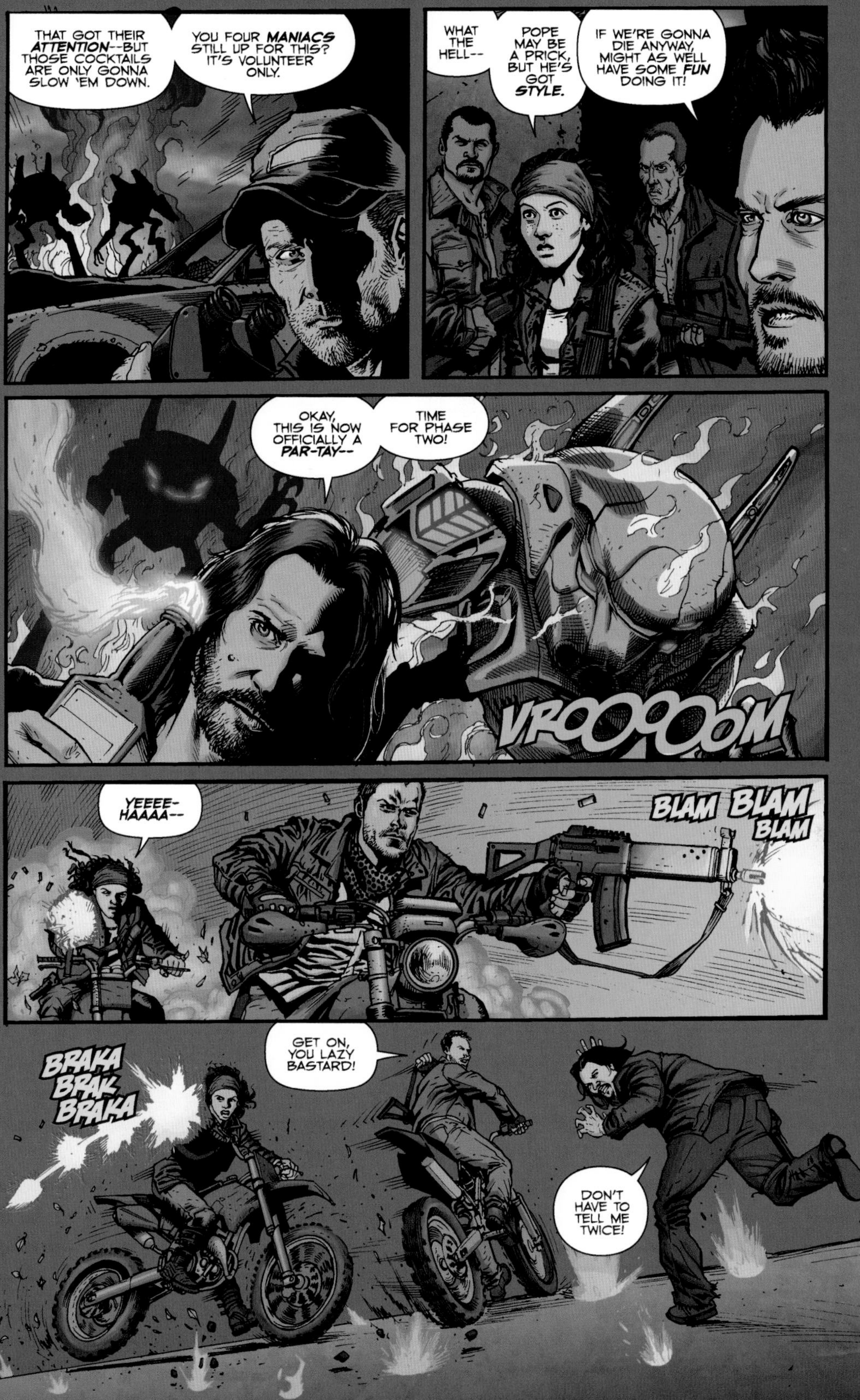
THAT GOT THEIR ATTENTION--BUT THOSE COCKTAILS ARE ONLY GONNA SLOW 'EM DOWN.
YOU FOUR MANIACS STILL UP FOR THIS? IT'S VOLUNTEER ONLY.
WHAT THE HELL--
POPE MAY BE A PRICK, BUT HE'S GOT STYLE.
IF WE'RE GONNA DIE ANYWAY, MIGHT AS WELL HAVE SOME FUN DOING IT!
OKAY, THIS IS NOW OFFICIALLY A PAR-TAY--
TIME FOR PHASE TWO!
VROOOOOOM
YEEEE-HAAAA--
BLAM BLAM BLAM
BRAKA BRAK BRAKA
GET ON, YOU LAZY BASTARD!
DON'T HAVE TO TELL ME TWICE!

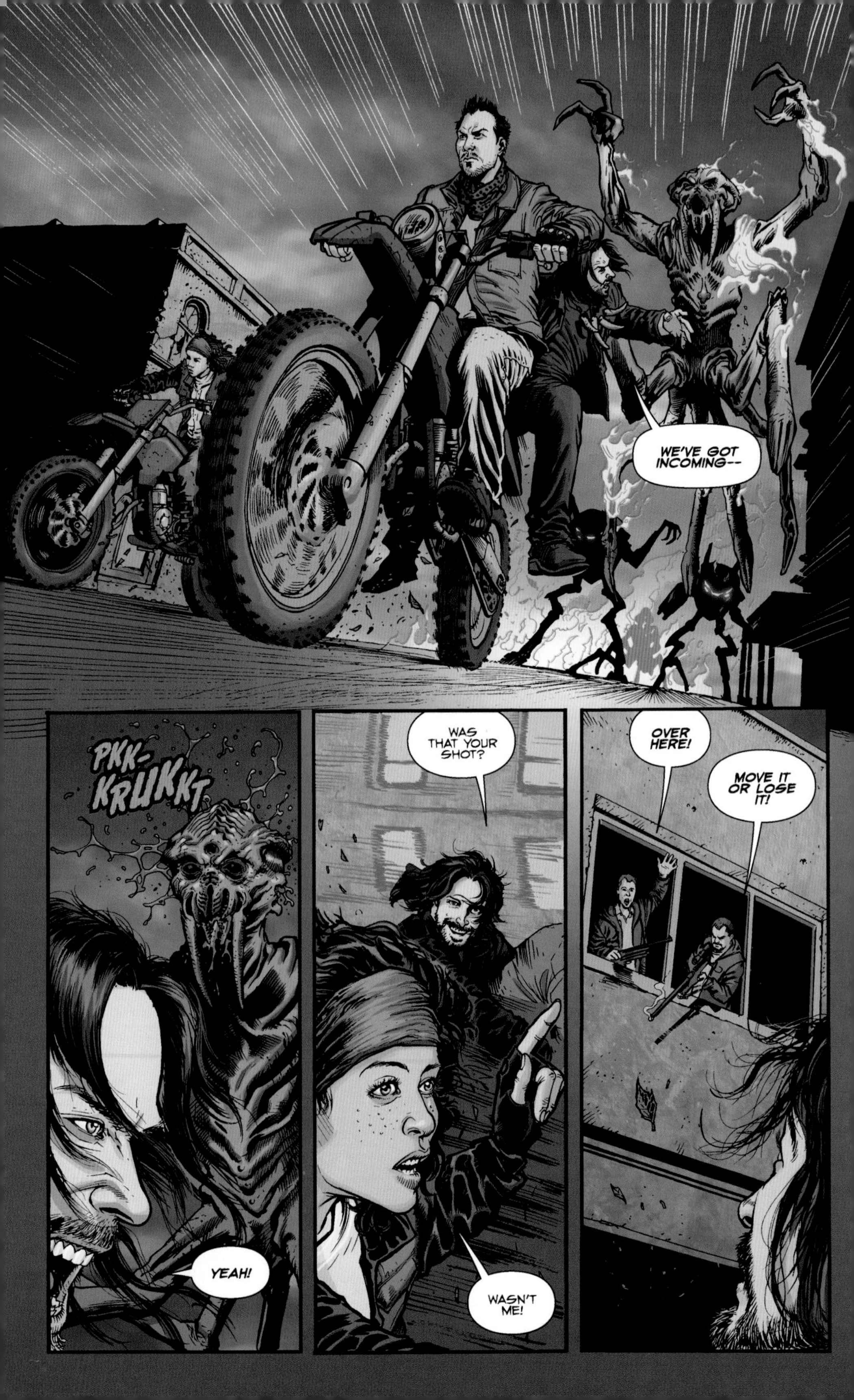
WE'VE GOT INCOMING--
PKK-KRUKKT
YEAH!
WAS THAT YOUR SHOT?
WASN'T ME!
OVER HERE!
MOVE IT OR LOSE IT!

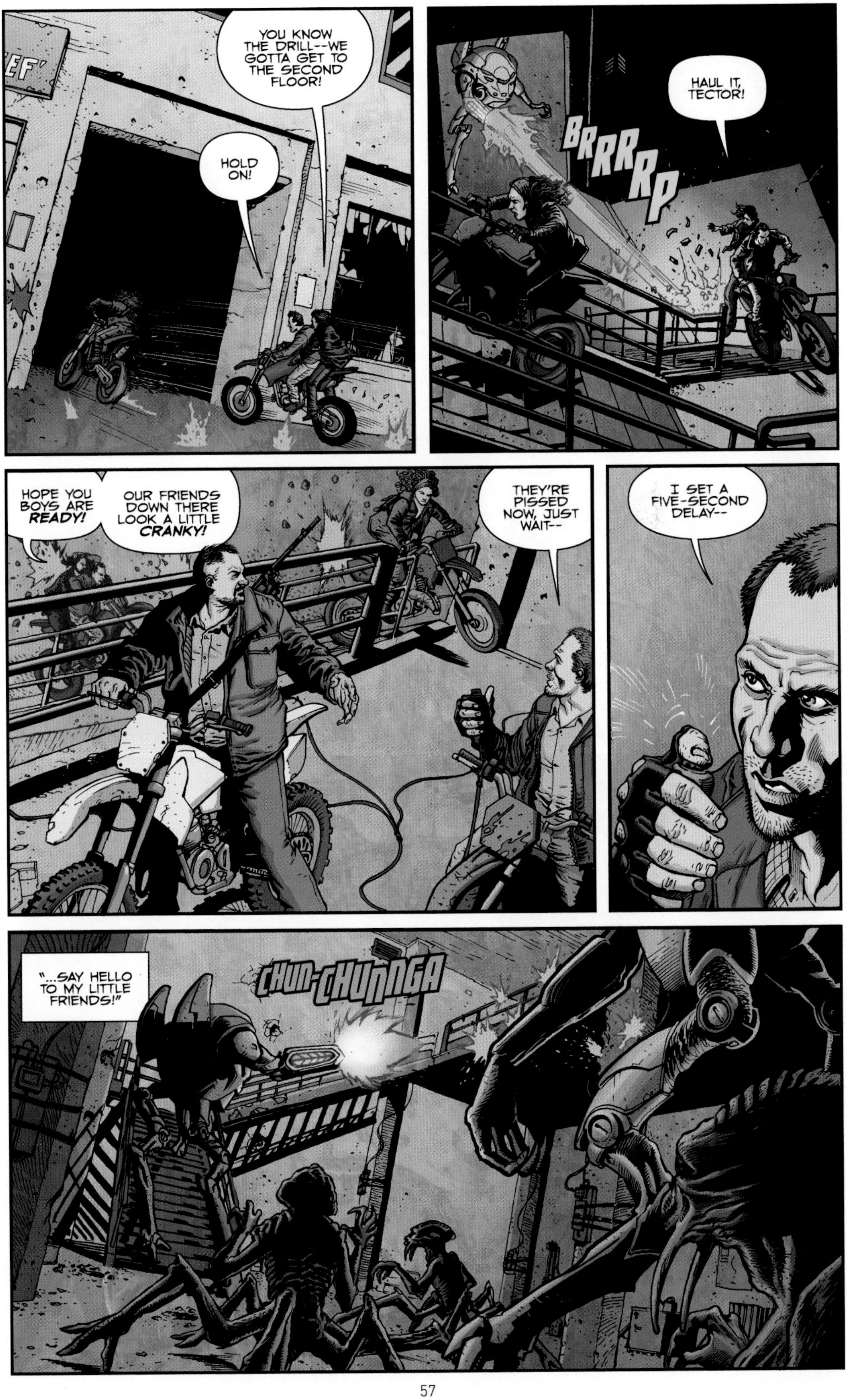
YOU KNOW THE DRILL--WE GOTTA GET TO THE SECOND FLOOR!
HOLD ON!
HAUL IT, TECTOR!
BRRRRP
HOPE YOU BOYS ARE *READY!*
OUR FRIENDS DOWN THERE LOOK A LITTLE *CRANKY!*
THEY'RE PISSED NOW, JUST WAIT--
I SET A FIVE-SECOND DELAY--
"...SAY HELLO TO MY LITTLE FRIENDS!"
CHUN-CHUNNGA

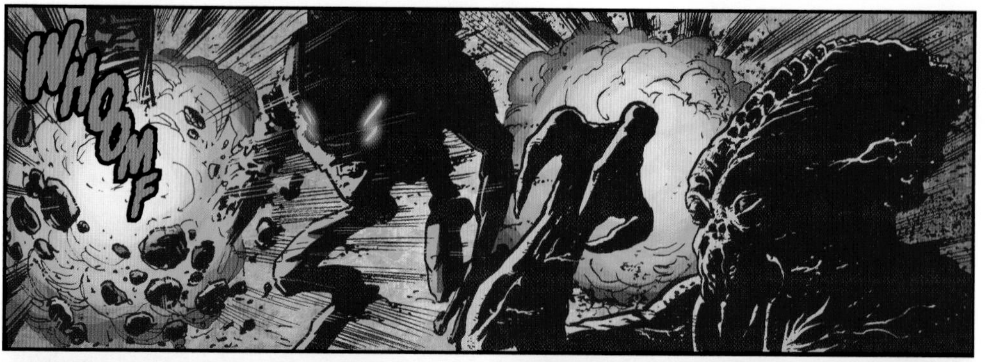
WHOOMF

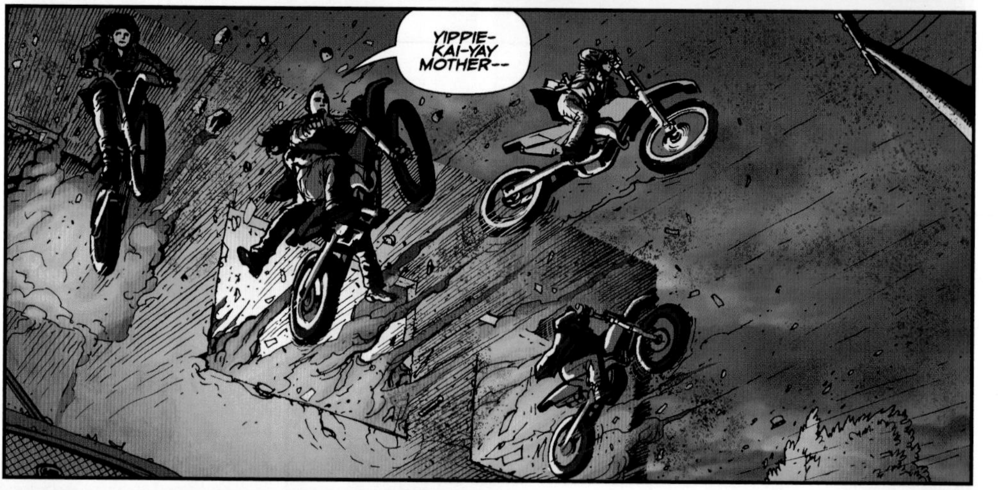
YIPPIE-KAI-YAY MOTHER--

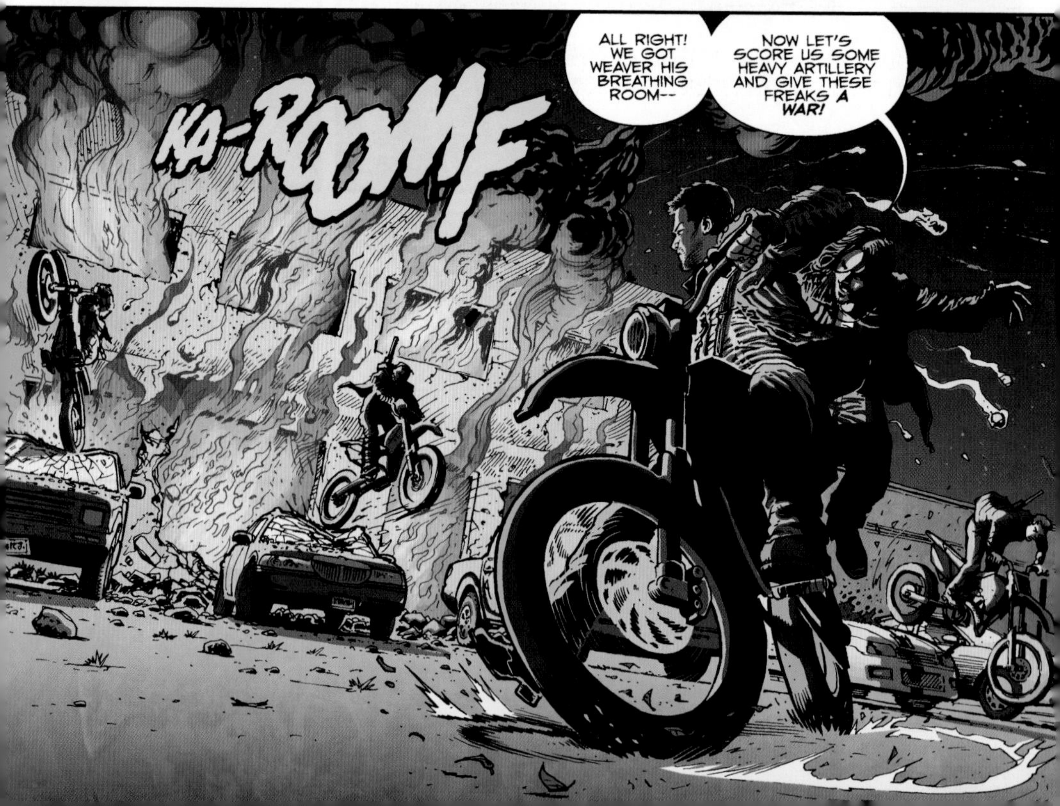
KA-ROOMF
ALL RIGHT! WE GOT WEAVER HIS BREATHING ROOM--
NOW LET'S SCORE US SOME HEAVY ARTILLERY AND GIVE THESE FREAKS A *WAR!*

THE BATTLE OF FITCHBURG

CHAPTER THREE

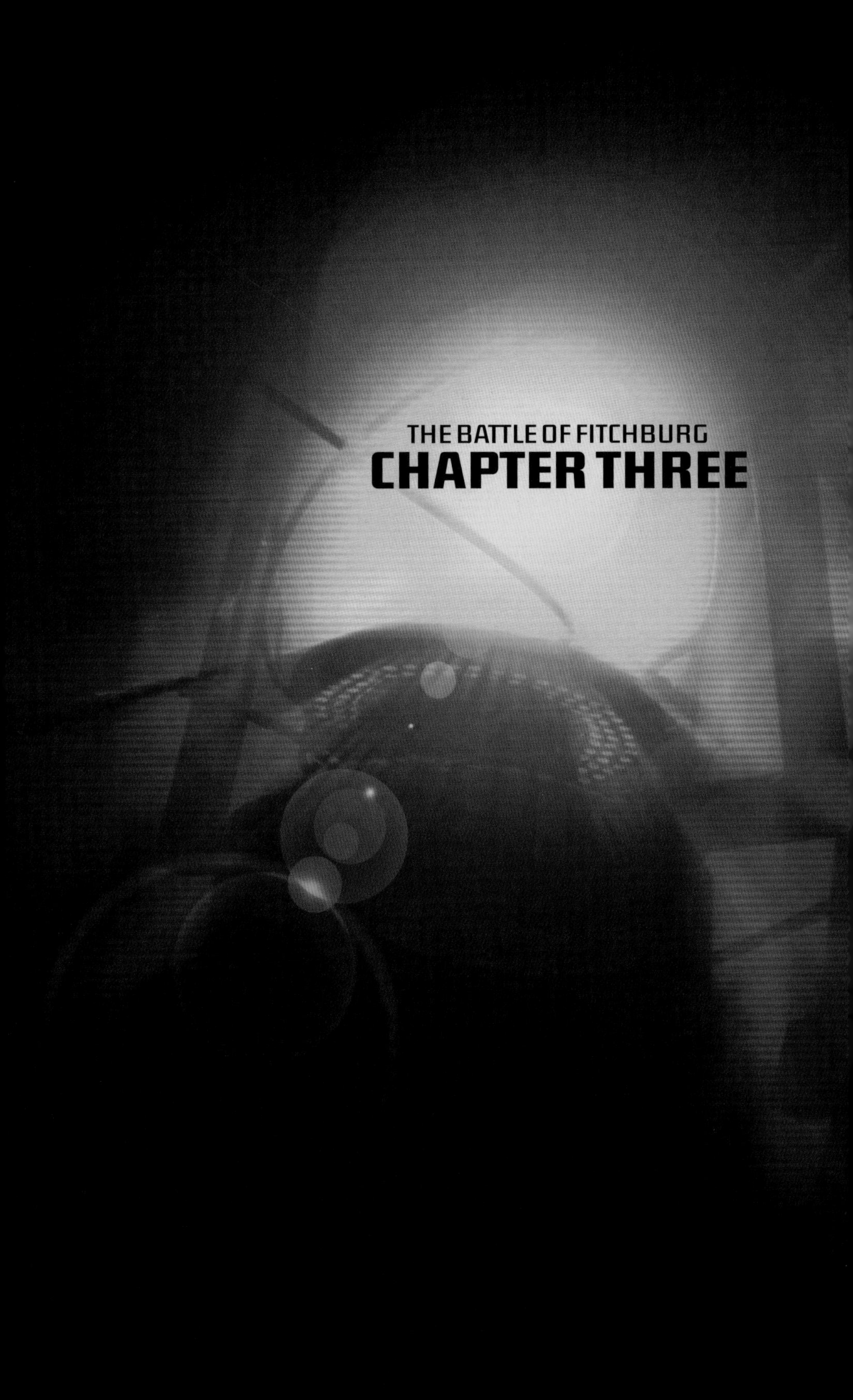

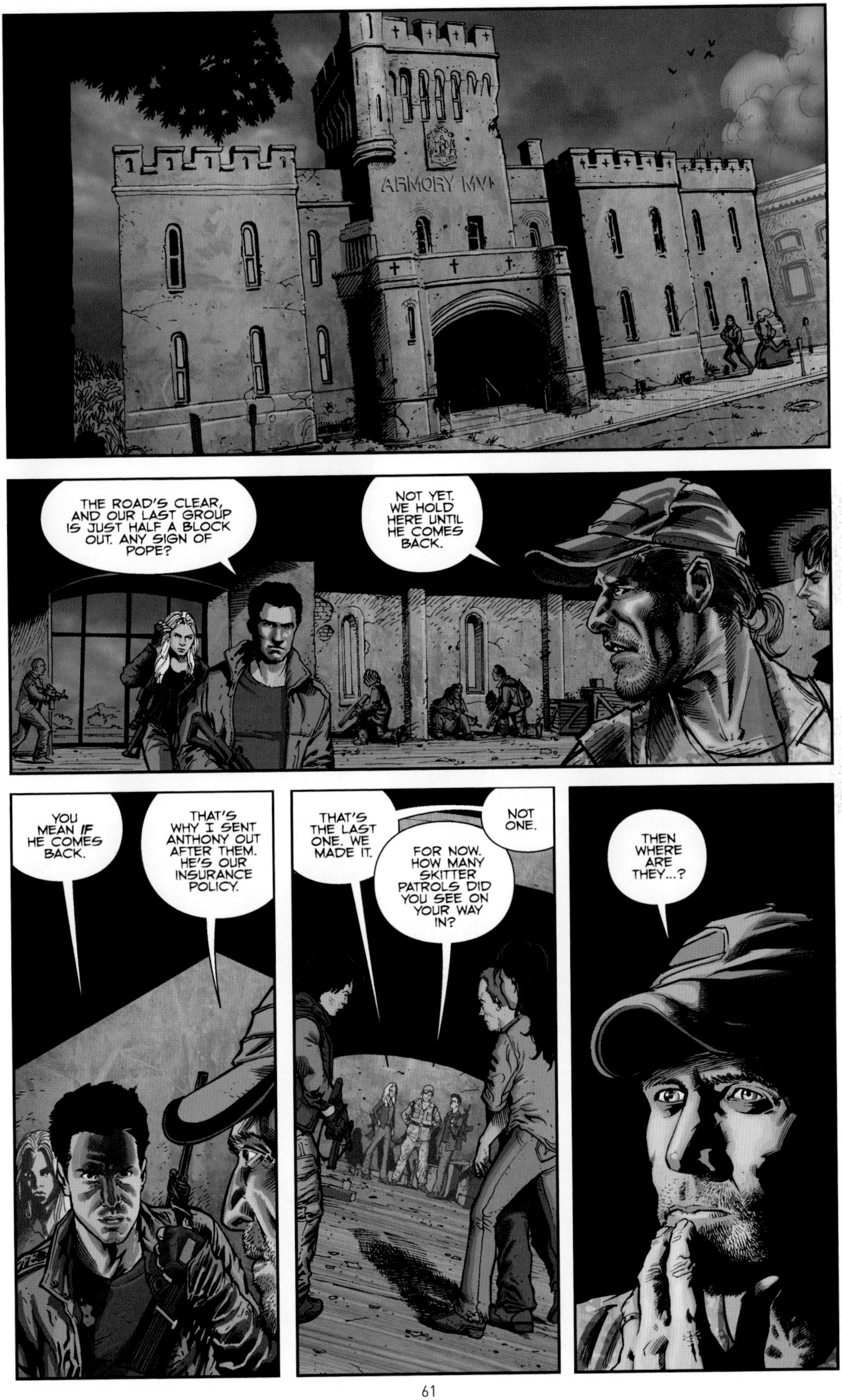
ARMORY MVI
THE ROAD'S CLEAR, AND OUR LAST GROUP IS JUST HALF A BLOCK OUT. ANY SIGN OF POPE?
NOT YET. WE HOLD HERE UNTIL HE COMES BACK.
YOU MEAN *IF* HE COMES BACK.
THAT'S WHY I SENT ANTHONY OUT AFTER THEM. HE'S OUR INSURANCE POLICY.
THAT'S THE LAST ONE. WE MADE IT.
FOR NOW. HOW MANY SKITTER PATROLS DID YOU SEE ON YOUR WAY IN?
NOT ONE.
THEN WHERE ARE THEY...?

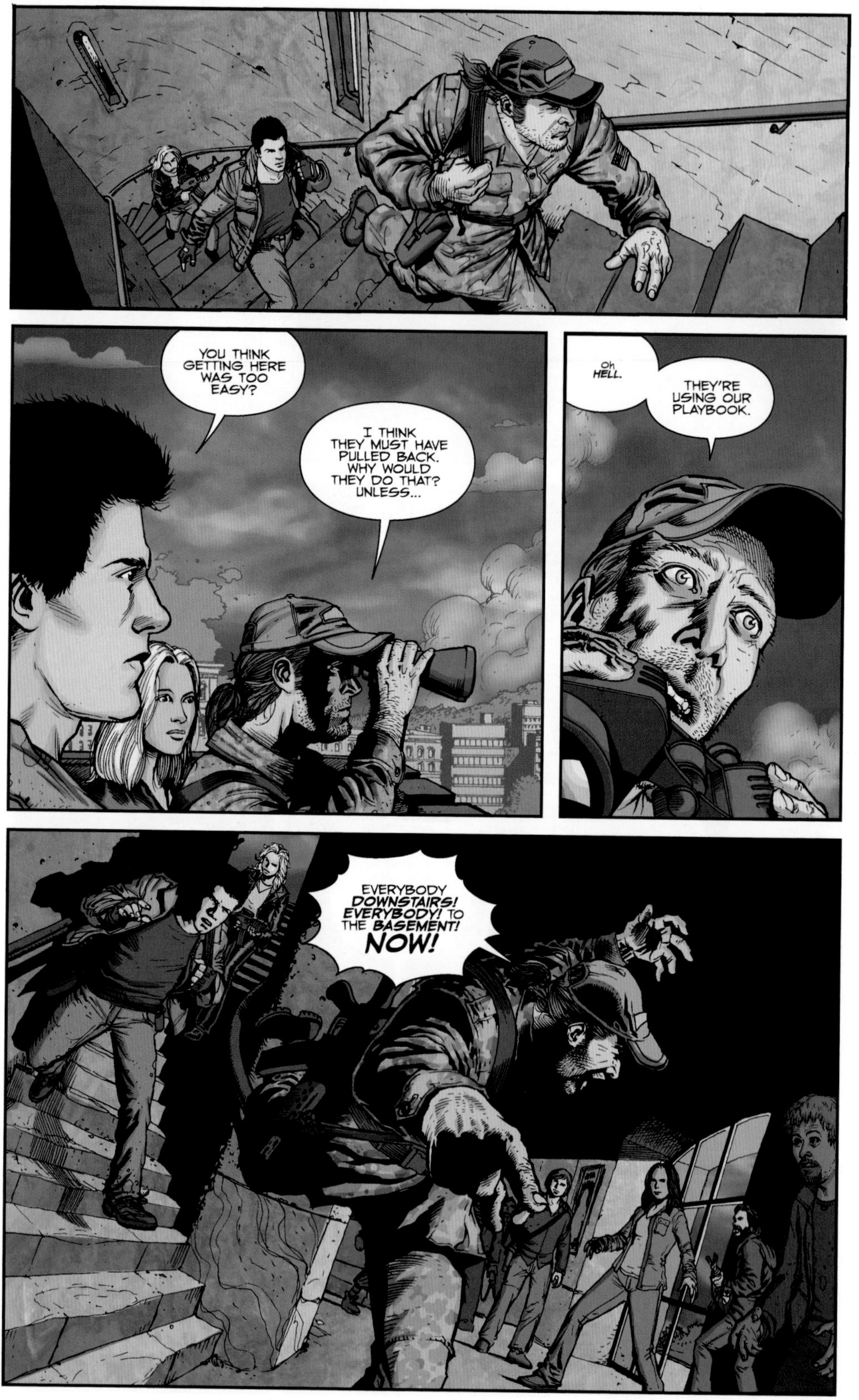
YOU THINK GETTING HERE WAS TOO EASY?
I THINK THEY MUST HAVE PULLED BACK. WHY WOULD THEY DO THAT? UNLESS...
Oh *HELL.*
THEY'RE USING OUR PLAYBOOK.
EVERYBODY *DOWNSTAIRS! EVERYBODY!* TO THE *BASEMENT!* **NOW!**

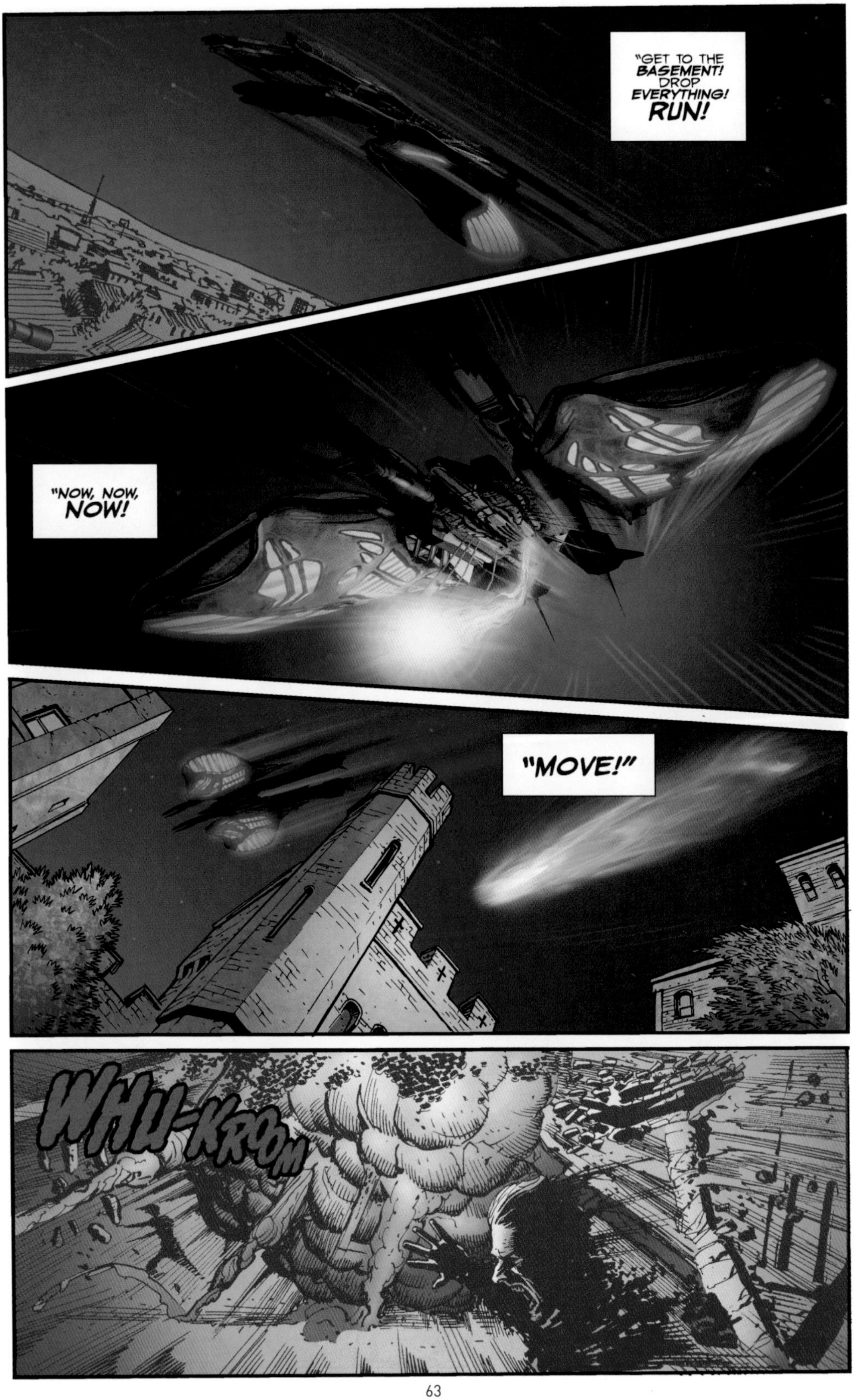
"GET TO THE BASEMENT! DROP EVERYTHING! RUN!
"NOW, NOW, NOW!
"MOVE!"
WHU-KROOM

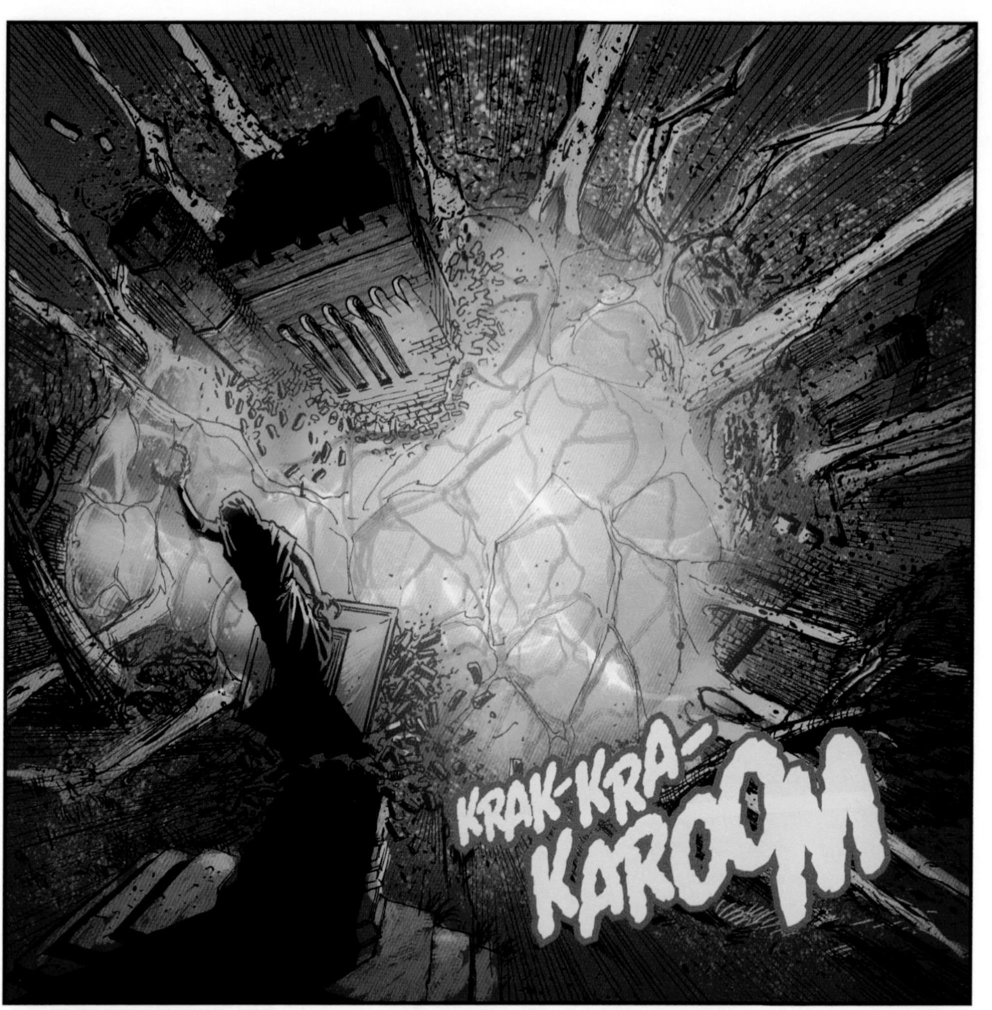
KRAK-KRA-
KAROOM

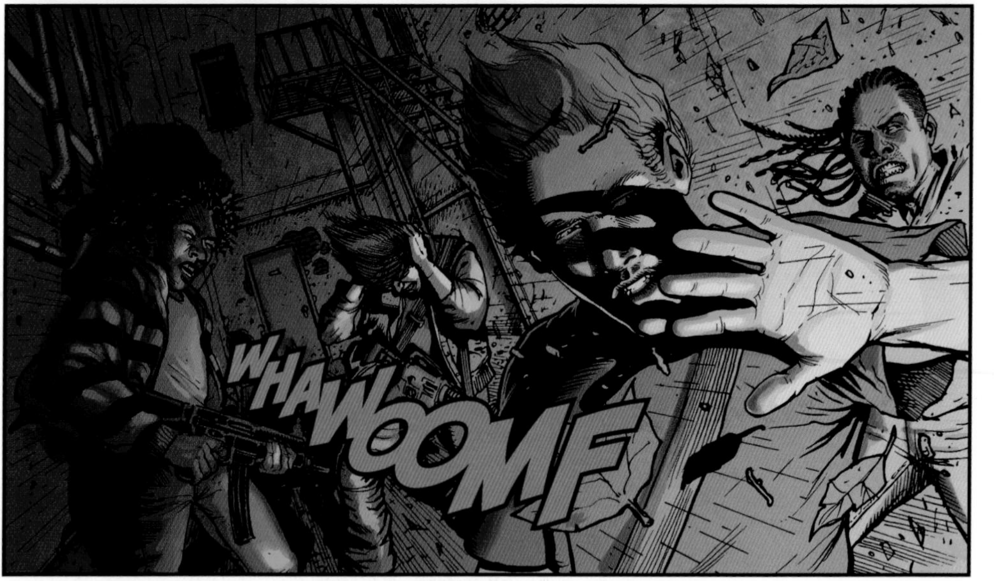
WHAWOOMF

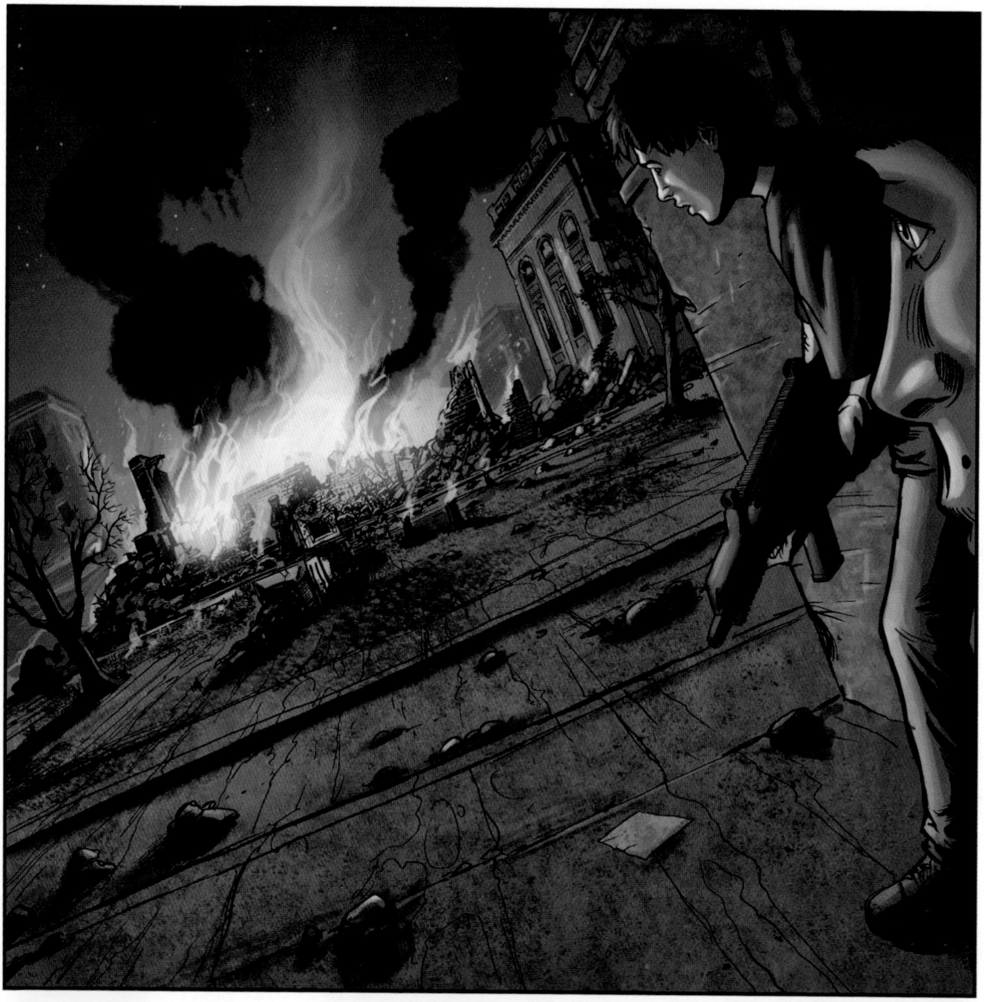

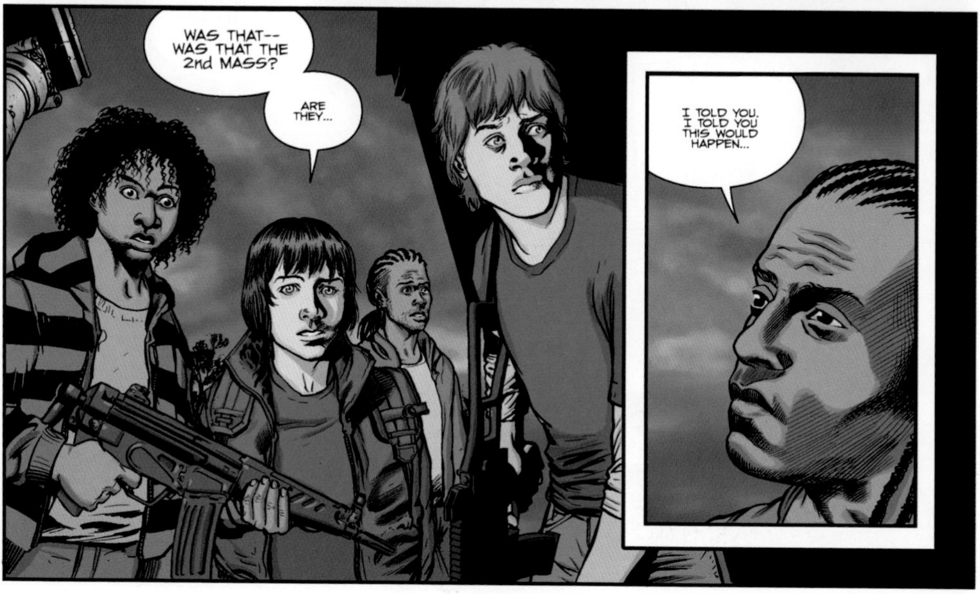
WAS THAT-- WAS THAT THE 2nd MASS?
ARE THEY...
I TOLD YOU. I TOLD YOU THIS WOULD HAPPEN...

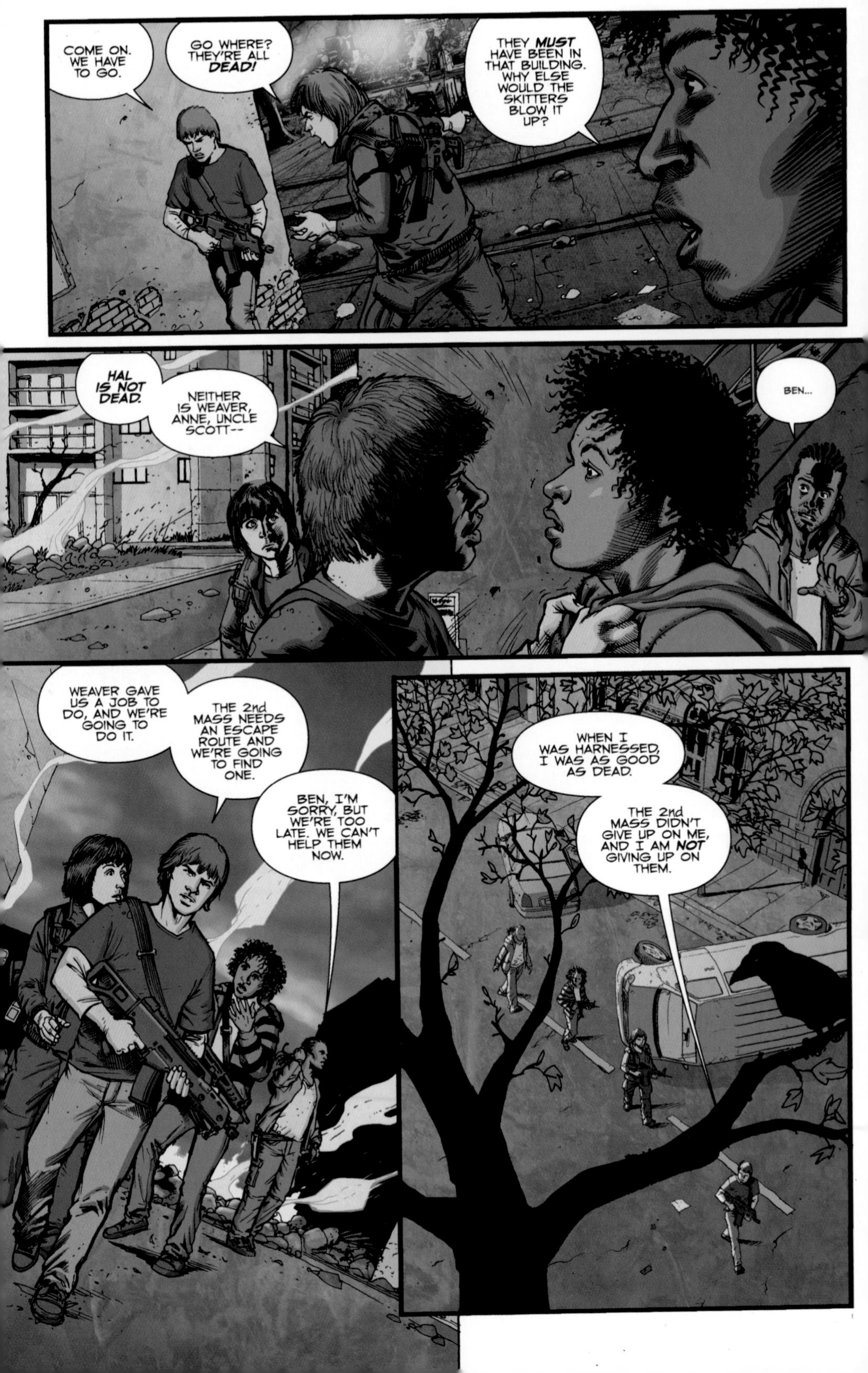
COME ON. WE HAVE TO GO.
GO WHERE? THEY'RE ALL DEAD!
THEY MUST HAVE BEEN IN THAT BUILDING. WHY ELSE WOULD THE SKITTERS BLOW IT UP?
HAL IS NOT DEAD.
NEITHER IS WEAVER, ANNE, UNCLE SCOTT--
BEN...
WEAVER GAVE US A JOB TO DO, AND WE'RE GOING TO DO IT.
THE 2nd MASS NEEDS AN ESCAPE ROUTE AND WE'RE GOING TO FIND ONE.
BEN, I'M SORRY, BUT WE'RE TOO LATE. WE CAN'T HELP THEM NOW.
WHEN I WAS HARNESSED, I WAS AS GOOD AS DEAD.
THE 2nd MASS DIDN'T GIVE UP ON ME, AND I AM NOT GIVING UP ON THEM.

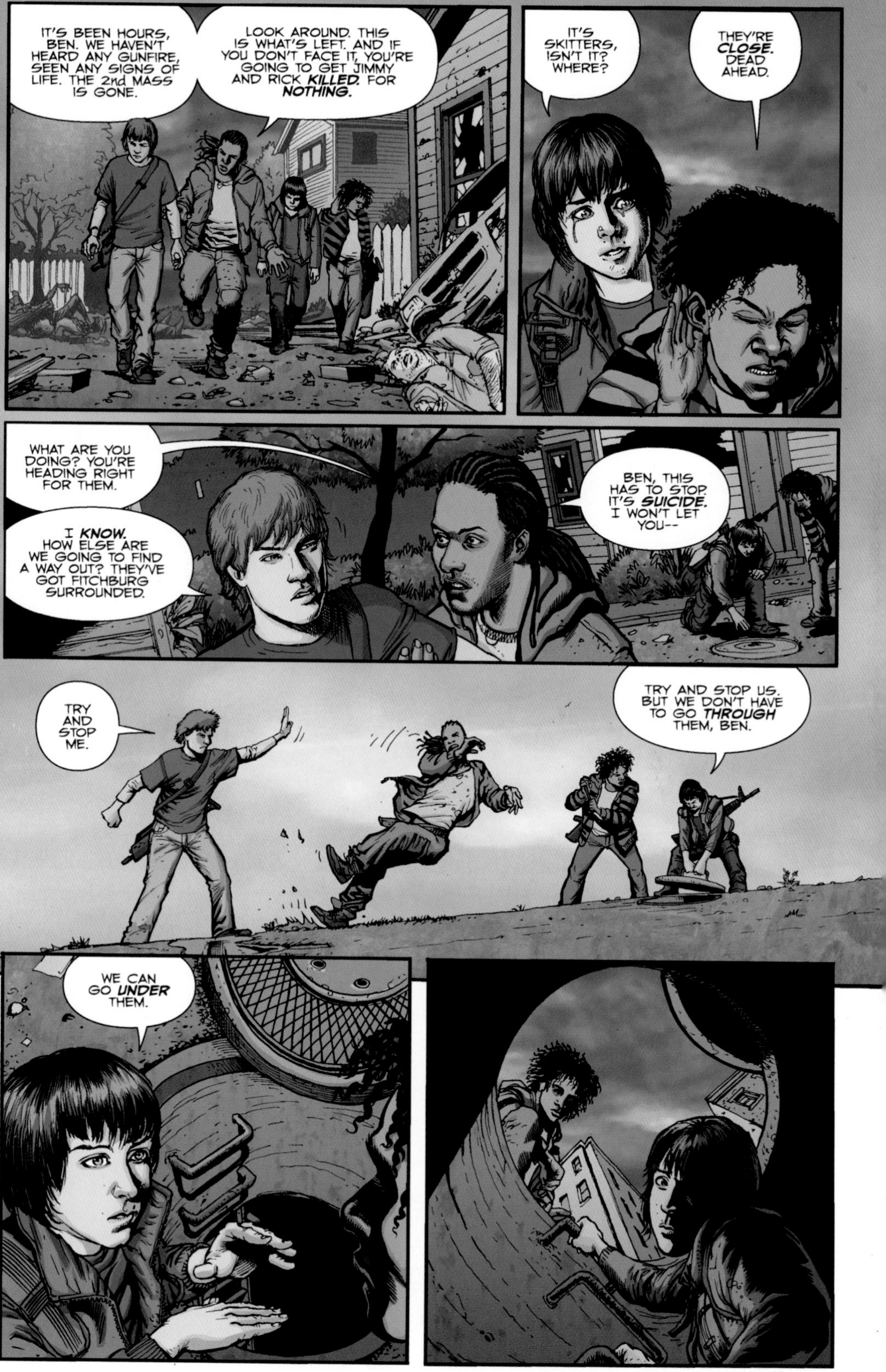
IT'S BEEN HOURS, BEN. WE HAVEN'T HEARD ANY GUNFIRE, SEEN ANY SIGNS OF LIFE. THE 2nd MASS IS GONE.
LOOK AROUND. THIS IS WHAT'S LEFT. AND IF YOU DON'T FACE IT, YOU'RE GOING TO GET JIMMY AND RICK **KILLED.** FOR **NOTHING.**
IT'S SKITTERS, ISN'T IT? WHERE?
THEY'RE **CLOSE.** DEAD AHEAD.
WHAT ARE YOU DOING? YOU'RE HEADING RIGHT FOR THEM.
I **KNOW.** HOW ELSE ARE WE GOING TO FIND A WAY OUT? THEY'VE GOT FITCHBURG SURROUNDED.
BEN, THIS HAS TO STOP. IT'S **SUICIDE.** I WON'T LET YOU--
TRY AND STOP ME.
TRY AND STOP US. BUT WE DON'T HAVE TO GO **THROUGH** THEM, BEN.
WE CAN GO **UNDER** THEM.

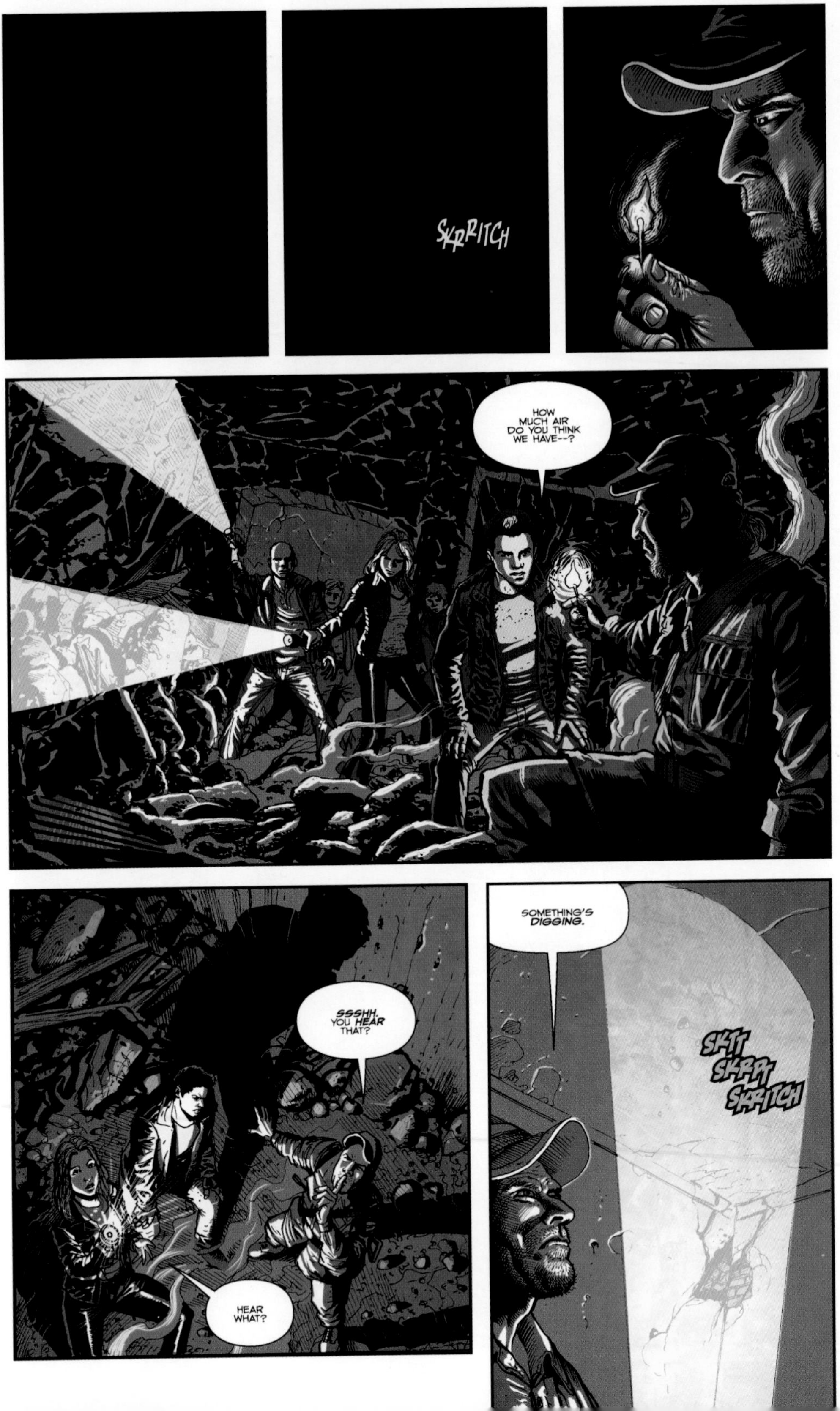
SKRRITCH
HOW MUCH AIR DO YOU THINK WE HAVE--?
SSSHH. YOU HEAR THAT?
HEAR WHAT?
SOMETHING'S DIGGING.
SKTT SKRRT SKRITCH

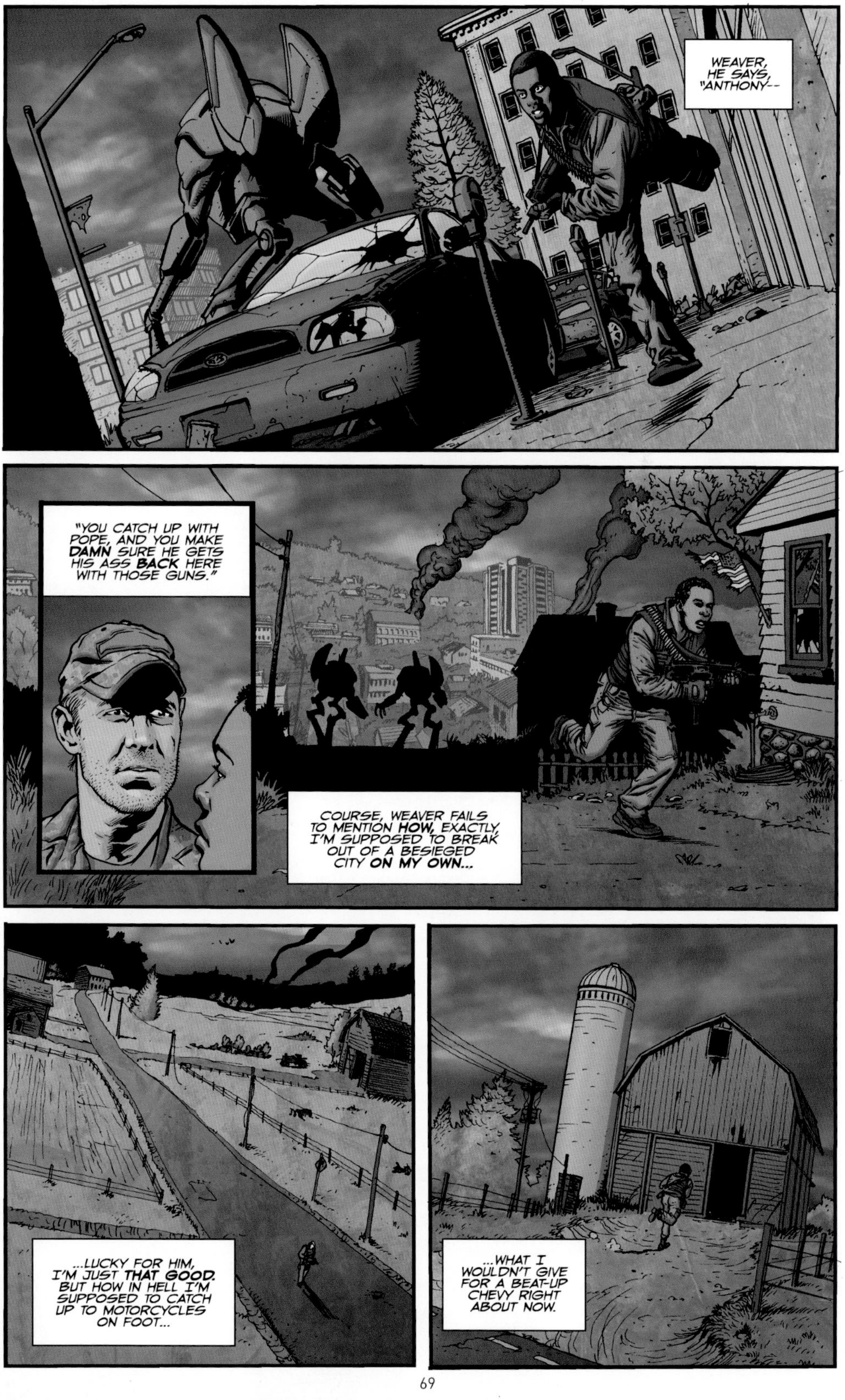
WEAVER, HE SAYS, "ANTHONY--
"YOU CATCH UP WITH POPE, AND YOU MAKE DAMN SURE HE GETS HIS ASS BACK HERE WITH THOSE GUNS."
COURSE, WEAVER FAILS TO MENTION HOW, EXACTLY, I'M SUPPOSED TO BREAK OUT OF A BESIEGED CITY ON MY OWN...
...LUCKY FOR HIM, I'M JUST THAT GOOD. BUT HOW IN HELL I'M SUPPOSED TO CATCH UP TO MOTORCYCLES ON FOOT...
...WHAT I WOULDN'T GIVE FOR A BEAT-UP CHEVY RIGHT ABOUT NOW.

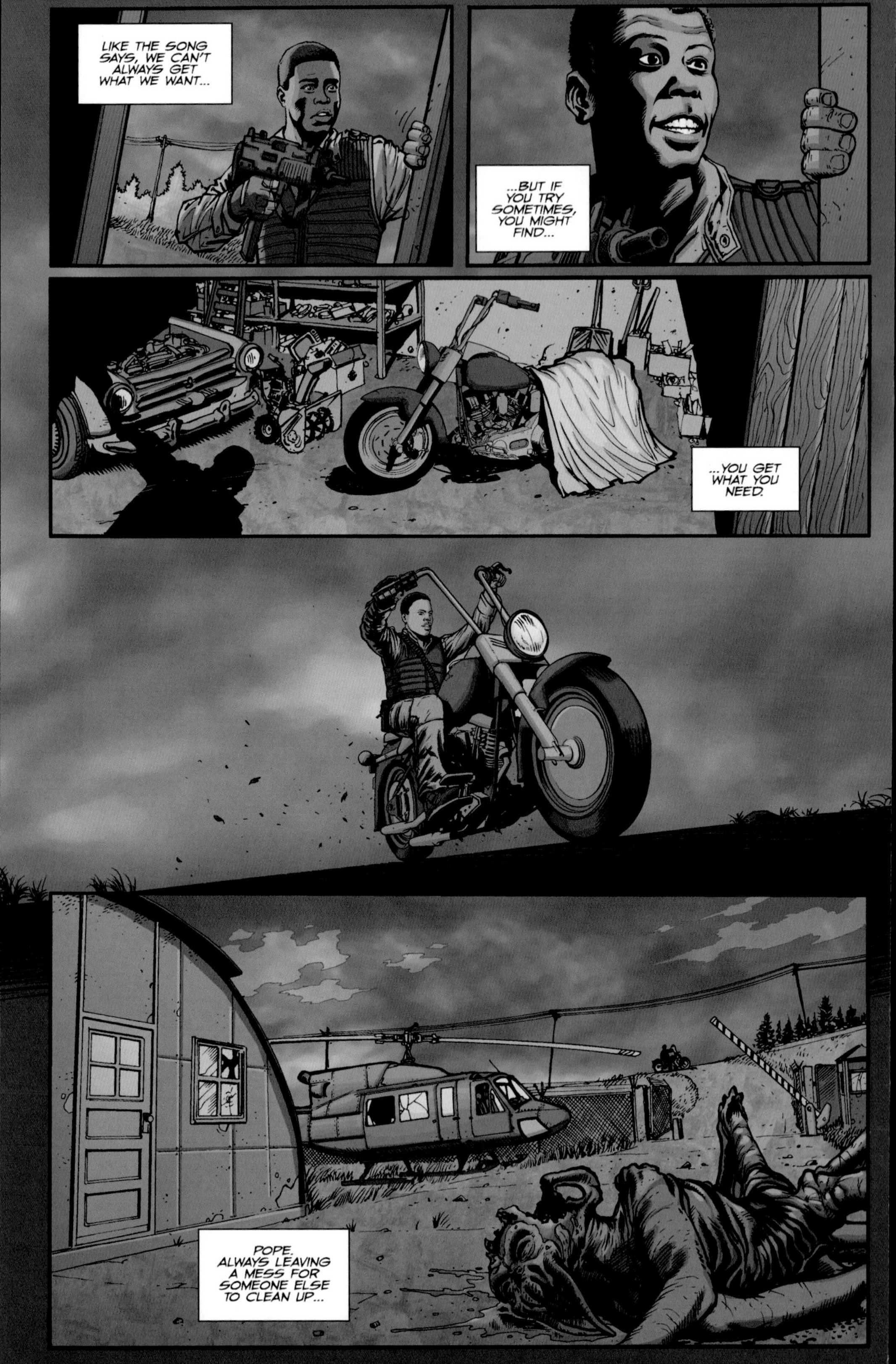
LIKE THE SONG SAYS, WE CAN'T ALWAYS GET WHAT WE WANT...
...BUT IF YOU TRY SOMETIMES, YOU MIGHT FIND...
...YOU GET WHAT YOU NEED.
POPE. ALWAYS LEAVING A MESS FOR SOMEONE ELSE TO CLEAN UP...

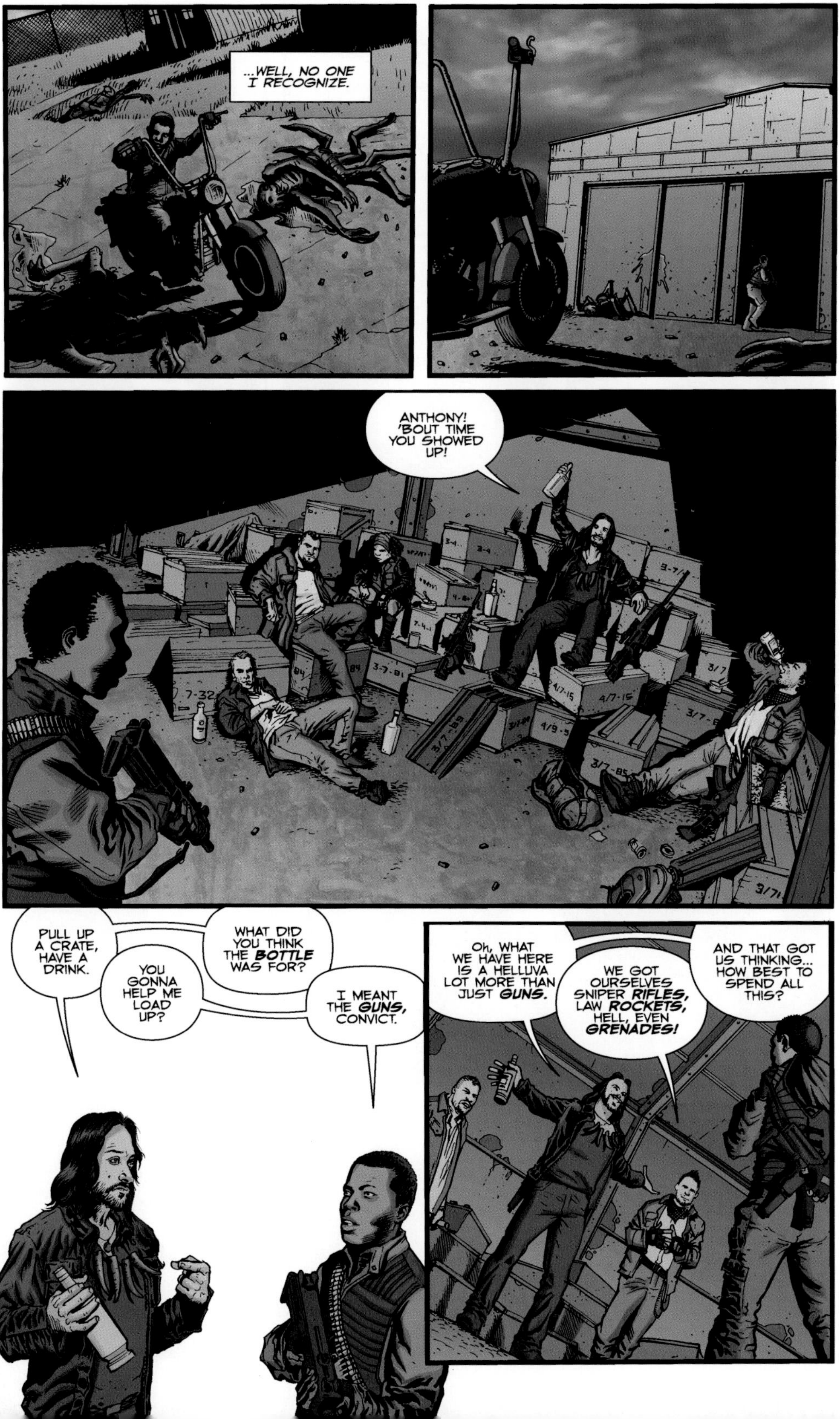
...WELL, NO ONE I RECOGNIZE.
ANTHONY! 'BOUT TIME YOU SHOWED UP!
PULL UP A CRATE, HAVE A DRINK.
YOU GONNA HELP ME LOAD UP?
WHAT DID YOU THINK THE BOTTLE WAS FOR?
I MEANT THE GUNS, CONVICT.
Oh, WHAT WE HAVE HERE IS A HELLUVA LOT MORE THAN JUST GUNS.
WE GOT OURSELVES SNIPER RIFLES, LAW ROCKETS, HELL, EVEN GRENADES!
AND THAT GOT US THINKING... HOW BEST TO SPEND ALL THIS?

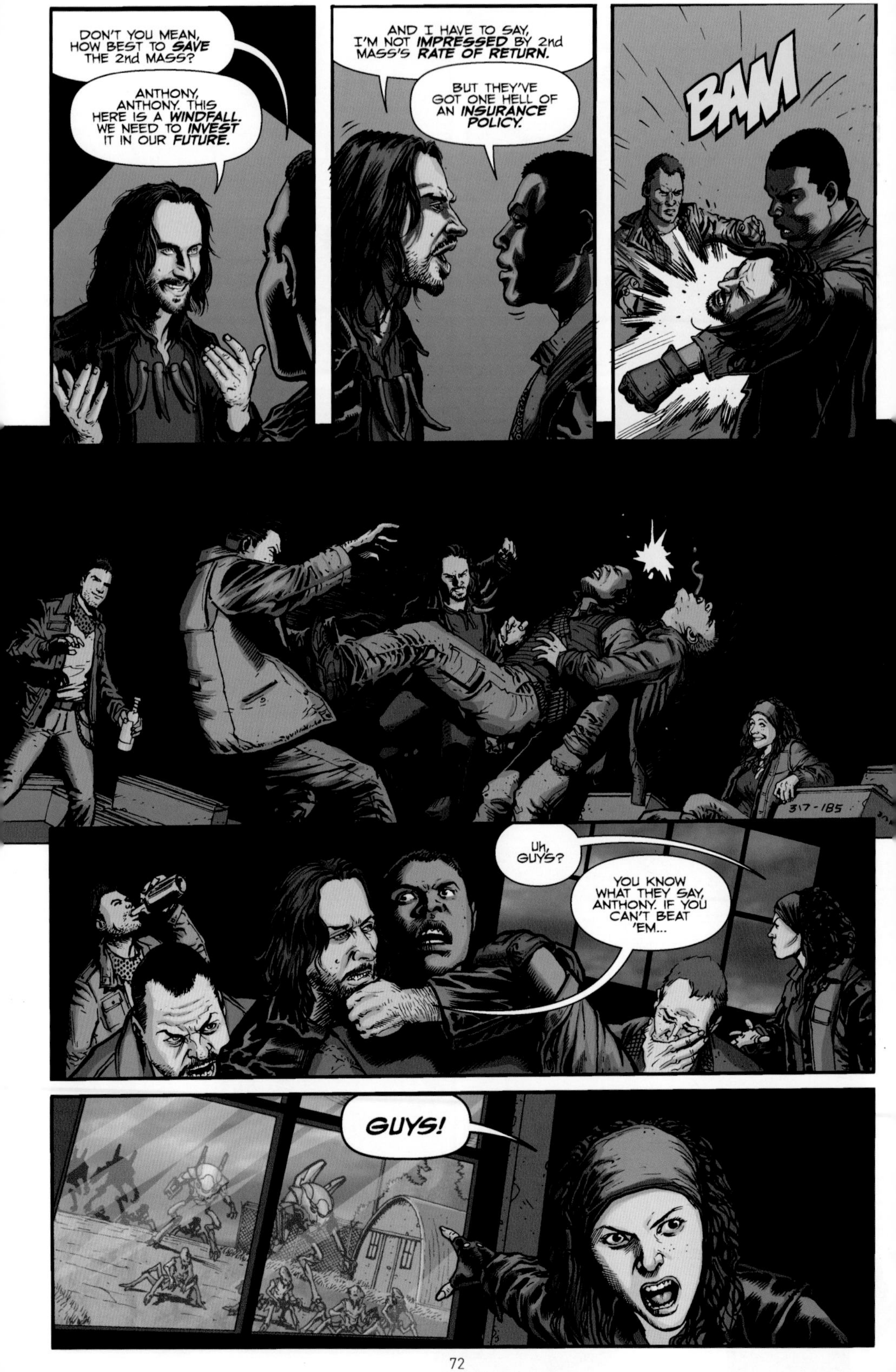

DON'T YOU MEAN, HOW BEST TO SAVE THE 2nd MASS?
ANTHONY, ANTHONY. THIS HERE IS A WINDFALL. WE NEED TO INVEST IT IN OUR FUTURE.
AND I HAVE TO SAY, I'M NOT IMPRESSED BY 2nd MASS'S RATE OF RETURN.
BUT THEY'VE GOT ONE HELL OF AN INSURANCE POLICY.
BAM
UH, GUYS?
YOU KNOW WHAT THEY SAY, ANTHONY. IF YOU CAN'T BEAT 'EM...
GUYS!

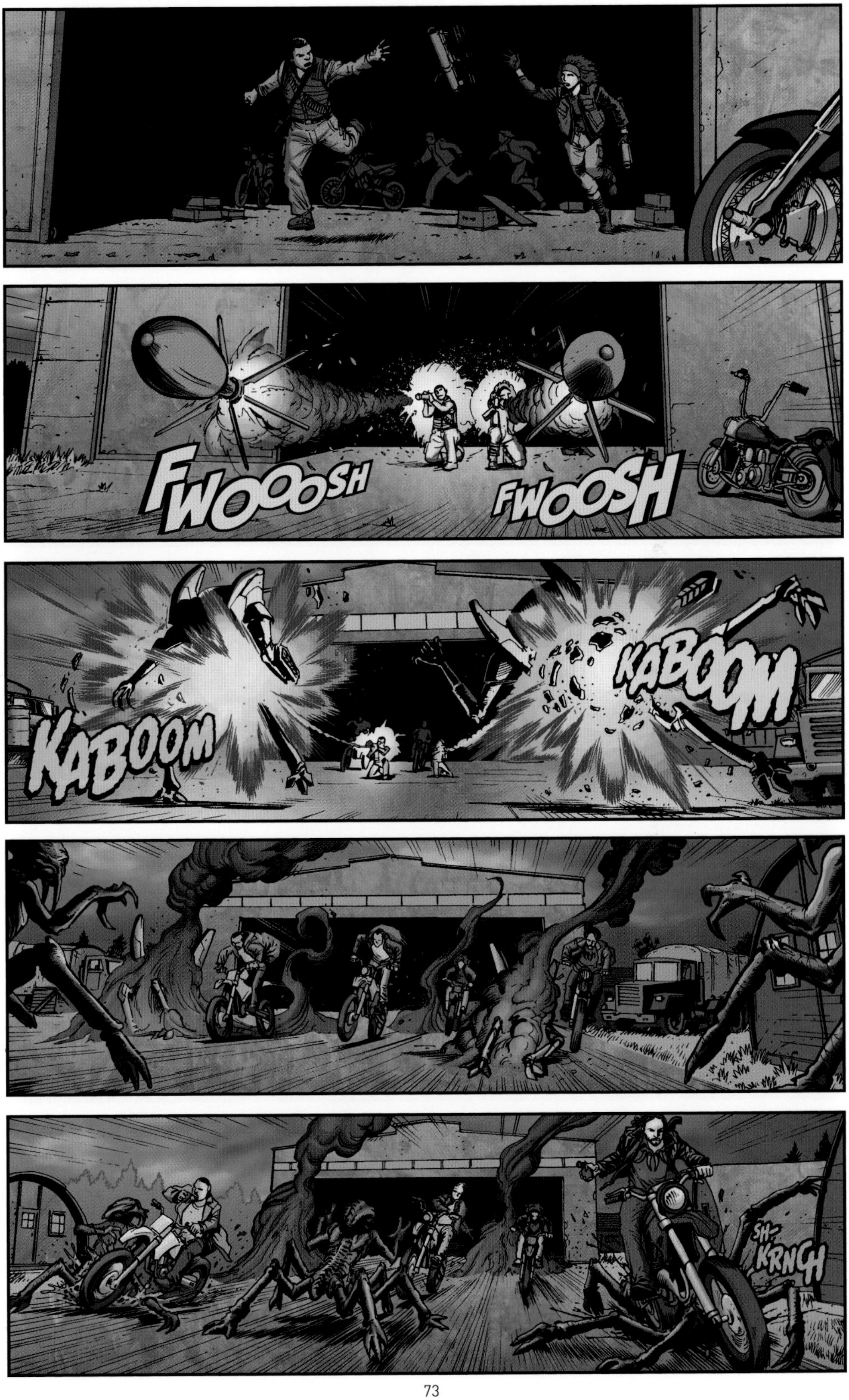
FWOOOSH
FWOOSH
KABOOM
KABOOM
SH-
KRNCH

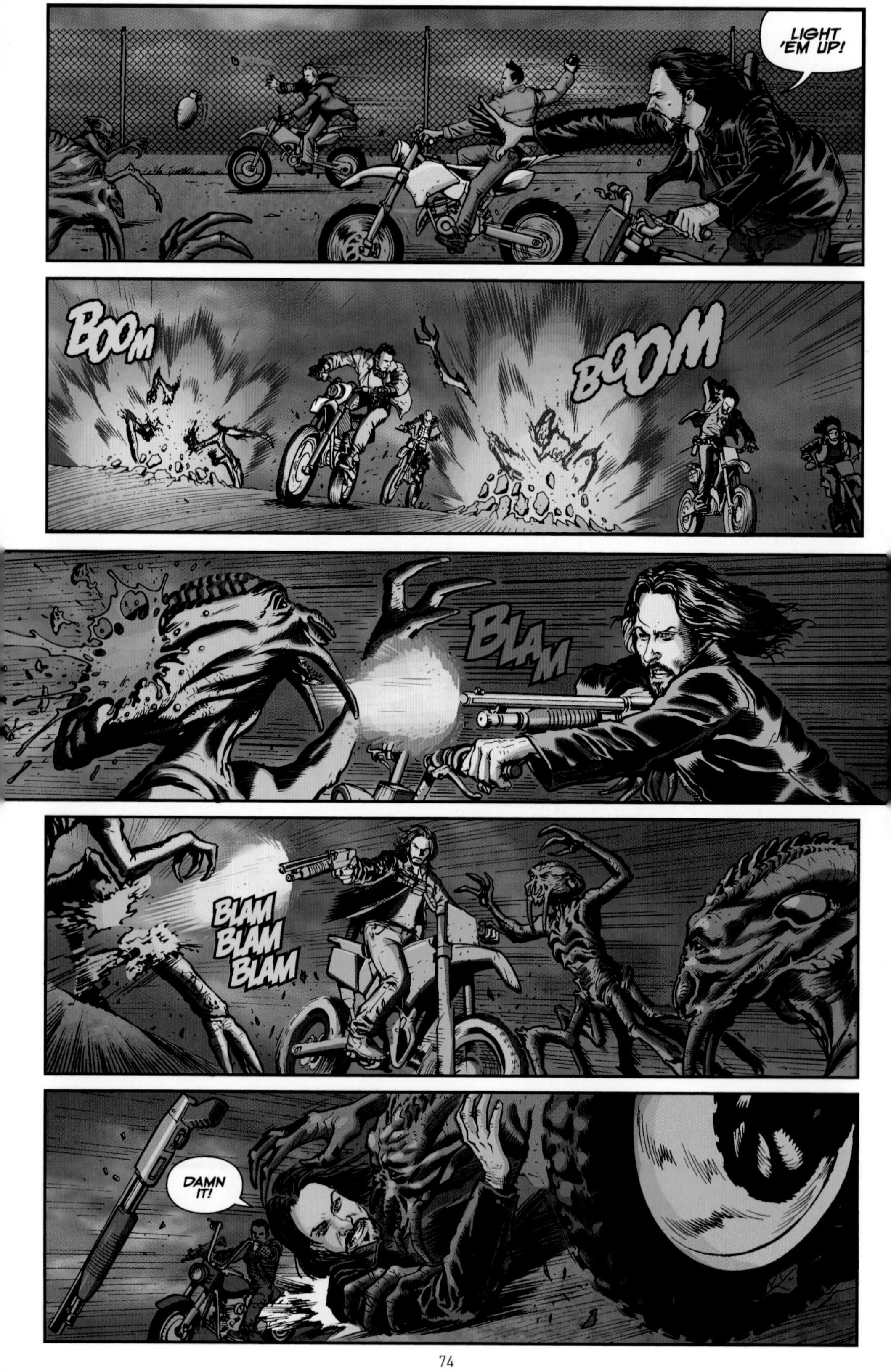
LIGHT 'EM UP!
BOOM
BOOM
BLAM
BLAM BLAM BLAM
DAMN IT!

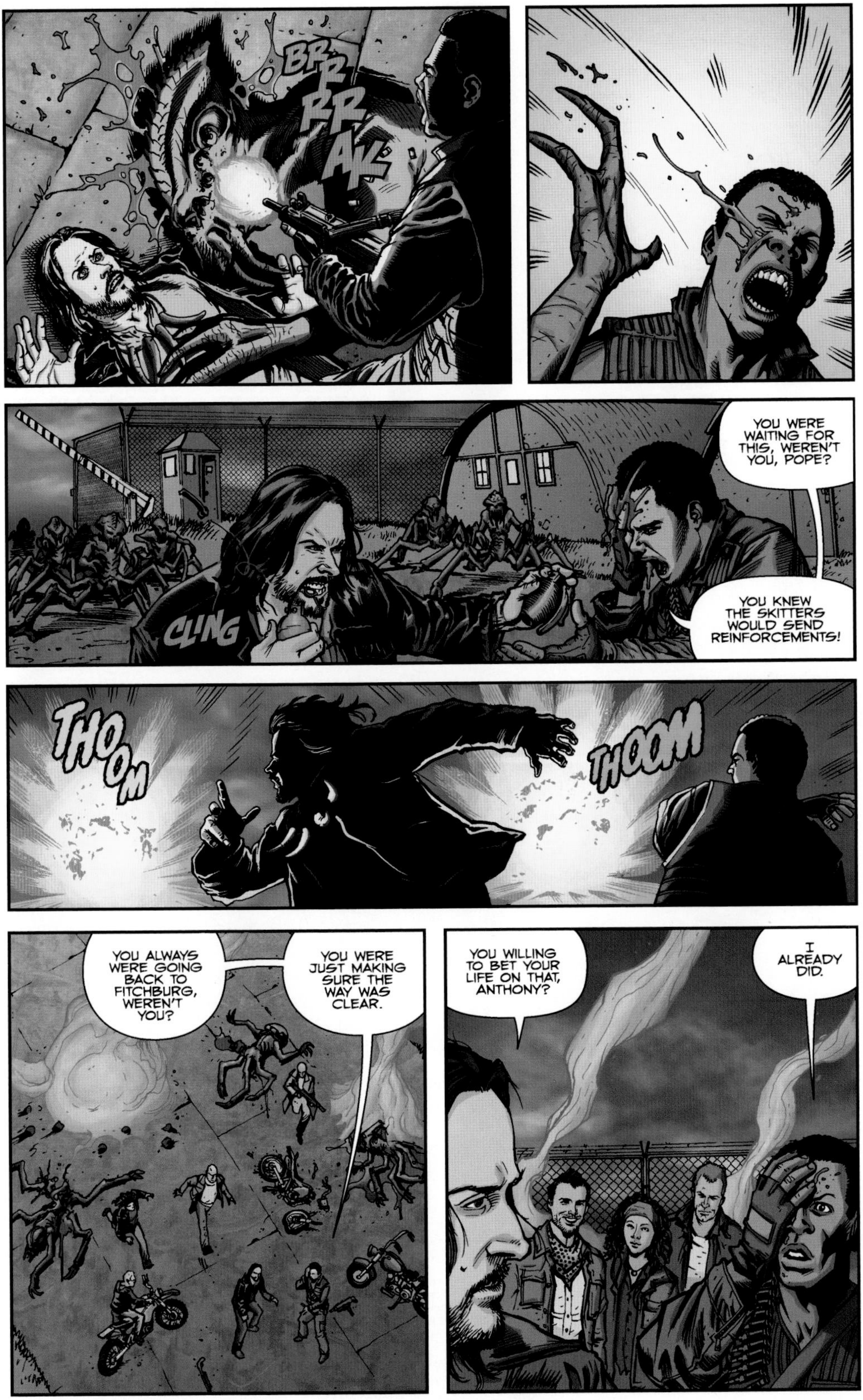
BRRRRAK
YOU WERE WAITING FOR THIS, WEREN'T YOU, POPE?
YOU KNEW THE SKITTERS WOULD SEND REINFORCEMENTS!
CLING
THOOM
THOOM
YOU ALWAYS WERE GOING BACK TO FITCHBURG, WEREN'T YOU?
YOU WERE JUST MAKING SURE THE WAY WAS CLEAR.
YOU WILLING TO BET YOUR LIFE ON THAT, ANTHONY?
I ALREADY DID.

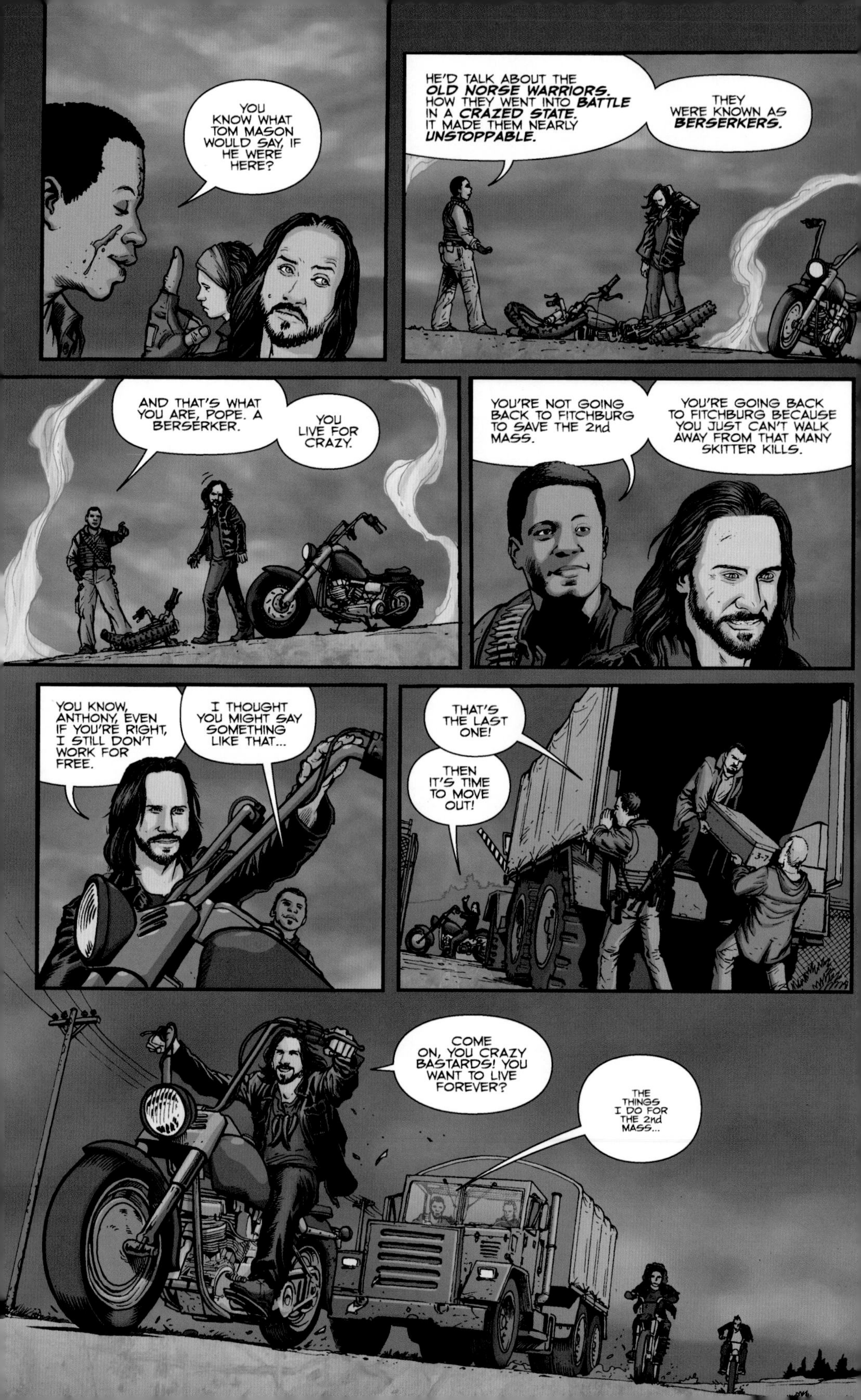
YOU KNOW WHAT TOM MASON WOULD SAY, IF HE WERE HERE?
HE'D TALK ABOUT THE OLD NORSE WARRIORS. HOW THEY WENT INTO BATTLE IN A CRAZED STATE. IT MADE THEM NEARLY UNSTOPPABLE.
THEY WERE KNOWN AS BERSERKERS.
AND THAT'S WHAT YOU ARE, POPE. A BERSERKER.
YOU LIVE FOR CRAZY.
YOU'RE NOT GOING BACK TO FITCHBURG TO SAVE THE 2nd MASS.
YOU'RE GOING BACK TO FITCHBURG BECAUSE YOU JUST CAN'T WALK AWAY FROM THAT MANY SKITTER KILLS.
YOU KNOW, ANTHONY, EVEN IF YOU'RE RIGHT, I STILL DON'T WORK FOR FREE.
I THOUGHT YOU MIGHT SAY SOMETHING LIKE THAT...
THAT'S THE LAST ONE!
THEN IT'S TIME TO MOVE OUT!
COME ON, YOU CRAZY BASTARDS! YOU WANT TO LIVE FOREVER?
THE THINGS I DO FOR THE 2nd MASS...

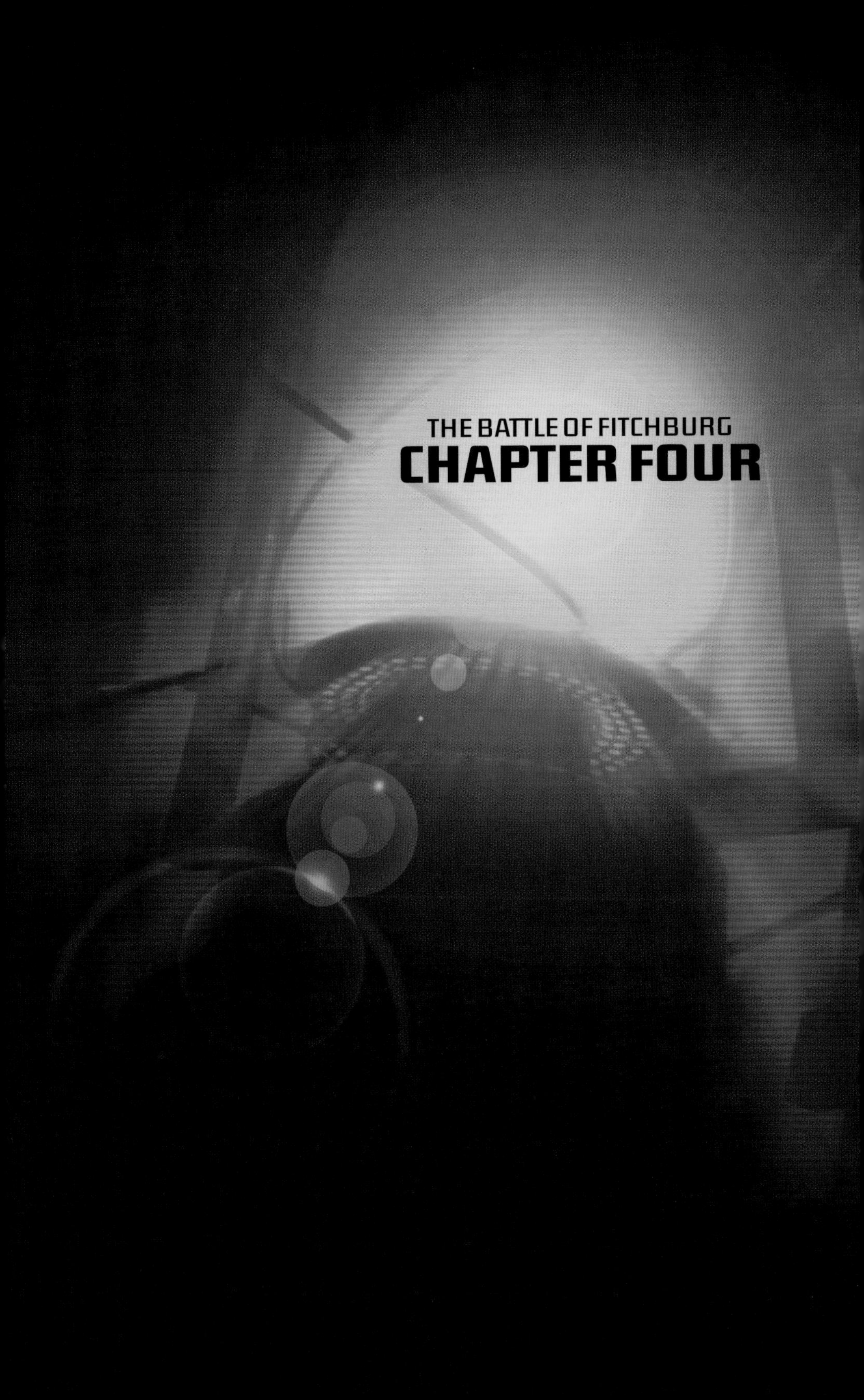

THE BATTLE OF FITCHBURG

CHAPTER FOUR

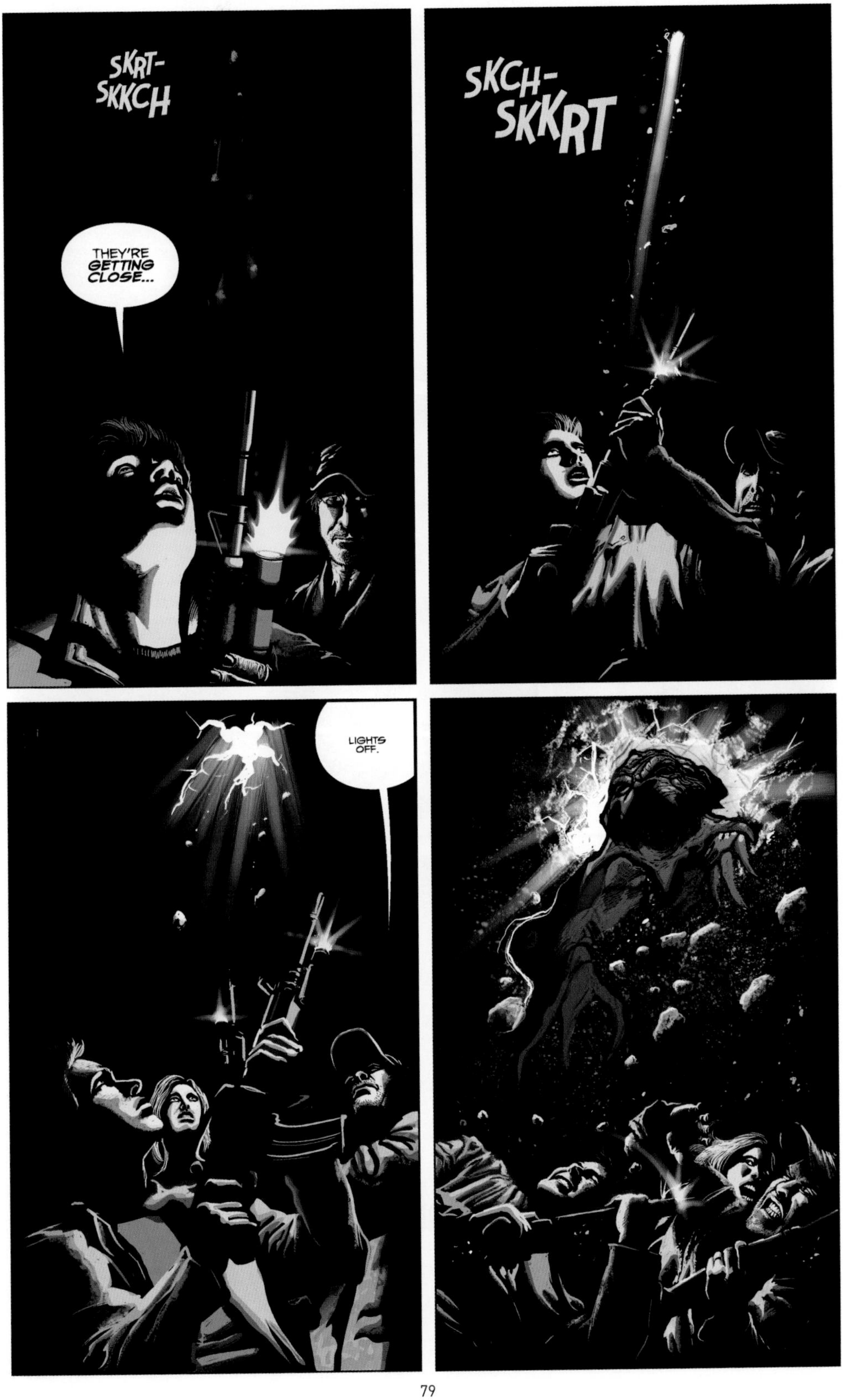
SKRT-
SKKCH
THEY'RE GETTING CLOSE...
SKCH-
SKKRT
LIGHTS OFF.

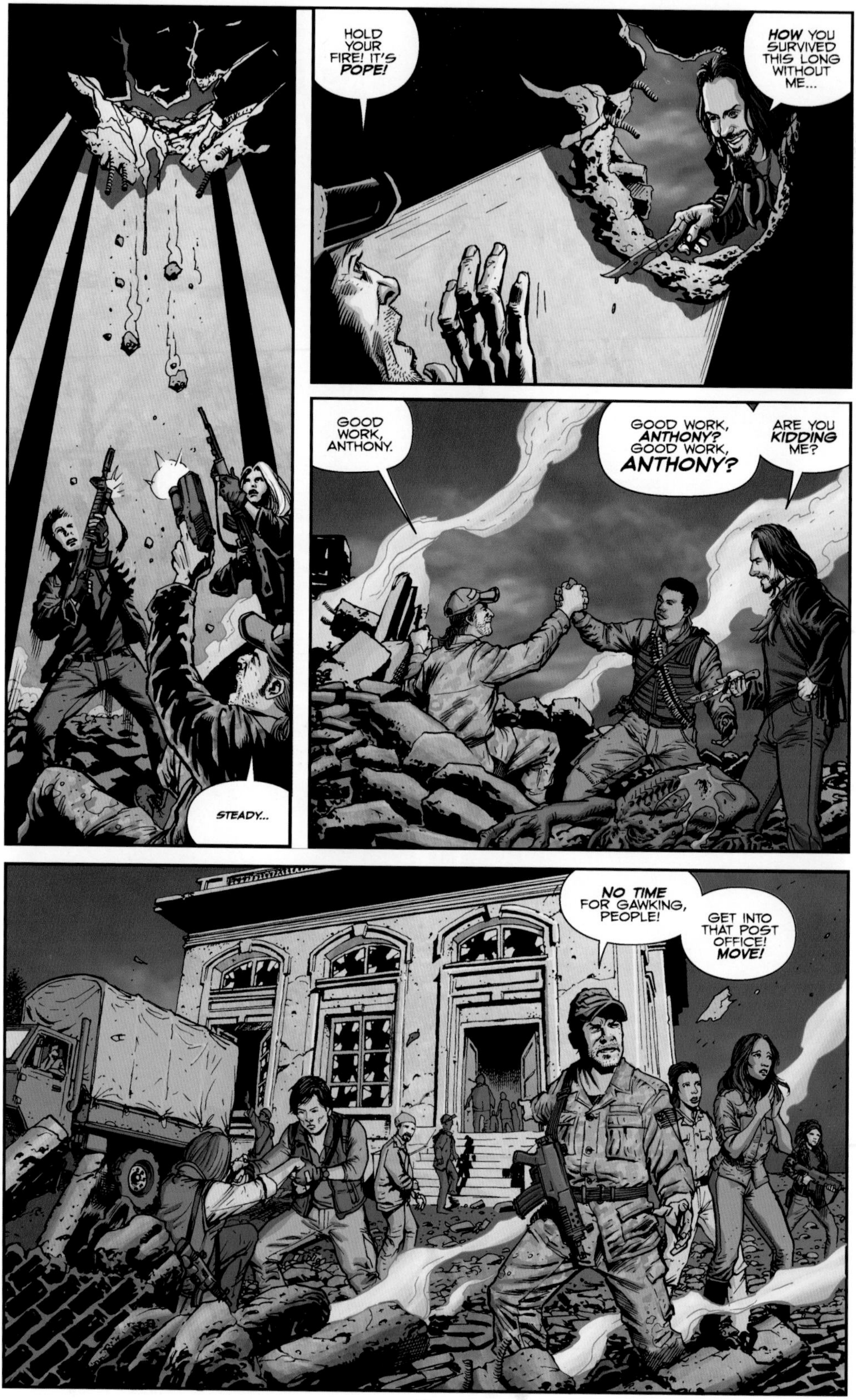
STEADY...
HOLD YOUR FIRE! IT'S POPE!
HOW YOU SURVIVED THIS LONG WITHOUT ME...
GOOD WORK, ANTHONY.
GOOD WORK, ANTHONY? GOOD WORK, ANTHONY?
ARE YOU KIDDING ME?
NO TIME FOR GAWKING, PEOPLE!
GET INTO THAT POST OFFICE! MOVE!

I WANT TWO-MAN TEAMS ON THE WINDOWS! SNIPERS ON THE ROOF!
WE'VE GOT INCOMING!
GOOD THING SOMEBODY BROUGHT BACK ALL THESE GUNS, ISN'T IT?
PAKT
PAKK
PAK
PAKT
PAKT
PAK
PAK
PAK
THEY'RE ON THE RUN!
DAMN IT. IF THEY RETREAT, THEY'LL CALL IN ANOTHER AIRSTRIKE.
WE KEEP THEM IN THE SQUARE, NO MATTER WHAT IT TAKES!

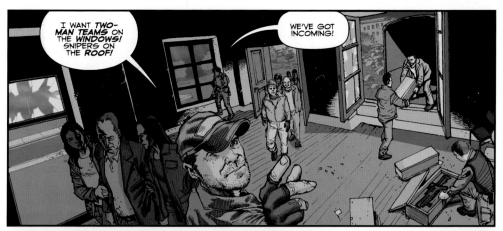

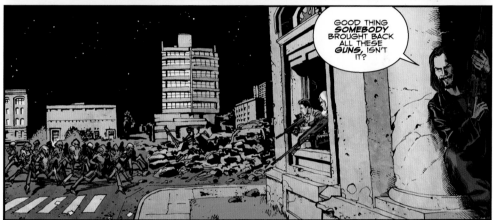

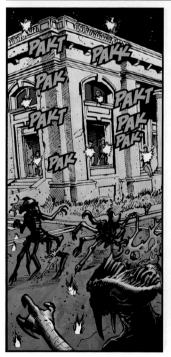

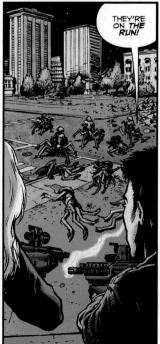

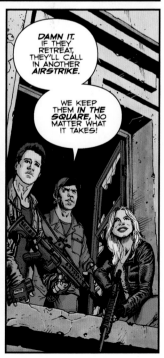

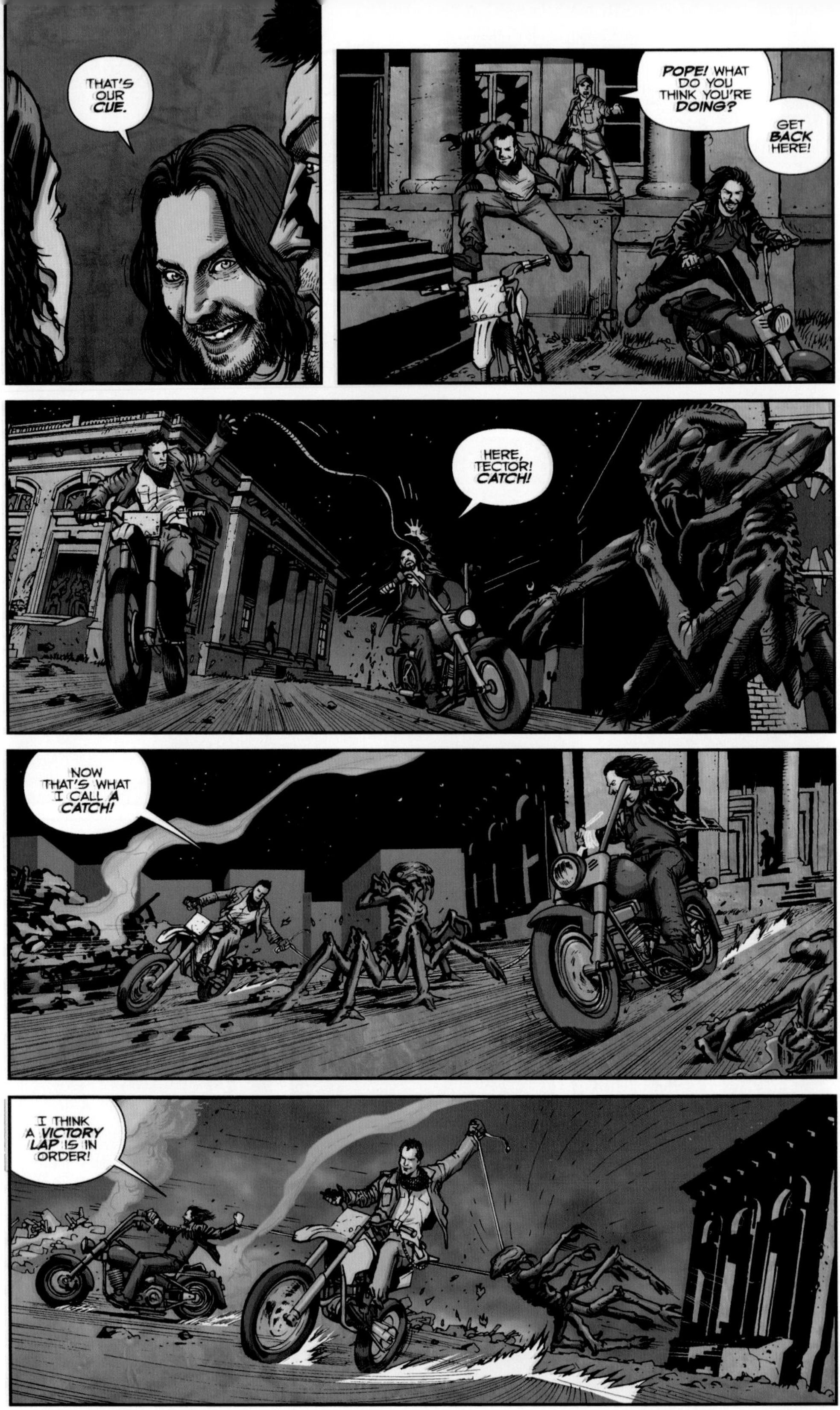
THAT'S OUR CUE.
POPE! WHAT DO YOU THINK YOU'RE DOING?
GET BACK HERE!
HERE, TECTOR! CATCH!
NOW THAT'S WHAT I CALL A CATCH!
I THINK A VICTORY LAP IS IN ORDER!

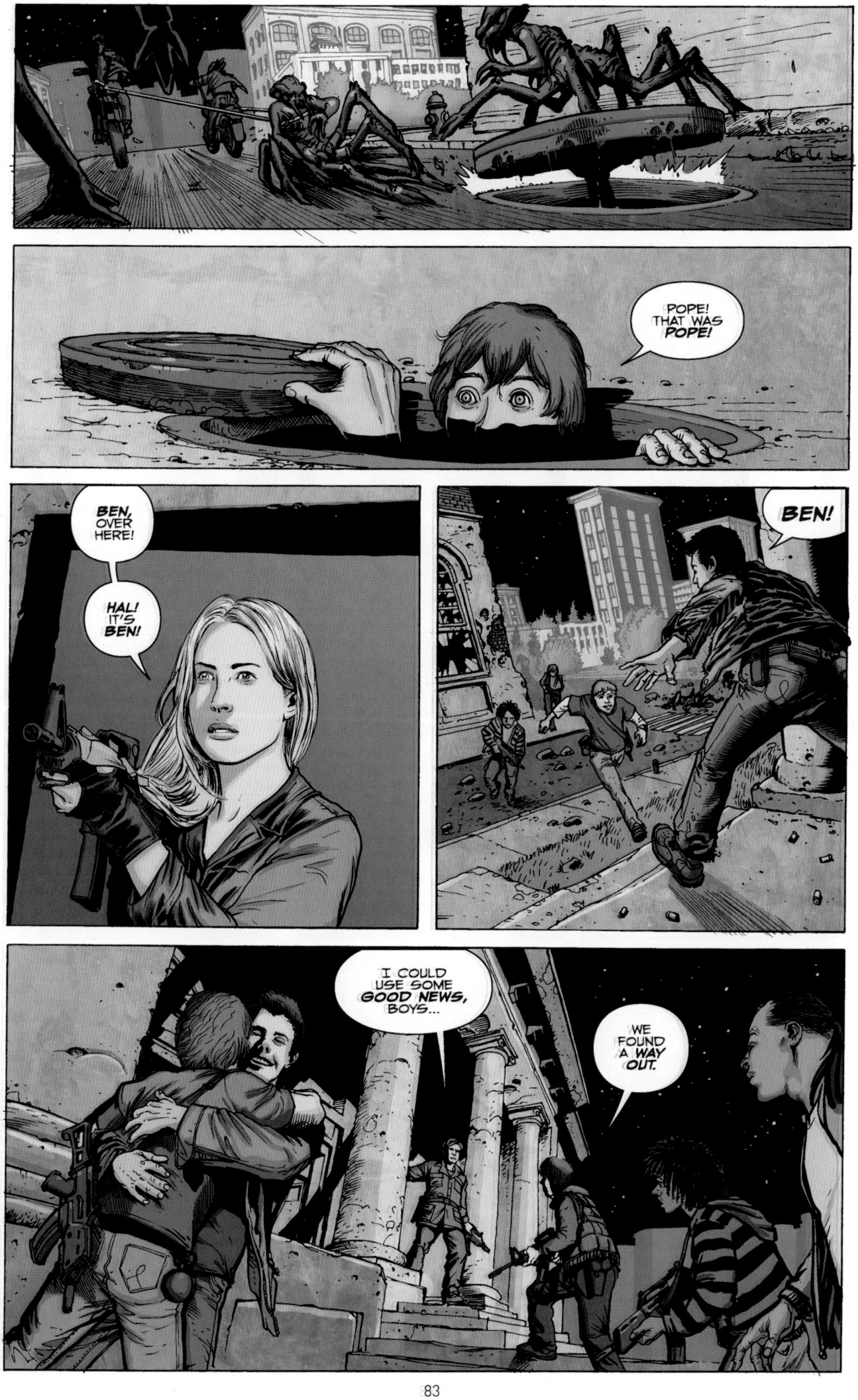
POPE! THAT WAS POPE!
BEN, OVER HERE!
HAL! IT'S BEN!
BEN!
I COULD USE SOME GOOD NEWS, BOYS...
WE FOUND A WAY OUT.

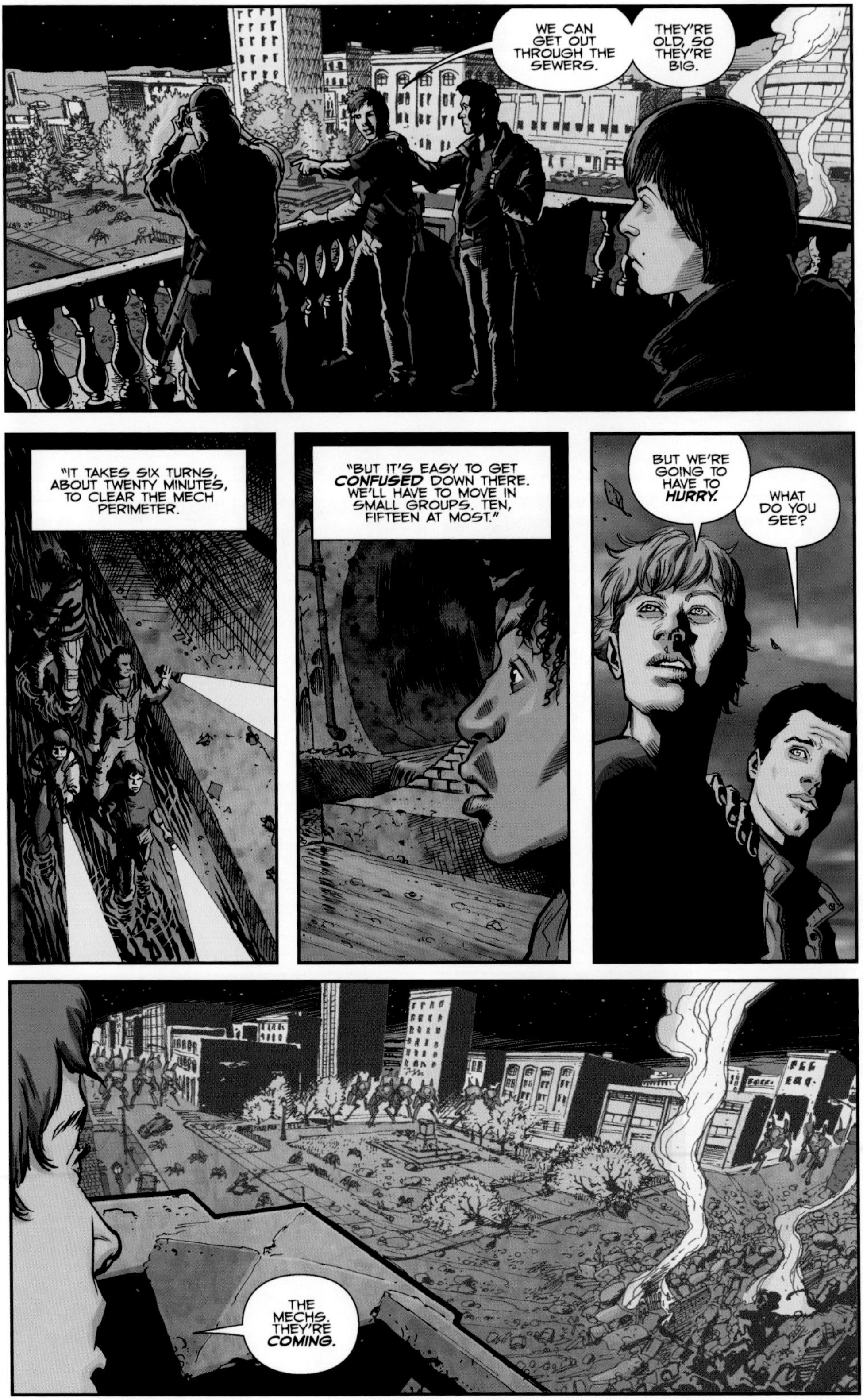
WE CAN GET OUT THROUGH THE SEWERS.
THEY'RE OLD, SO THEY'RE BIG.
"IT TAKES SIX TURNS, ABOUT TWENTY MINUTES, TO CLEAR THE MECH PERIMETER.
"BUT IT'S EASY TO GET CONFUSED DOWN THERE. WE'LL HAVE TO MOVE IN SMALL GROUPS. TEN, FIFTEEN AT MOST."
BUT WE'RE GOING TO HAVE TO HURRY.
WHAT DO YOU SEE?
THE MECHS. THEY'RE COMING.

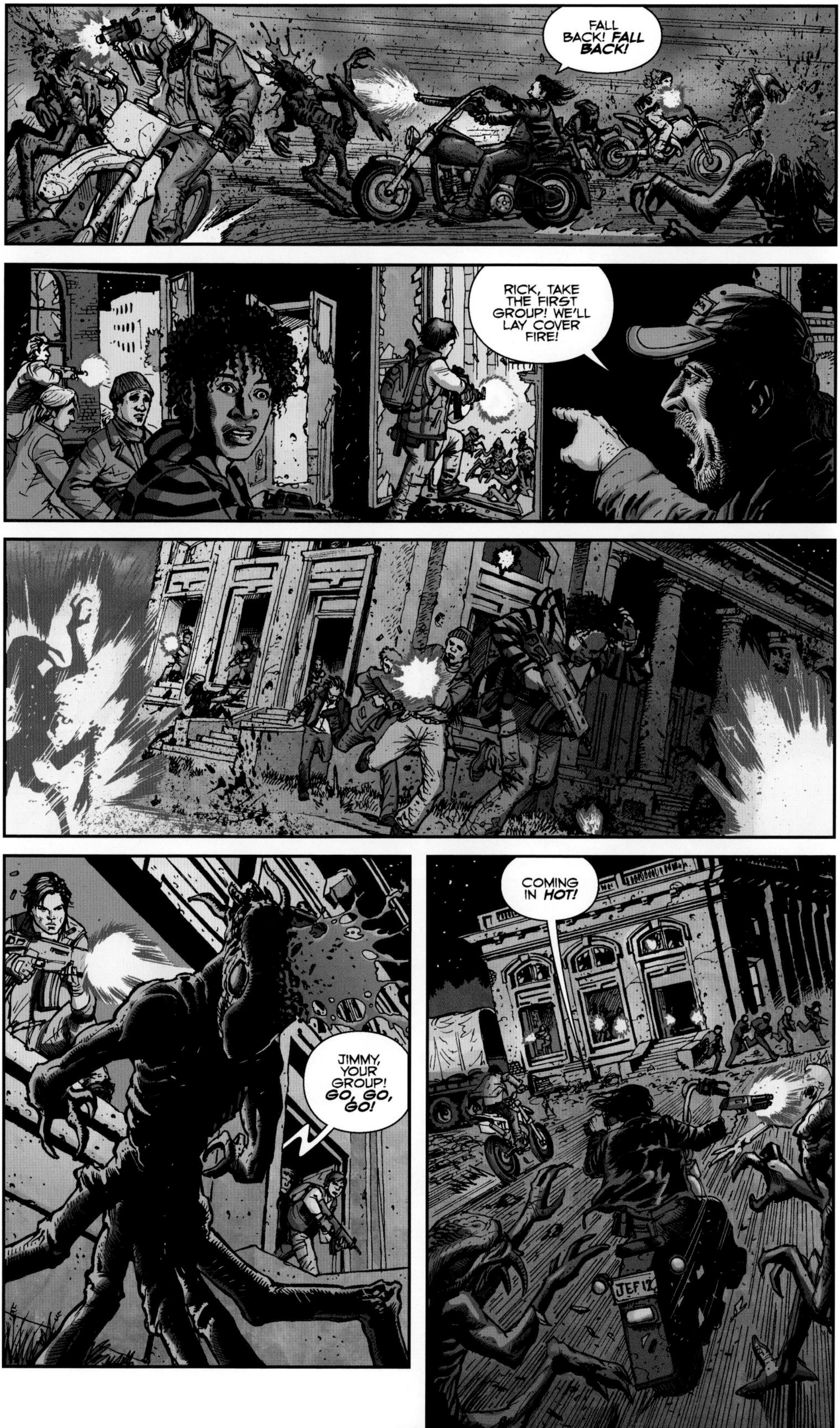
FALL BACK! **FALL BACK!**
RICK, TAKE THE FIRST GROUP! WE'LL LAY COVER FIRE!
JIMMY, YOUR GROUP! **GO, GO, GO!**
COMING IN **HOT!**

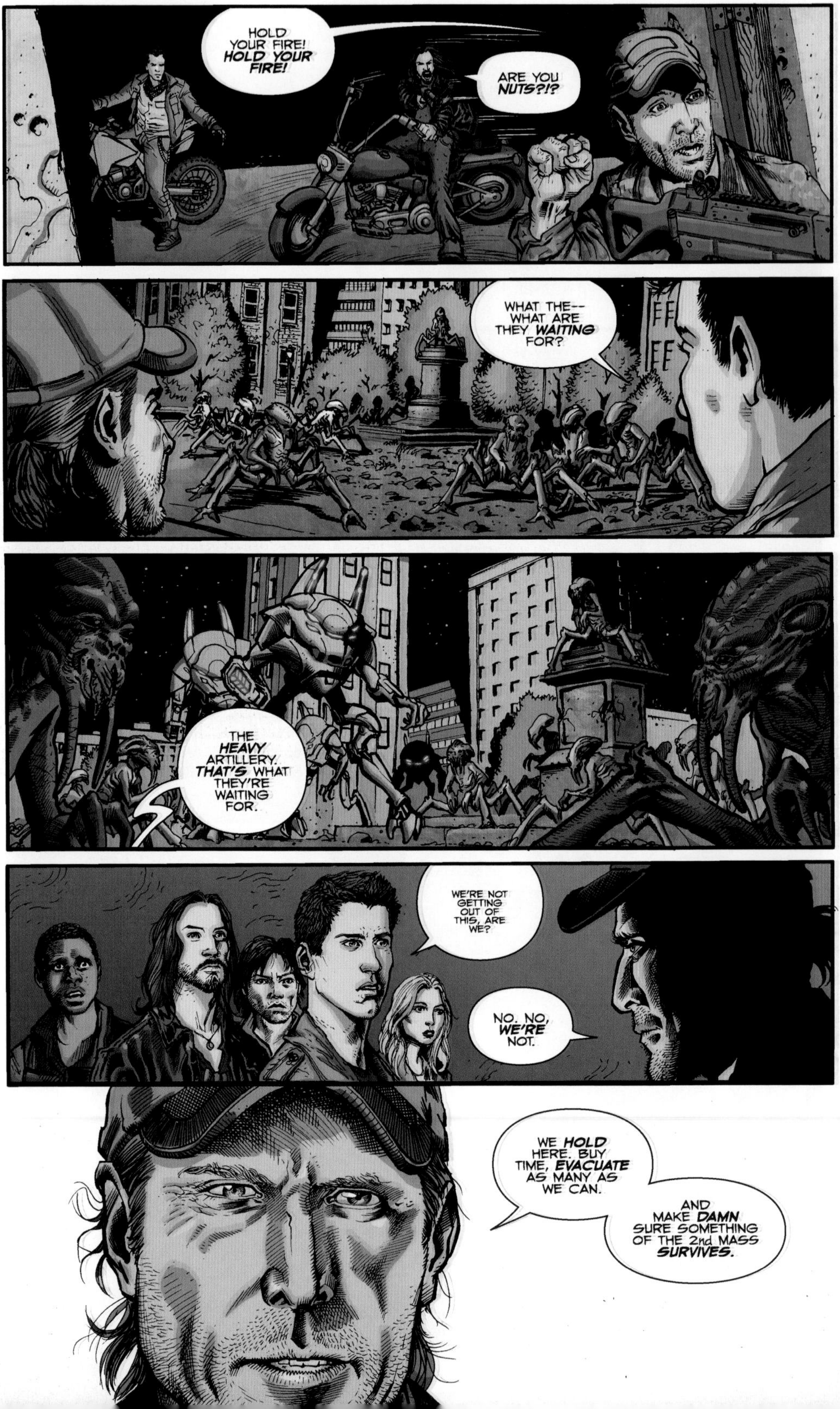
HOLD YOUR FIRE! HOLD YOUR FIRE!
ARE YOU NUTS?!?
WHAT THE-- WHAT ARE THEY WAITING FOR?
THE HEAVY ARTILLERY. THAT'S WHAT THEY'RE WAITING FOR.
WE'RE NOT GETTING OUT OF THIS, ARE WE?
NO. NO, WE'RE NOT.
WE HOLD HERE. BUY TIME, EVACUATE AS MANY AS WE CAN.
AND MAKE DAMN SURE SOMETHING OF THE 2nd MASS SURVIVES.

BEN! *RICK'S* GROUP IS RIGHT BEHIND US.

ONLY *TWO MORE* TO GO!

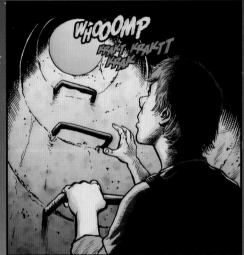

WHOOOMP

KRAKT KRAKTT KRAK

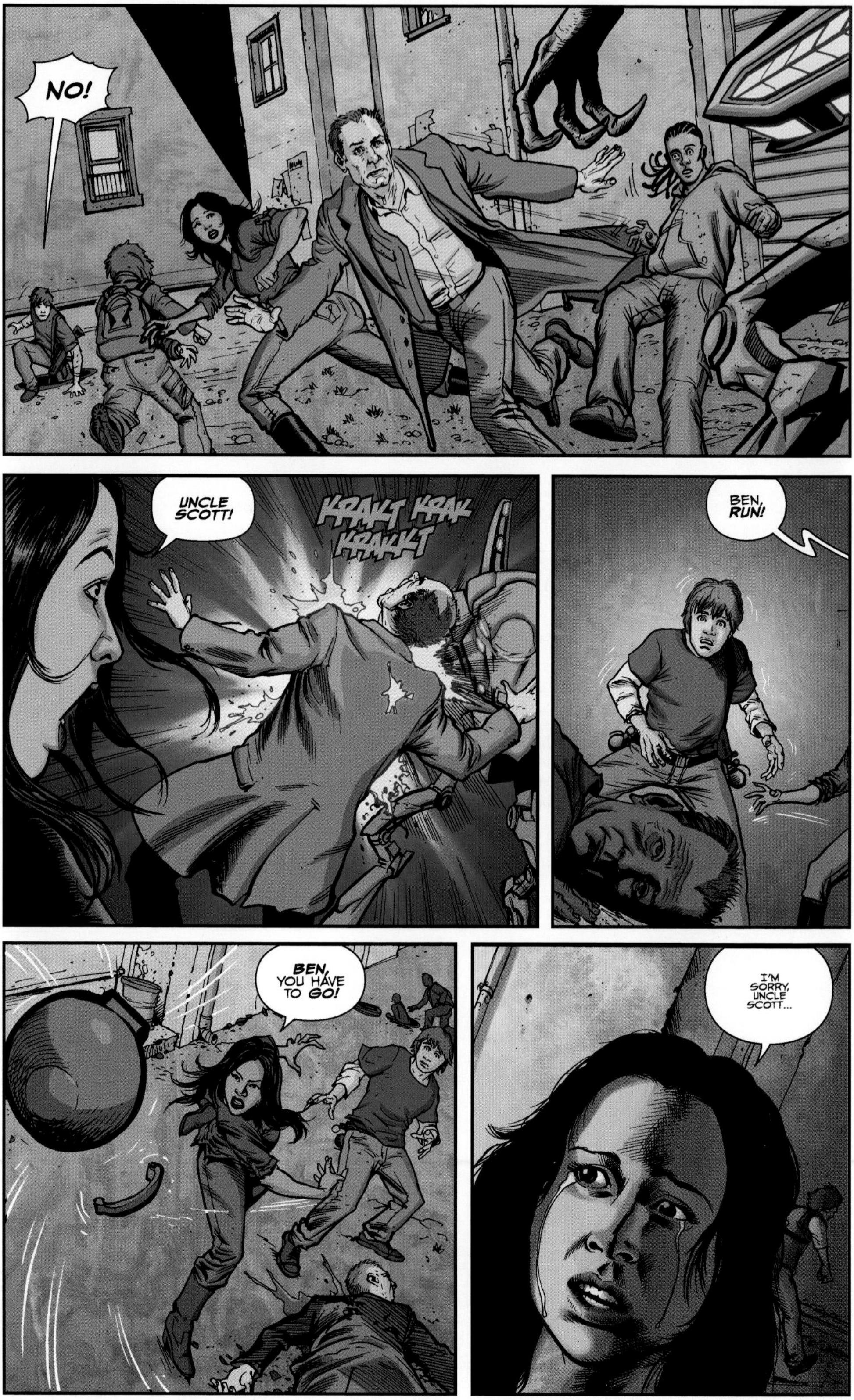
NO!
UNCLE SCOTT!
KRAKT KRAK KRAKKT
BEN, RUN!
BEN, YOU HAVE TO GO!
I'M SORRY, UNCLE SCOTT...

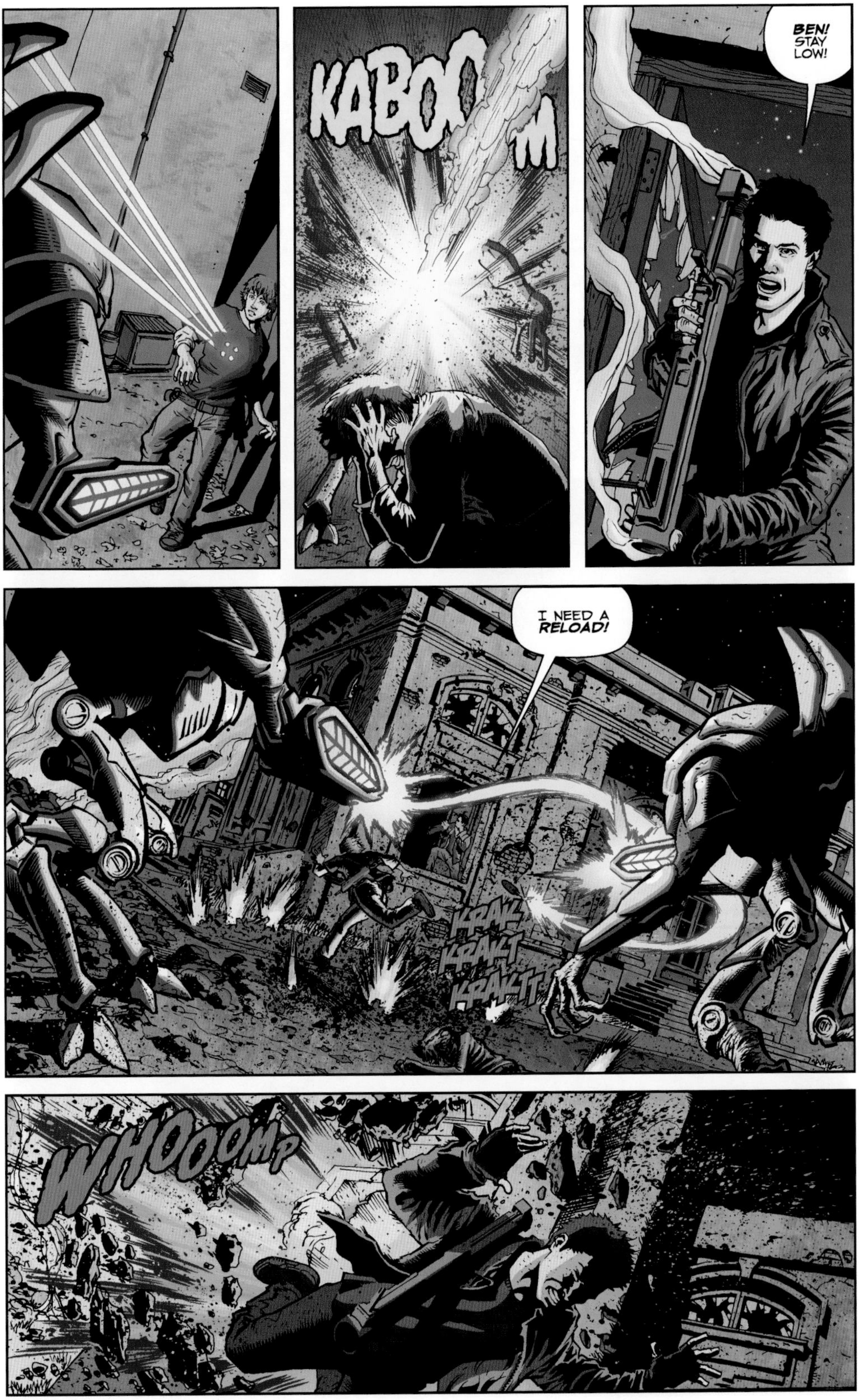
KABOOM
BEN! STAY LOW!
I NEED A RELOAD!
WHOOOMP

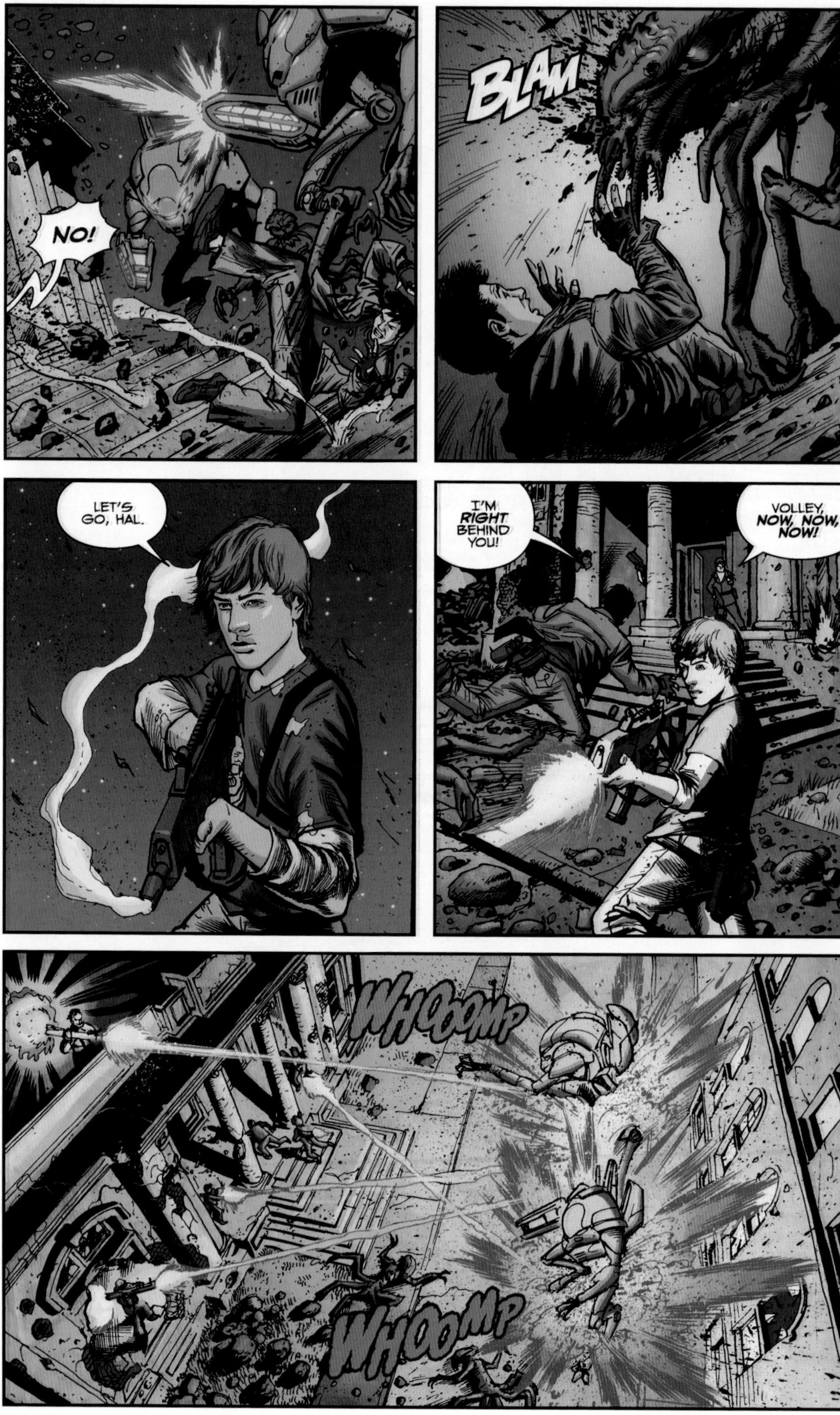

NO!
BLAM
LET'S GO, HAL.
I'M RIGHT BEHIND YOU!
VOLLEY, NOW, NOW, NOW!
WHOOOMP
WHOOMP

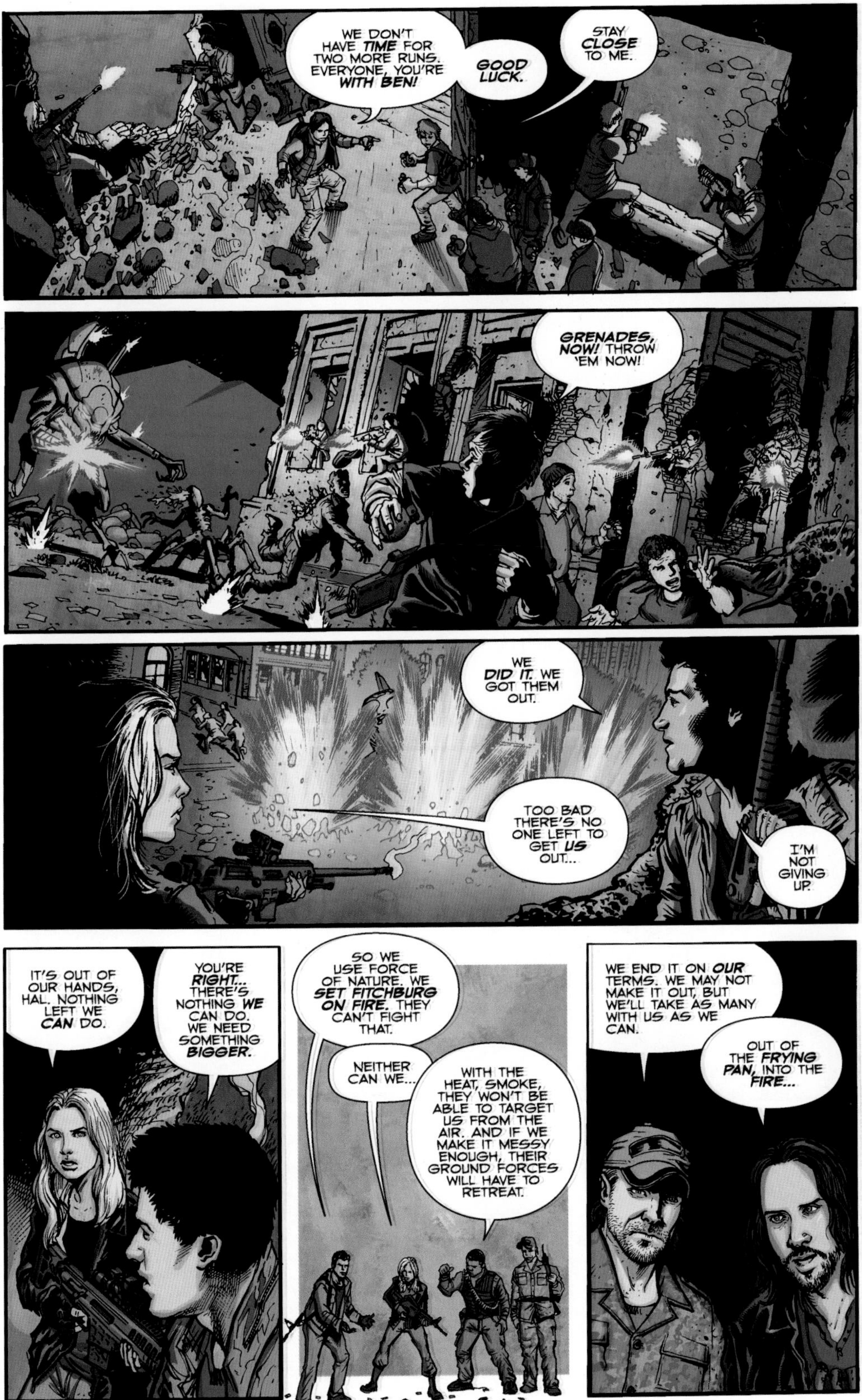
WE DON'T HAVE TIME FOR TWO MORE RUNS. EVERYONE, YOU'RE WITH BEN!
GOOD LUCK.
STAY CLOSE TO ME.
GRENADES, NOW! THROW 'EM NOW!
WE DID IT. WE GOT THEM OUT.
TOO BAD THERE'S NO ONE LEFT TO GET US OUT...
I'M NOT GIVING UP.
IT'S OUT OF OUR HANDS, HAL. NOTHING LEFT WE CAN DO.
YOU'RE RIGHT... THERE'S NOTHING WE CAN DO. WE NEED SOMETHING BIGGER.
SO WE USE FORCE OF NATURE. WE SET FITCHBURG ON FIRE. THEY CAN'T FIGHT THAT.
NEITHER CAN WE...
WITH THE HEAT, SMOKE, THEY WON'T BE ABLE TO TARGET US FROM THE AIR. AND IF WE MAKE IT MESSY ENOUGH, THEIR GROUND FORCES WILL HAVE TO RETREAT.
WE END IT ON OUR TERMS. WE MAY NOT MAKE IT OUT, BUT WE'LL TAKE AS MANY WITH US AS WE CAN.
OUT OF THE FRYING PAN, INTO THE FIRE...

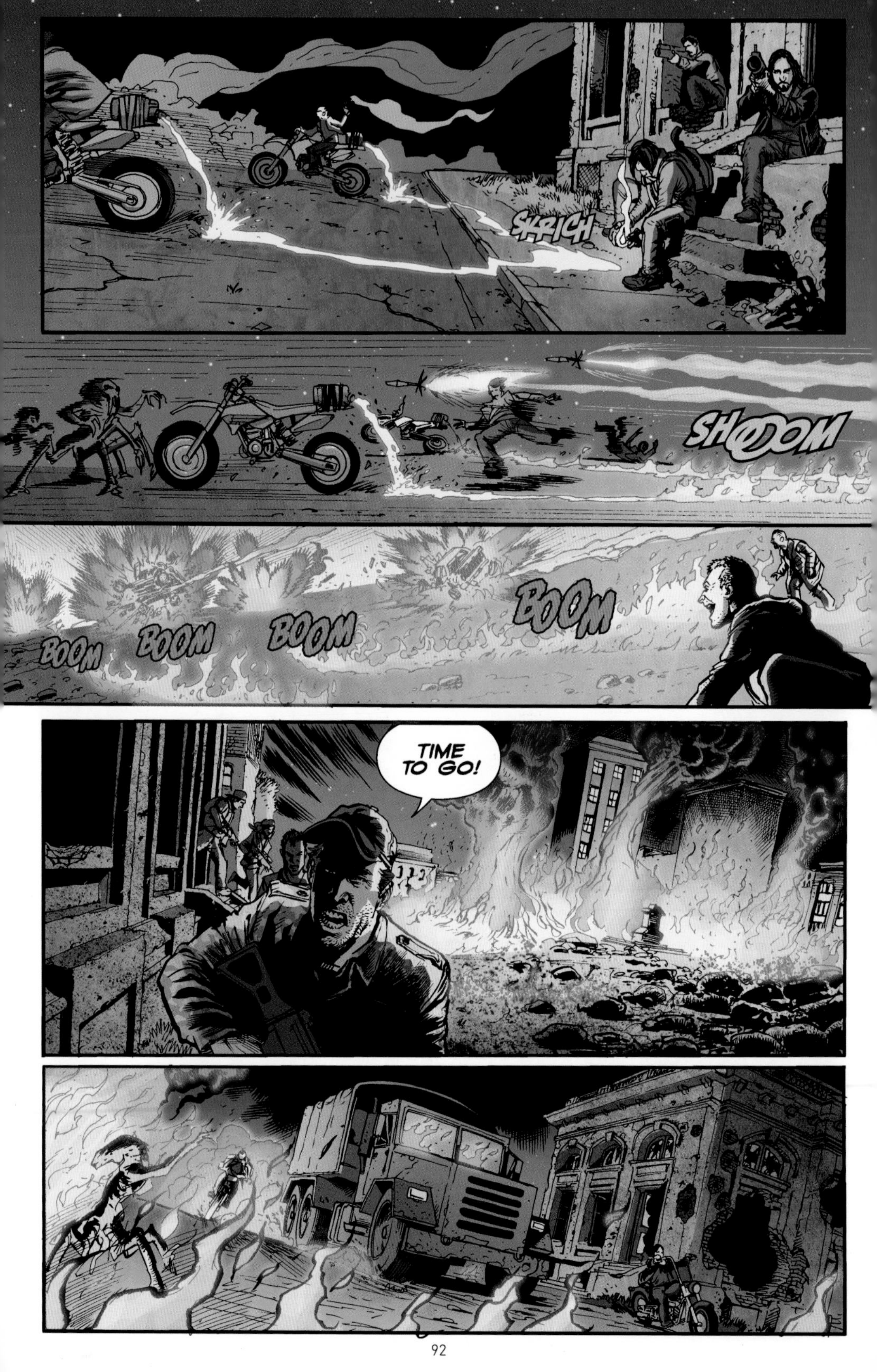
SKRICH
SHOOOM
BOOM
BOOM
BOOM
BOOM
TIME TO GO!

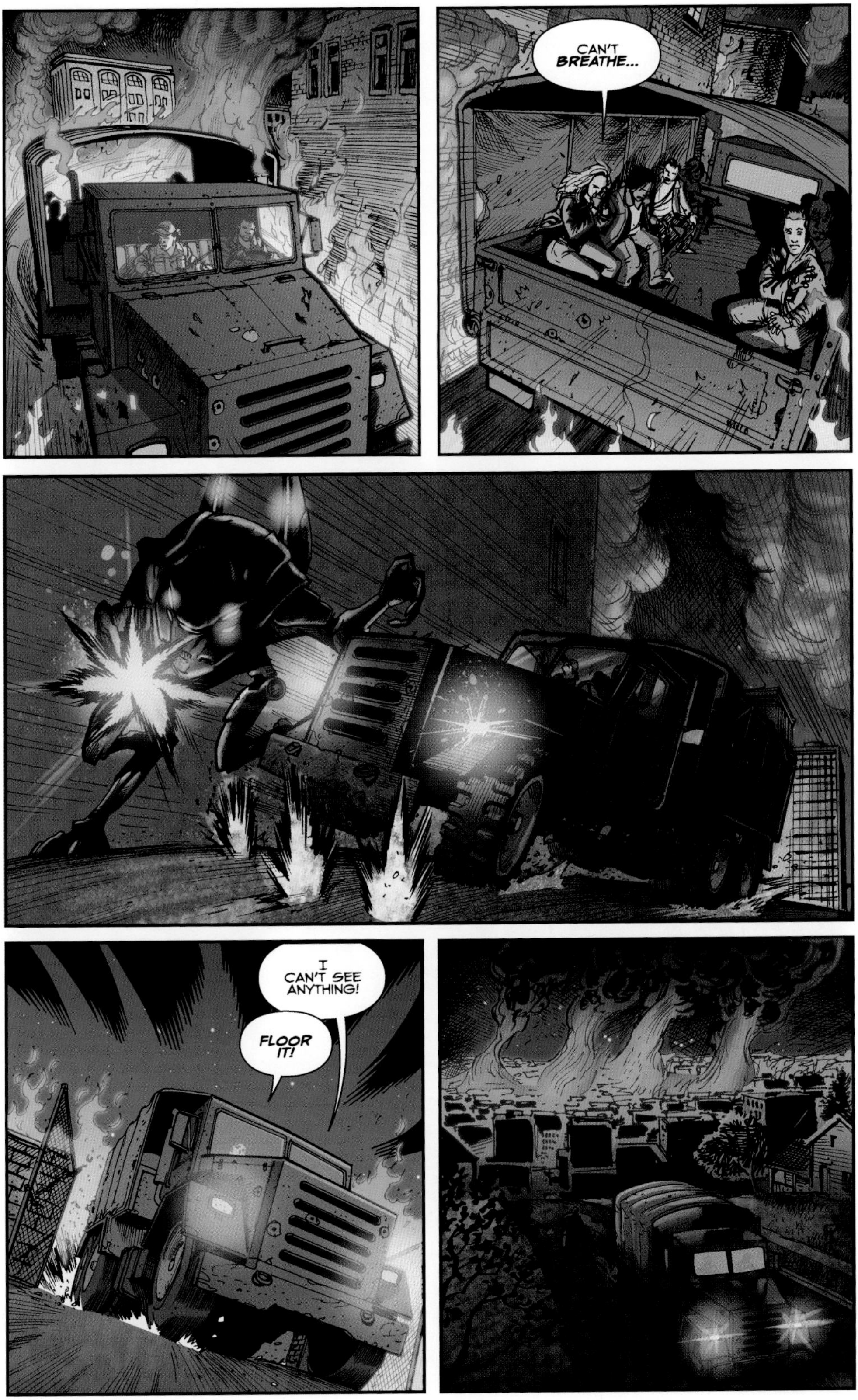
CAN'T BREATHE...
I CAN'T SEE ANYTHING!
FLOOR IT!

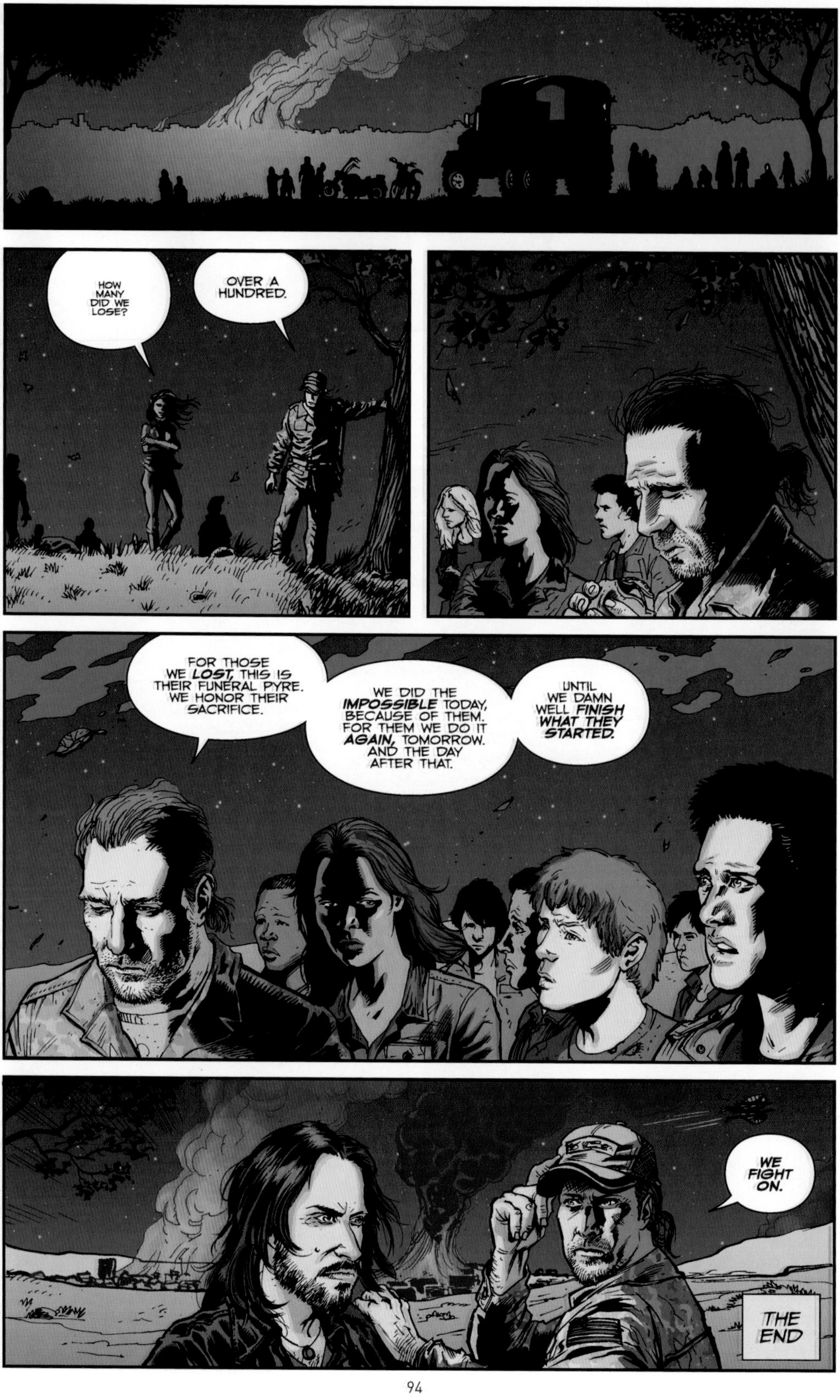
HOW MANY DID WE LOSE?
OVER A HUNDRED.
FOR THOSE WE LOST, THIS IS THEIR FUNERAL PYRE. WE HONOR THEIR SACRIFICE.
WE DID THE IMPOSSIBLE TODAY, BECAUSE OF THEM. FOR THEM WE DO IT AGAIN, TOMORROW. AND THE DAY AFTER THAT.
UNTIL WE DAMN WELL FINISH WHAT THEY STARTED.
WE FIGHT ON.
THE END

LUCK

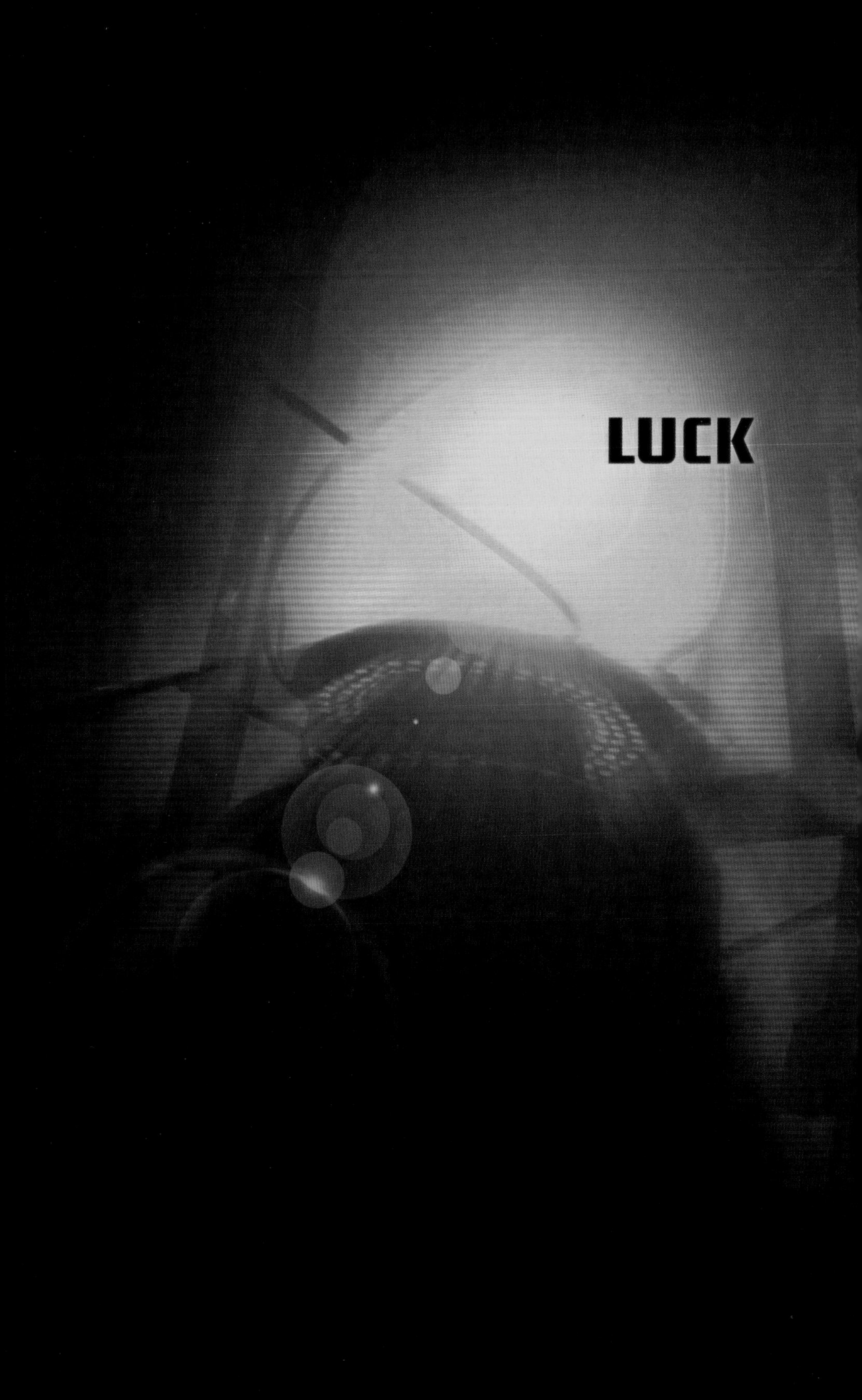

Script by **MARK VERHEIDEN** and **BRYAN OH**

Art by **MARK NELSON**

Lettering by **NATE PIEKOS OF BLAMBOT**®

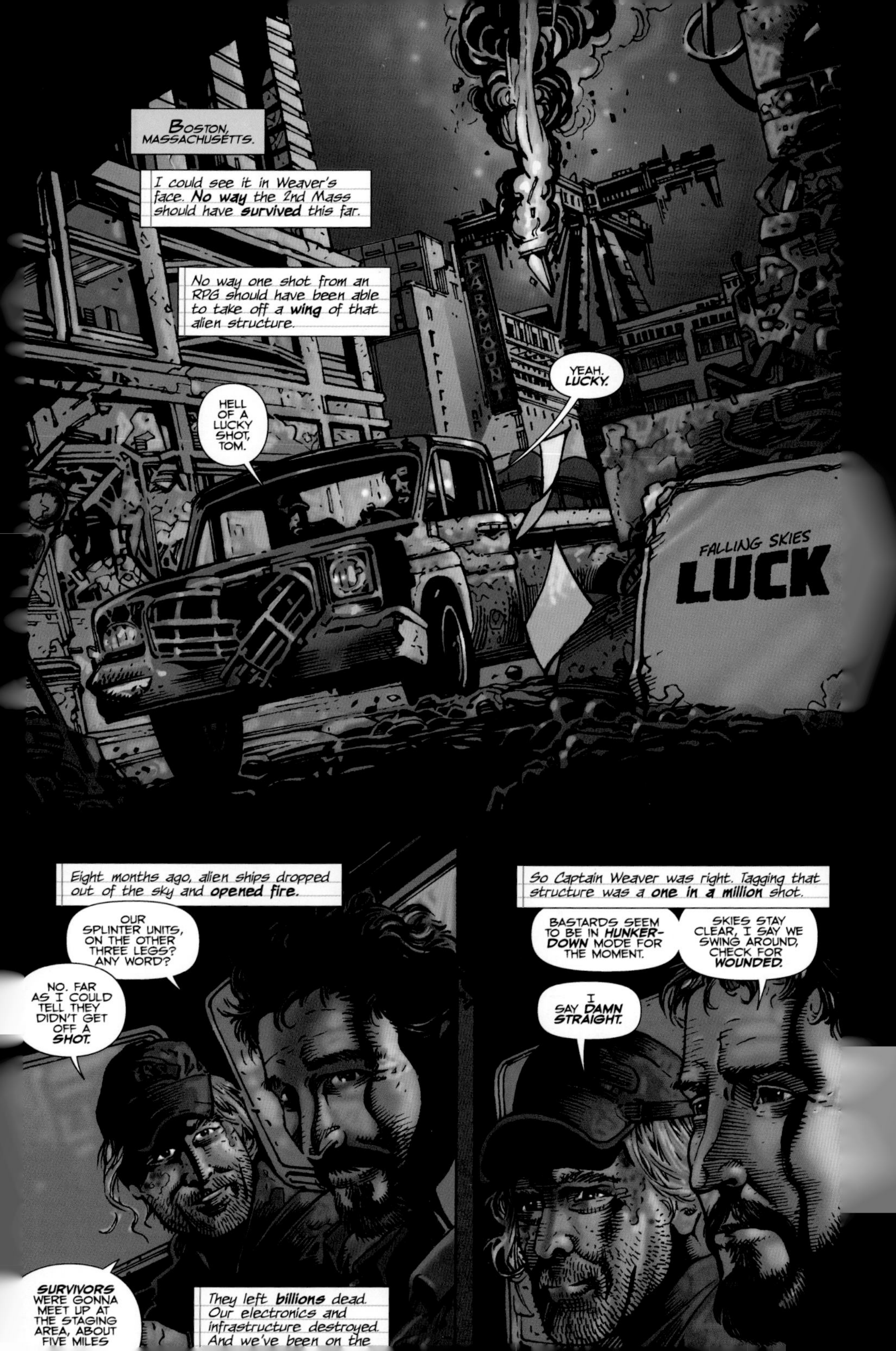

BOSTON, MASSACHUSETTS.
I could see it in Weaver's face. No way the 2nd Mass should have survived this far.
No way one shot from an RPG should have been able to take off a wing of that alien structure.
HELL OF A LUCKY SHOT, TOM.
YEAH. LUCKY.
FALLING SKIES
LUCK
Eight months ago, alien ships dropped out of the sky and opened fire.
OUR SPLINTER UNITS, ON THE OTHER THREE LEGS? ANY WORD?
NO. FAR AS I COULD TELL THEY DIDN'T GET OFF A SHOT.
SURVIVORS WERE GONNA MEET UP AT THE STAGING AREA, ABOUT FIVE MILES
They left billions dead. Our electronics and infrastructure destroyed. And we've been on the
So Captain Weaver was right. Tagging that structure was a one in a million shot.
BASTARDS SEEM TO BE IN HUNKER-DOWN MODE FOR THE MOMENT.
SKIES STAY CLEAR, I SAY WE SWING AROUND, CHECK FOR WOUNDED.
I SAY DAMN STRAIGHT.

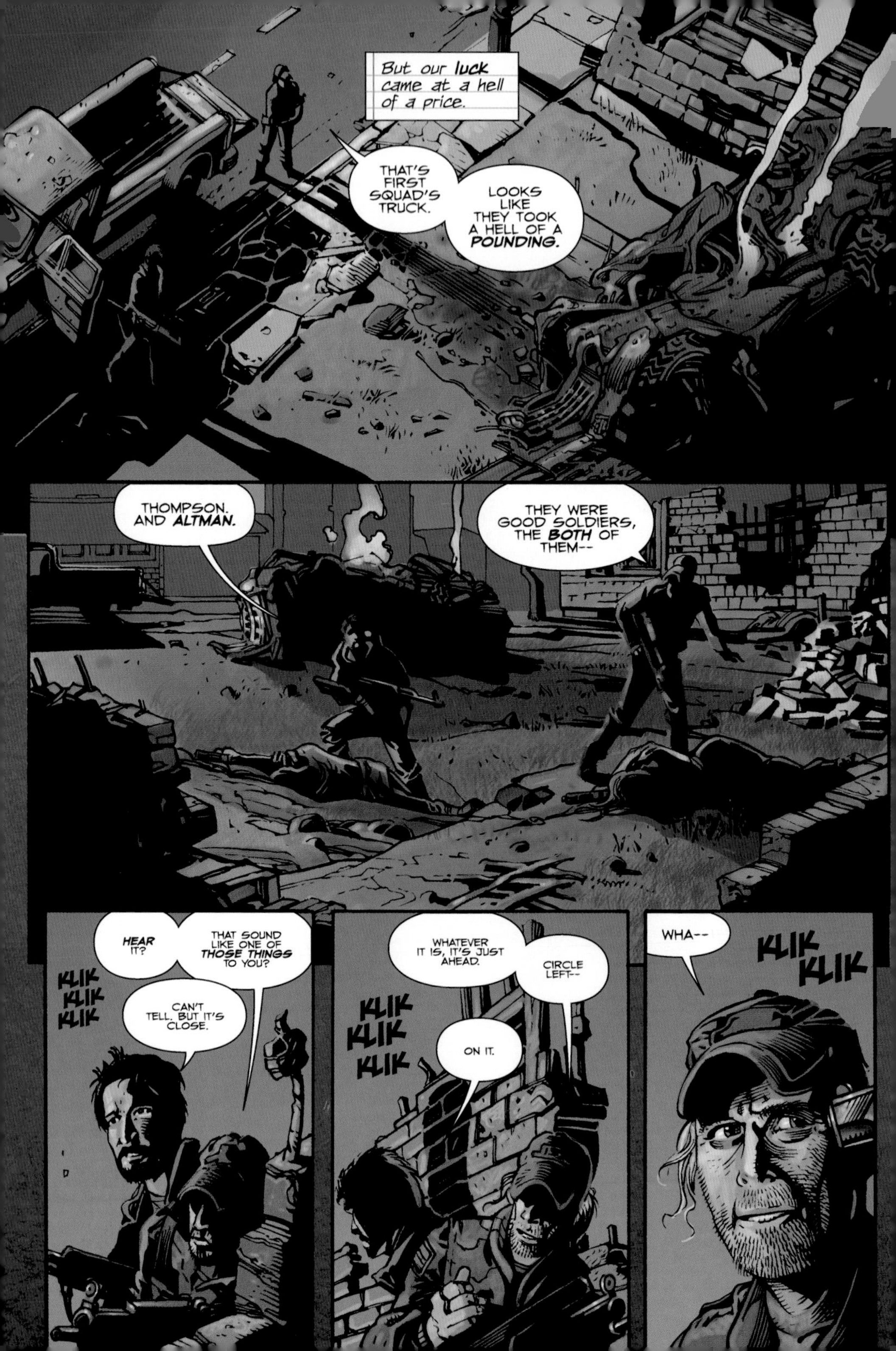

But our luck came at a hell of a price.
THAT'S FIRST SQUAD'S TRUCK.
LOOKS LIKE THEY TOOK A HELL OF A POUNDING.
THOMPSON. AND ALTMAN.
THEY WERE GOOD SOLDIERS, THE BOTH OF THEM--
HEAR IT?
THAT SOUND LIKE ONE OF THOSE THINGS TO YOU?
KLIK KLIK KLIK
CAN'T TELL. BUT IT'S CLOSE.
WHATEVER IT IS, IT'S JUST AHEAD.
CIRCLE LEFT--
KLIK KLIK KLIK
ON IT.
WHA--
KLIK KLIK

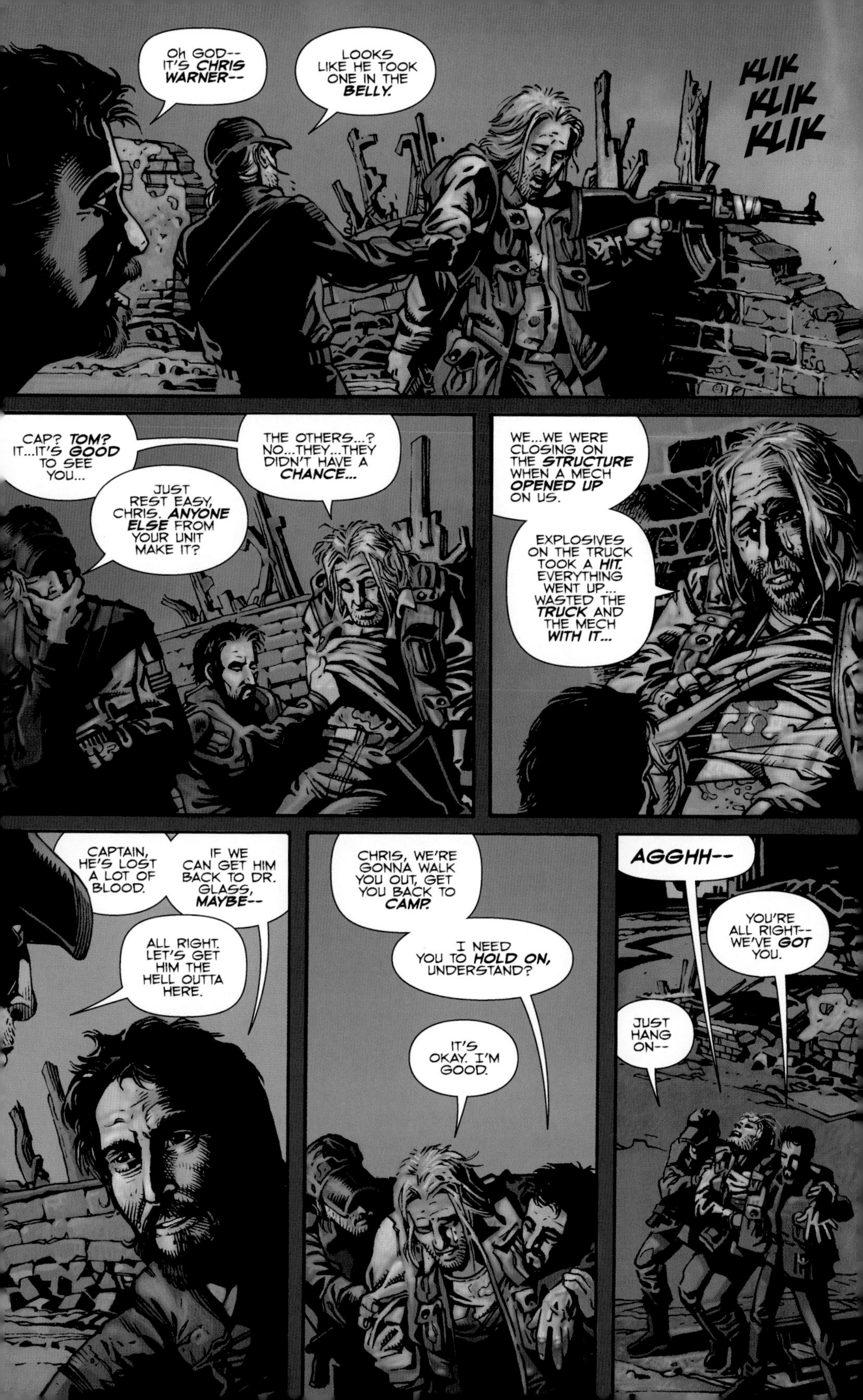

Oh GOD-- IT'S CHRIS WARNER--
LOOKS LIKE HE TOOK ONE IN THE BELLY.
KLIK KLIK KLIK
CAP? TOM? IT...IT'S GOOD TO SEE YOU...
JUST REST EASY, CHRIS. ANYONE ELSE FROM YOUR UNIT MAKE IT?
THE OTHERS...? NO...THEY...THEY DIDN'T HAVE A CHANCE...
WE...WE WERE CLOSING ON THE STRUCTURE WHEN A MECH OPENED UP ON US.
EXPLOSIVES ON THE TRUCK TOOK A HIT. EVERYTHING WENT UP... WASTED THE TRUCK AND THE MECH WITH IT...
CAPTAIN, HE'S LOST A LOT OF BLOOD.
IF WE CAN GET HIM BACK TO DR. GLASS, MAYBE--
ALL RIGHT. LET'S GET HIM THE HELL OUTTA HERE.
CHRIS, WE'RE GONNA WALK YOU OUT, GET YOU BACK TO CAMP.
I NEED YOU TO HOLD ON, UNDERSTAND?
IT'S OKAY. I'M GOOD.
AGGHH--
YOU'RE ALL RIGHT-- WE'VE GOT YOU.
JUST HANG ON--

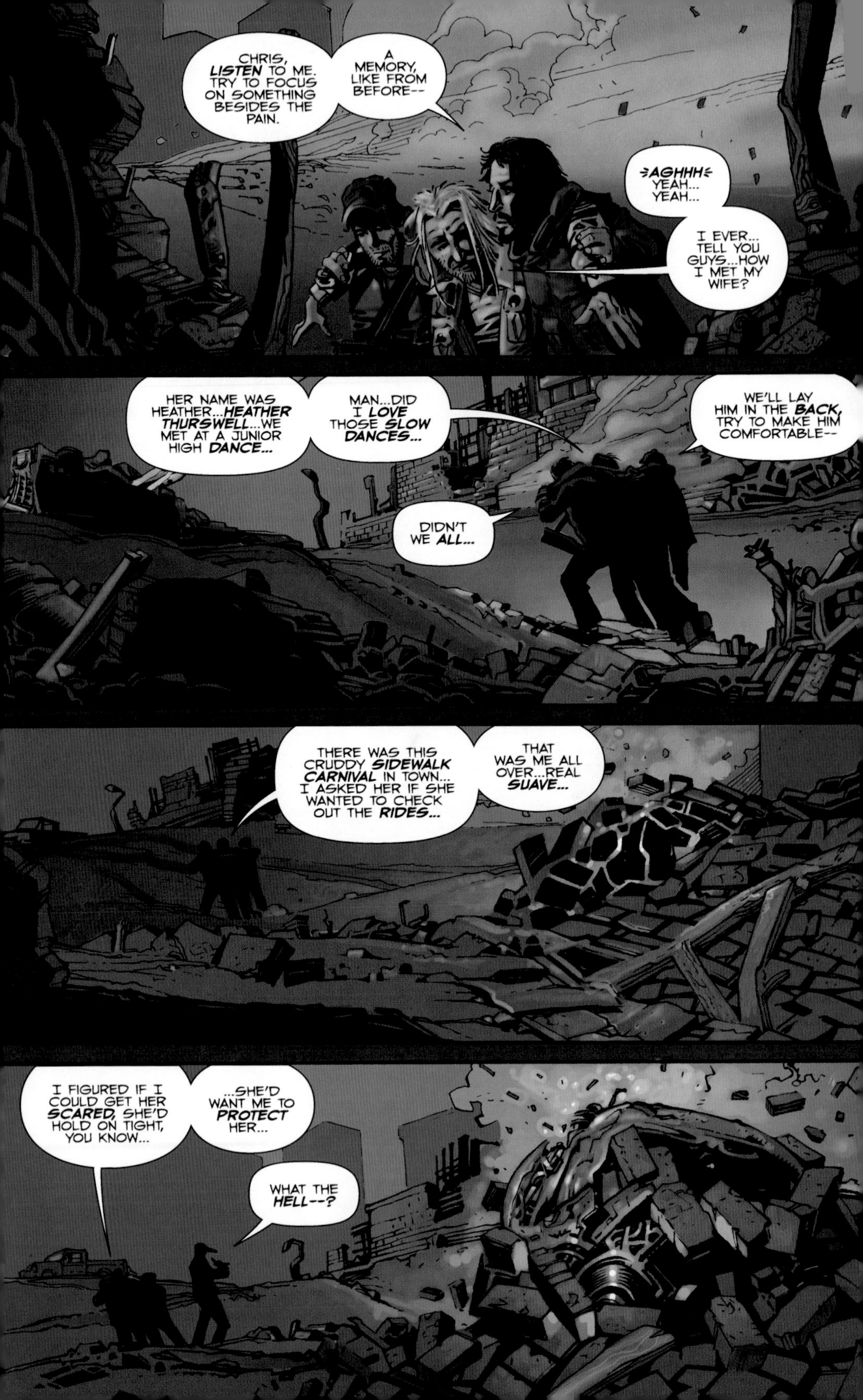
CHRIS, LISTEN TO ME. TRY TO FOCUS ON SOMETHING BESIDES THE PAIN.
A MEMORY, LIKE FROM BEFORE--
AGHHH YEAH... YEAH...
I EVER... TELL YOU GUYS...HOW I MET MY WIFE?
HER NAME WAS HEATHER...HEATHER THURSWELL...WE MET AT A JUNIOR HIGH DANCE...
MAN...DID I LOVE THOSE SLOW DANCES...
WE'LL LAY HIM IN THE BACK, TRY TO MAKE HIM COMFORTABLE--
DIDN'T WE ALL...
THERE WAS THIS CRUDDY SIDEWALK CARNIVAL IN TOWN... I ASKED HER IF SHE WANTED TO CHECK OUT THE RIDES...
THAT WAS ME ALL OVER...REAL SUAVE...
I FIGURED IF I COULD GET HER SCARED, SHE'D HOLD ON TIGHT, YOU KNOW...
...SHE'D WANT ME TO PROTECT HER...
WHAT THE HELL--?

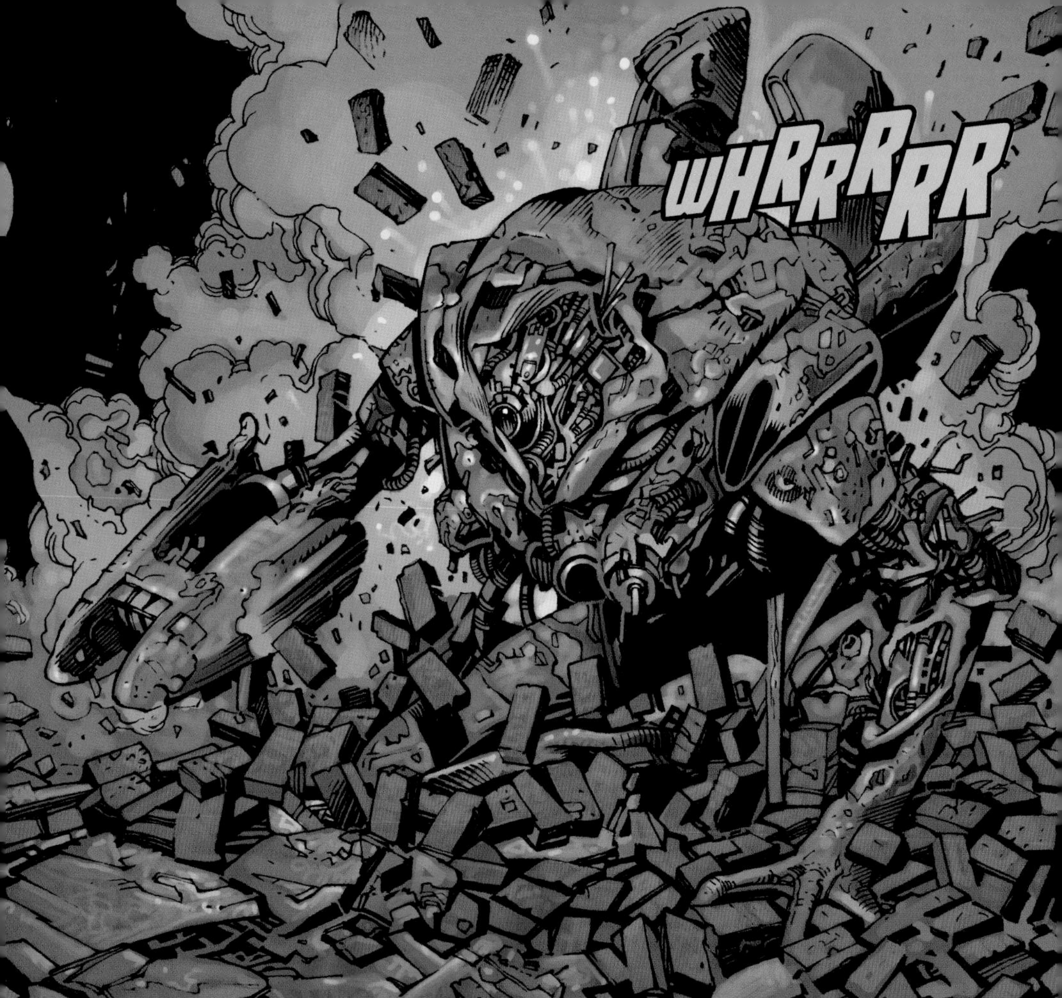
WHRRRRR

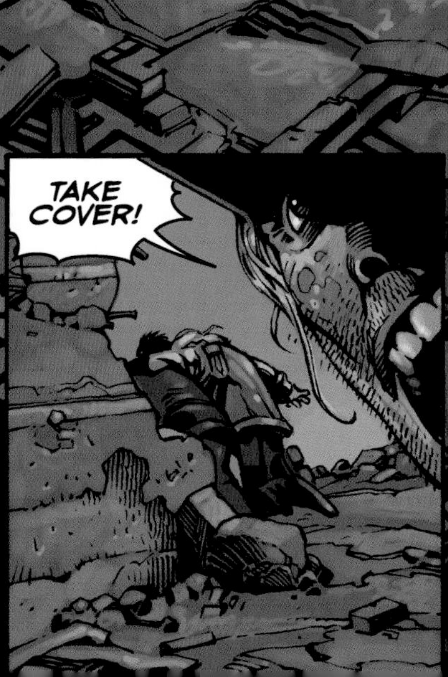
TAKE COVER!

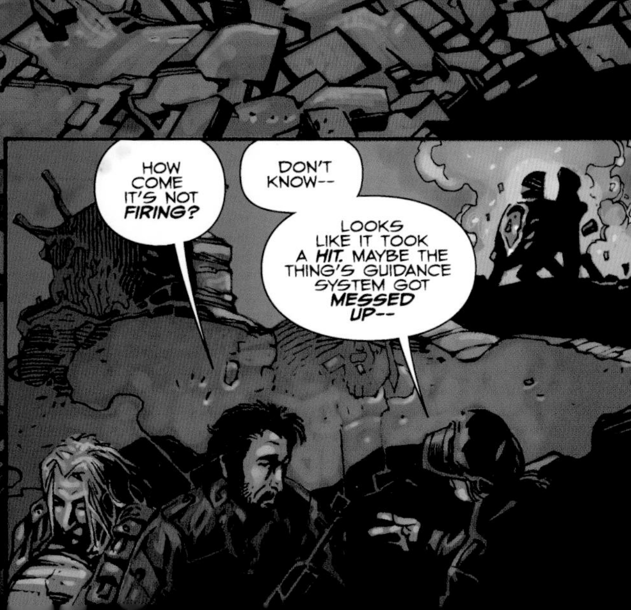
HOW COME IT'S NOT FIRING?
DON'T KNOW--
LOOKS LIKE IT TOOK A HIT. MAYBE THE THING'S GUIDANCE SYSTEM GOT MESSED UP--

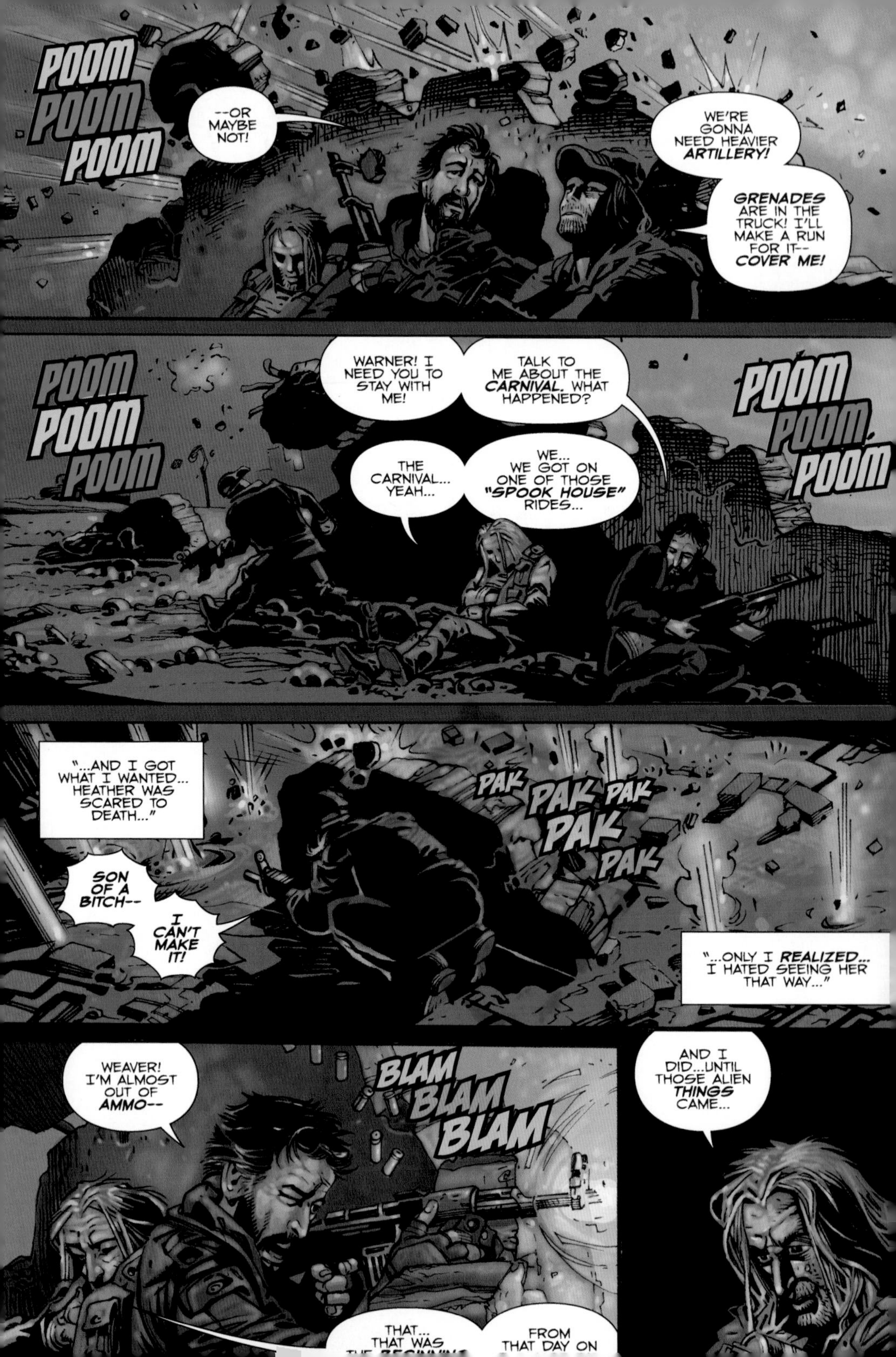
POOM POOM POOM
--OR MAYBE NOT!
WE'RE GONNA NEED HEAVIER ARTILLERY!
GRENADES ARE IN THE TRUCK! I'LL MAKE A RUN FOR IT-- COVER ME!
POOM POOM POOM
WARNER! I NEED YOU TO STAY WITH ME!
TALK TO ME ABOUT THE CARNIVAL. WHAT HAPPENED?
POOM POOM POOM
THE CARNIVAL... YEAH...
WE... WE GOT ON ONE OF THOSE "SPOOK HOUSE" RIDES...
"...AND I GOT WHAT I WANTED... HEATHER WAS SCARED TO DEATH..."
PAK PAK PAK PAK PAK
SON OF A BITCH--
I CAN'T MAKE IT!
"...ONLY I REALIZED... I HATED SEEING HER THAT WAY..."
WEAVER! I'M ALMOST OUT OF AMMO--
BLAM BLAM BLAM
AND I DID...UNTIL THOSE ALIEN THINGS CAME...
THAT... THAT WAS
FROM THAT DAY ON

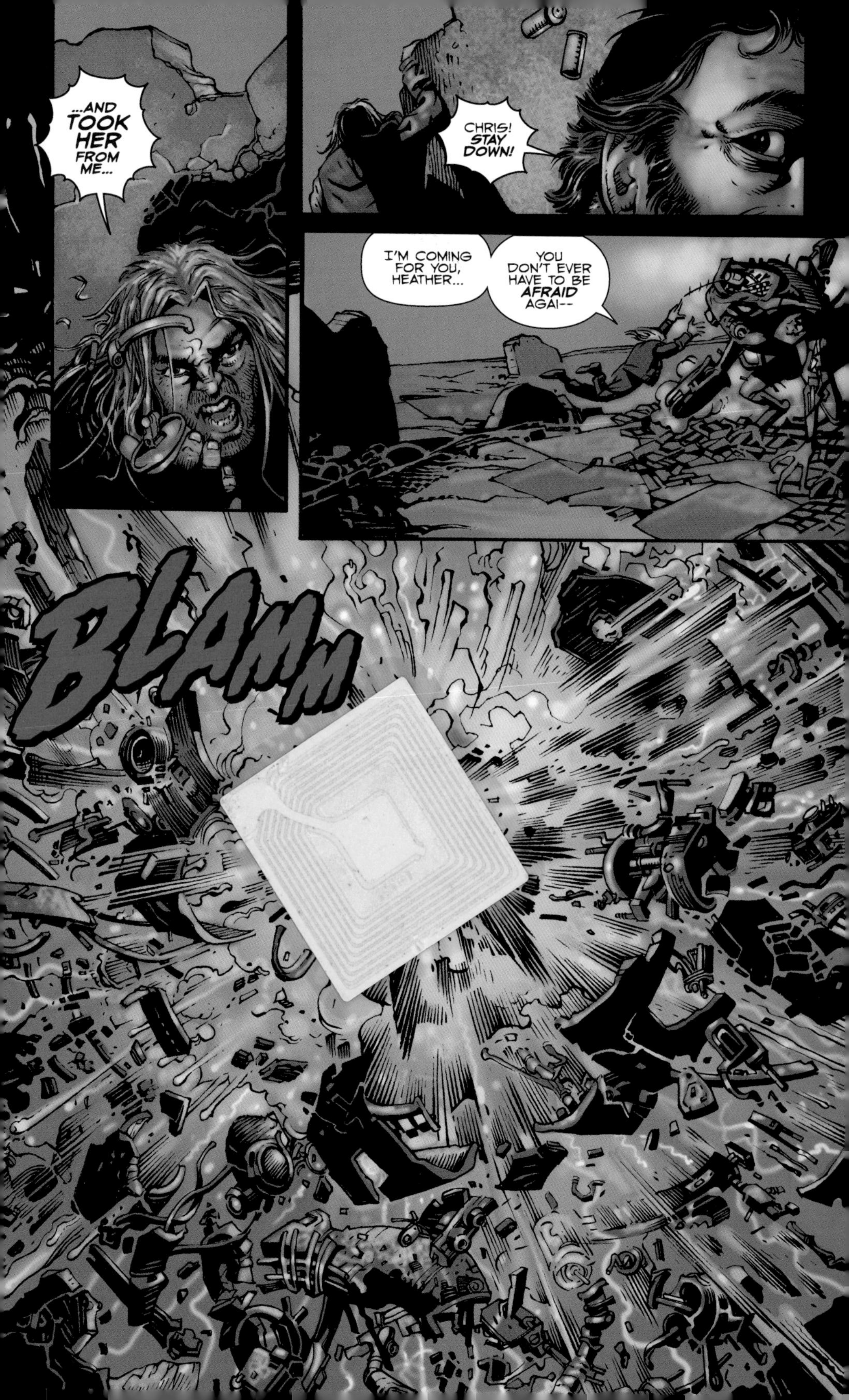
...AND TOOK HER FROM ME...
CHRIS! STAY DOWN!
I'M COMING FOR YOU, HEATHER...
YOU DON'T EVER HAVE TO BE AFRAID AGAI--
BLAMM

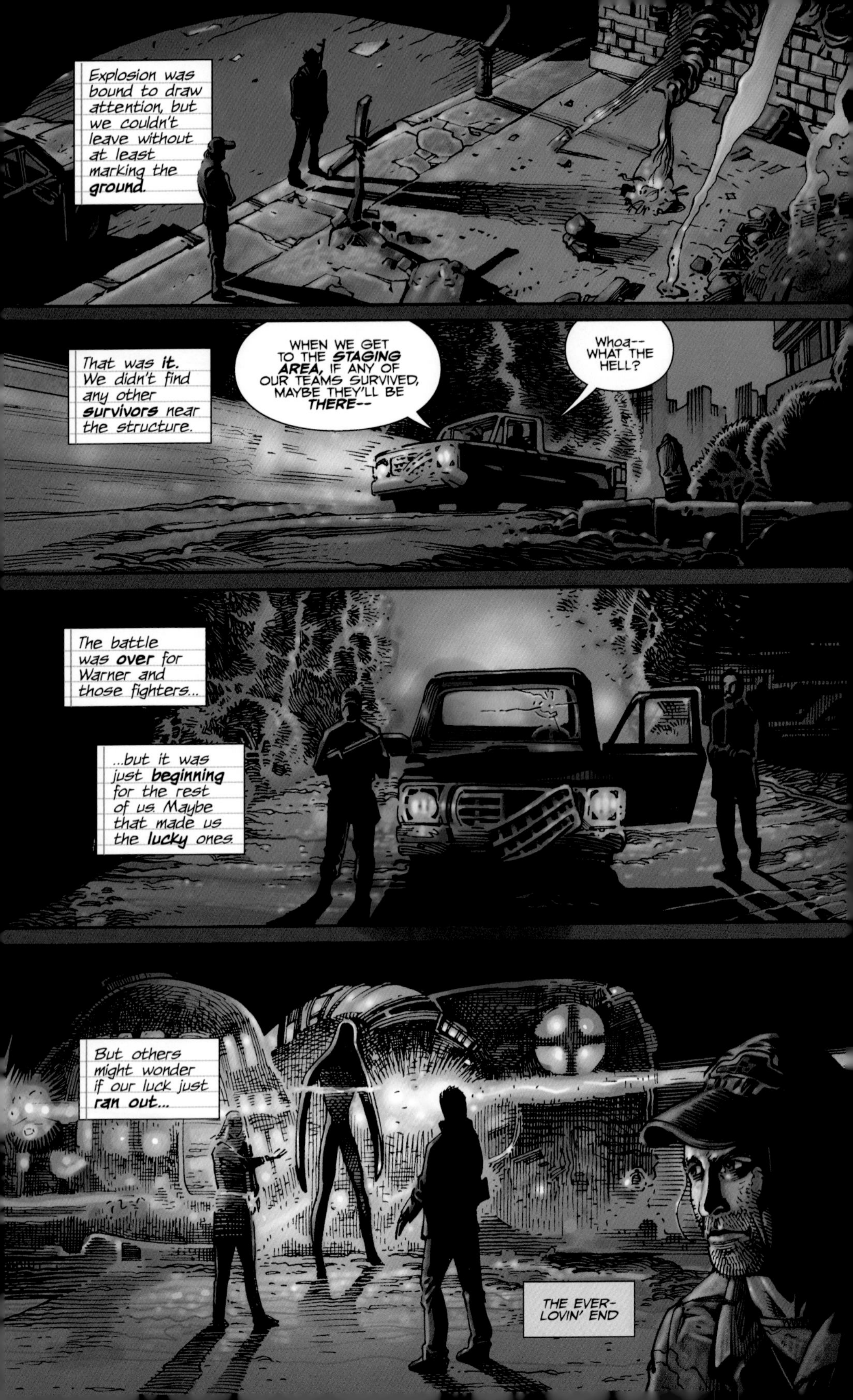

Explosion was bound to draw attention, but we couldn't leave without at least marking the **ground**.
That was **it.** We didn't find any other **survivors** near the structure.
WHEN WE GET TO THE **STAGING AREA,** IF ANY OF OUR TEAMS SURVIVED, MAYBE THEY'LL BE **THERE--**
Whoa-- WHAT THE HELL?
The battle was **over** for Warner and those fighters...
...but it was just **beginning** for the rest of us. Maybe that made us the **lucky** ones.
But others might wonder if our luck just **ran out...**
THE EVER-LOVIN' END

A BOY WITHOUT TOYS

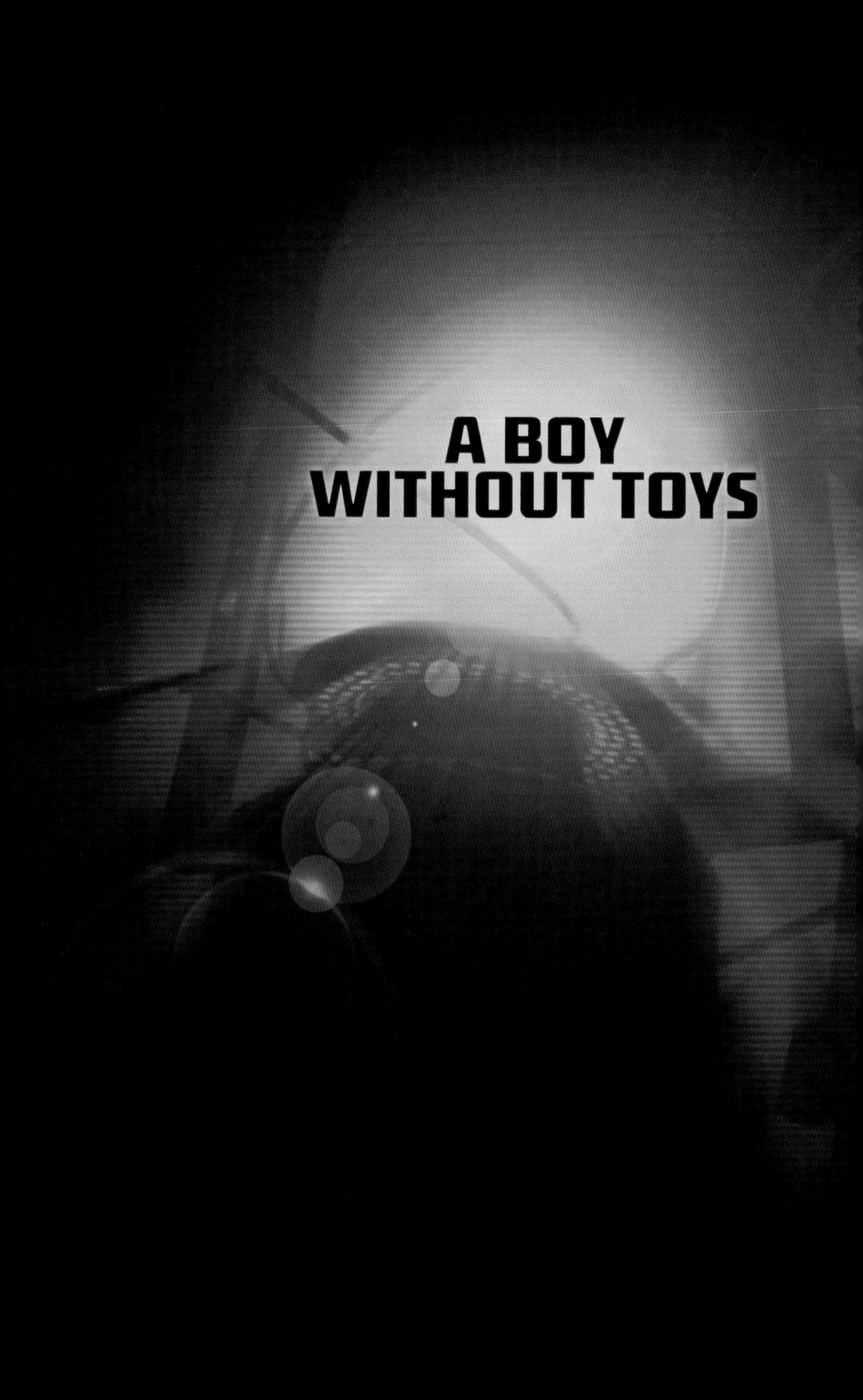

Script and Art by **DANILO BEYRUTH**

Colors by **CRIS PETER**

Lettering by **STEVEN FINCH**

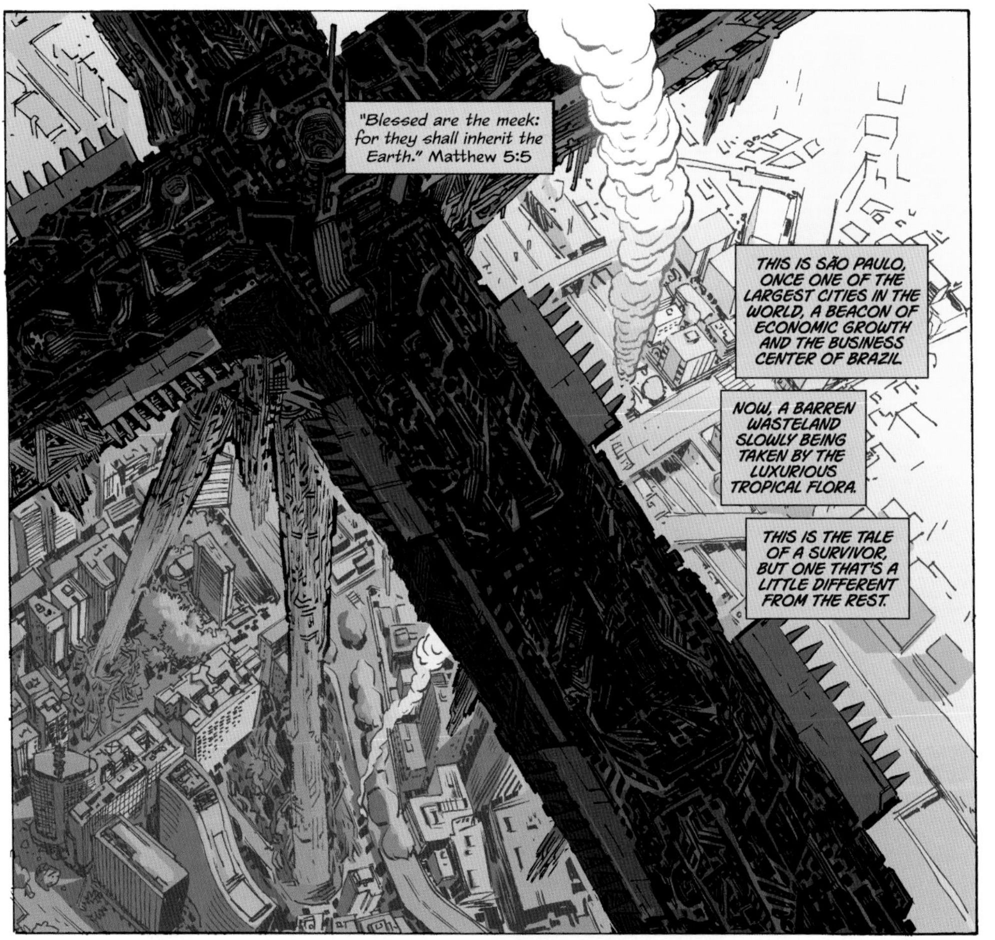
"Blessed are the meek: for they shall inherit the Earth." Matthew 5:5
THIS IS SÃO PAULO, ONCE ONE OF THE LARGEST CITIES IN THE WORLD, A BEACON OF ECONOMIC GROWTH AND THE BUSINESS CENTER OF BRAZIL.
NOW, A BARREN WASTELAND SLOWLY BEING TAKEN BY THE LUXURIOUS TROPICAL FLORA.
THIS IS THE TALE OF A SURVIVOR, BUT ONE THAT'S A LITTLE DIFFERENT FROM THE REST.

A BOY WITHOUT TOYS

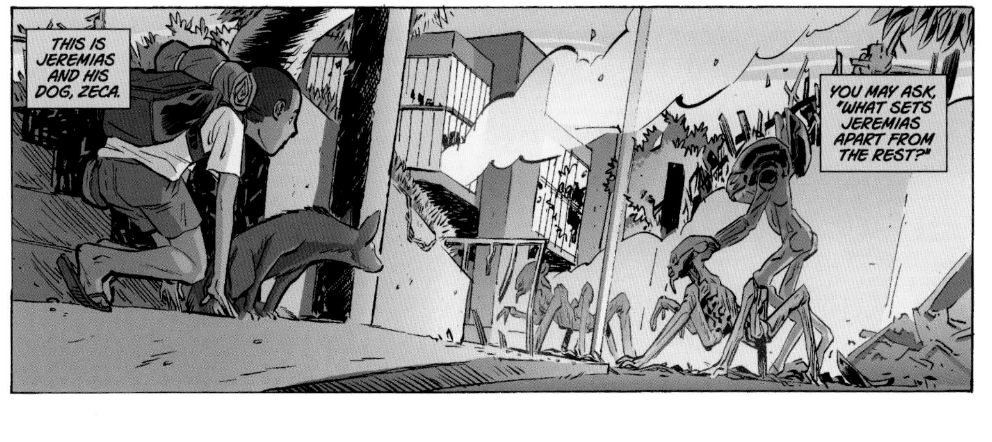
THIS IS JEREMIAS AND HIS DOG, ZECA.
YOU MAY ASK, "WHAT SETS JEREMIAS APART FROM THE REST?"

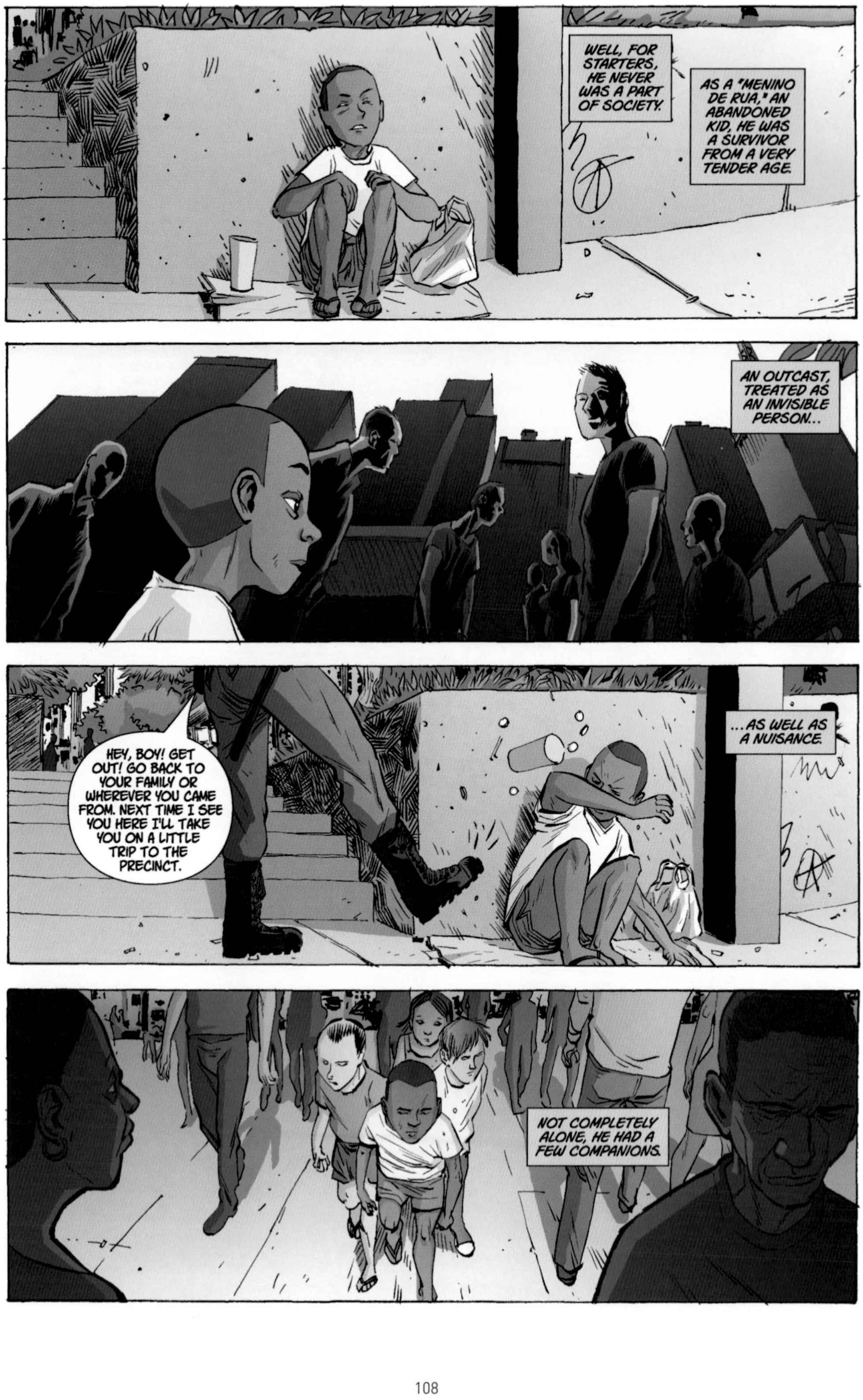
WELL, FOR STARTERS, HE NEVER WAS A PART OF SOCIETY.
AS A "MENINO DE RUA," AN ABANDONED KID, HE WAS A SURVIVOR FROM A VERY TENDER AGE.
AN OUTCAST, TREATED AS AN INVISIBLE PERSON...
HEY, BOY! GET OUT! GO BACK TO YOUR FAMILY OR WHEREVER YOU CAME FROM. NEXT TIME I SEE YOU HERE I'LL TAKE YOU ON A LITTLE TRIP TO THE PRECINCT.
...AS WELL AS A NUISANCE.
NOT COMPLETELY ALONE, HE HAD A FEW COMPANIONS.

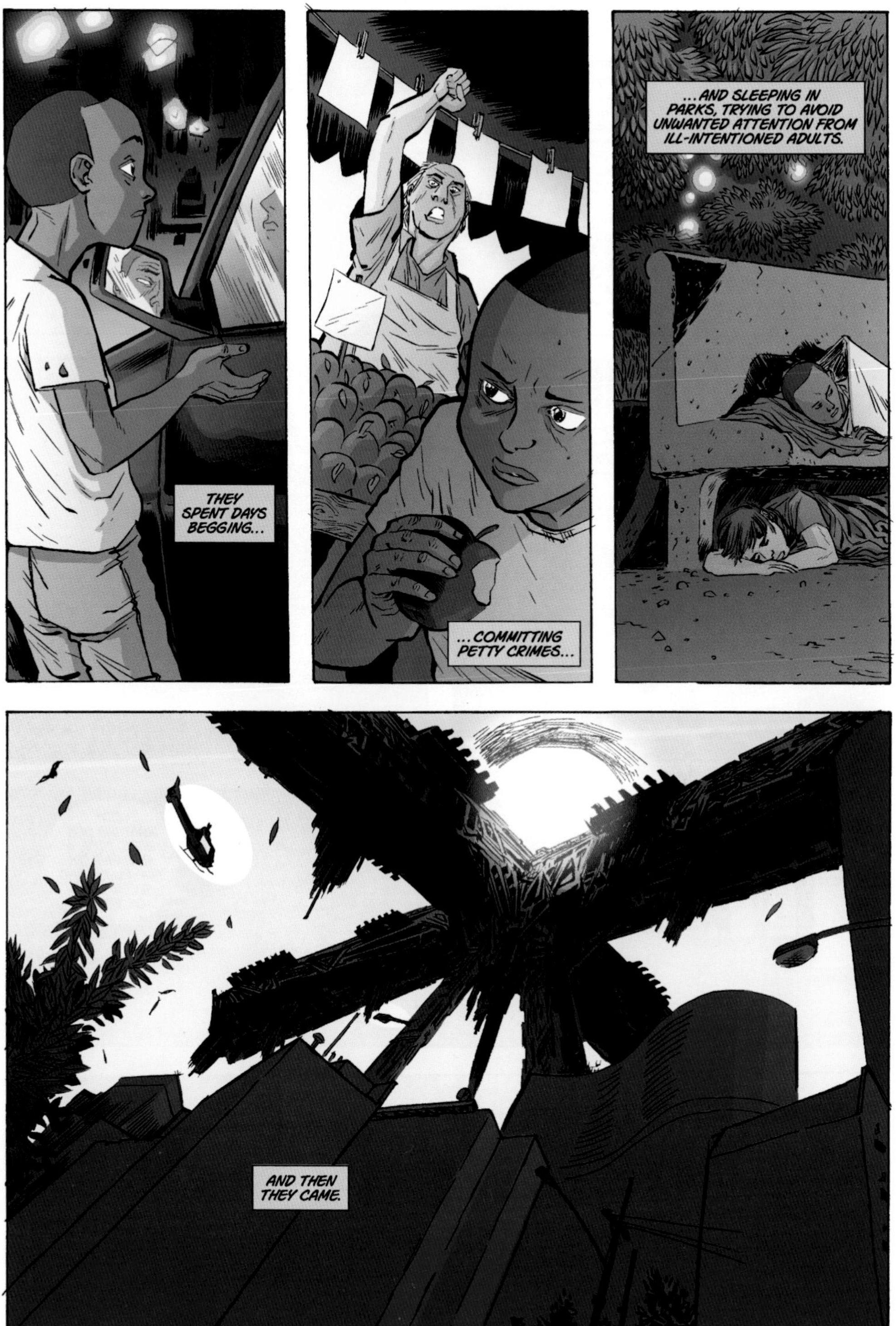
THEY SPENT DAYS BEGGING...
...COMMITTING PETTY CRIMES...
...AND SLEEPING IN PARKS, TRYING TO AVOID UNWANTED ATTENTION FROM ILL-INTENTIONED ADULTS.
AND THEN THEY CAME.

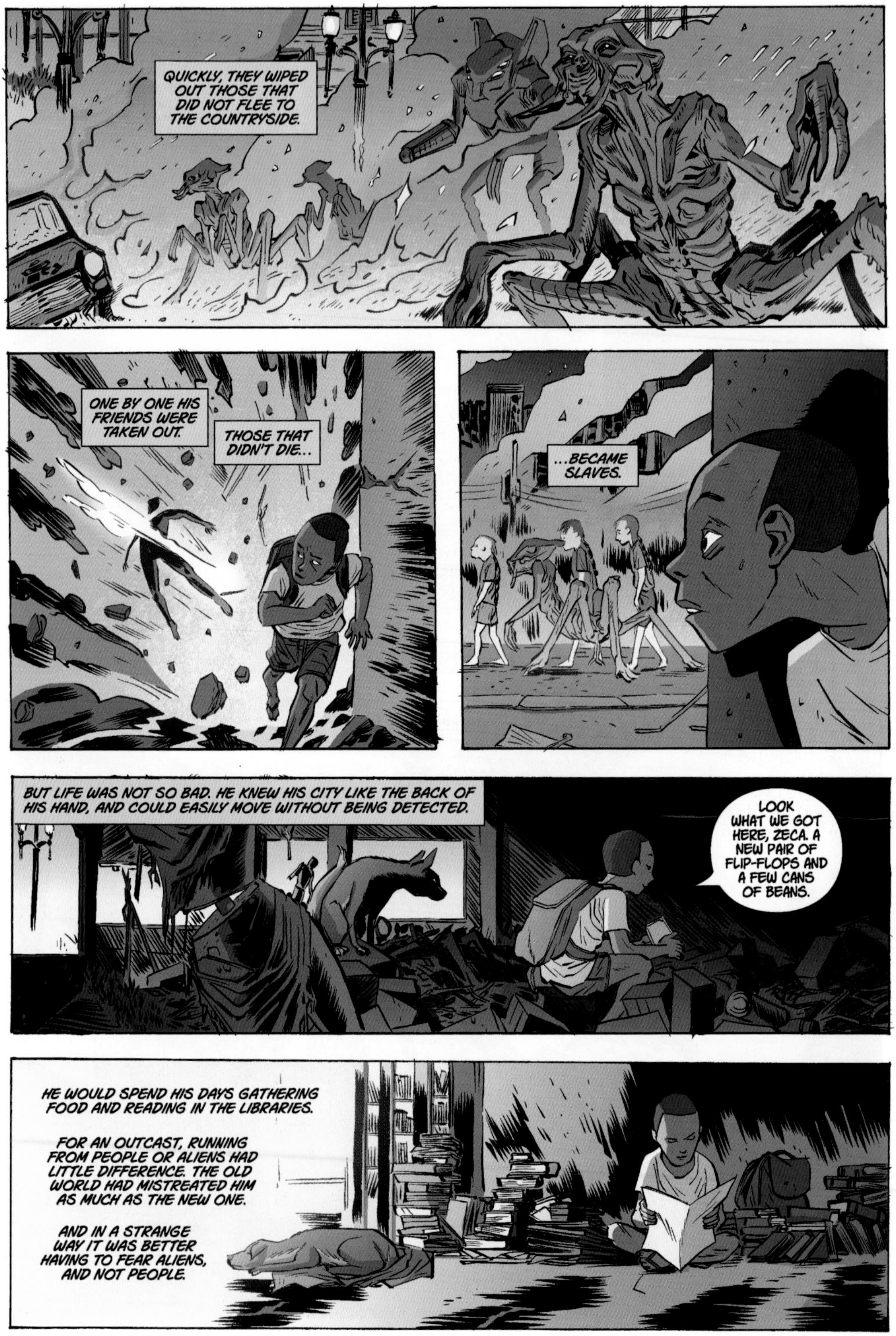
QUICKLY, THEY WIPED OUT THOSE THAT DID NOT FLEE TO THE COUNTRYSIDE.
ONE BY ONE HIS FRIENDS WERE TAKEN OUT.
THOSE THAT DIDN'T DIE...
...BECAME SLAVES.
BUT LIFE WAS NOT SO BAD. HE KNEW HIS CITY LIKE THE BACK OF HIS HAND, AND COULD EASILY MOVE WITHOUT BEING DETECTED.
LOOK WHAT WE GOT HERE, ZECA. A NEW PAIR OF FLIP-FLOPS AND A FEW CANS OF BEANS.
HE WOULD SPEND HIS DAYS GATHERING FOOD AND READING IN THE LIBRARIES.
FOR AN OUTCAST, RUNNING FROM PEOPLE OR ALIENS HAD LITTLE DIFFERENCE. THE OLD WORLD HAD MISTREATED HIM AS MUCH AS THE NEW ONE.
AND IN A STRANGE WAY IT WAS BETTER HAVING TO FEAR ALIENS, AND NOT PEOPLE.

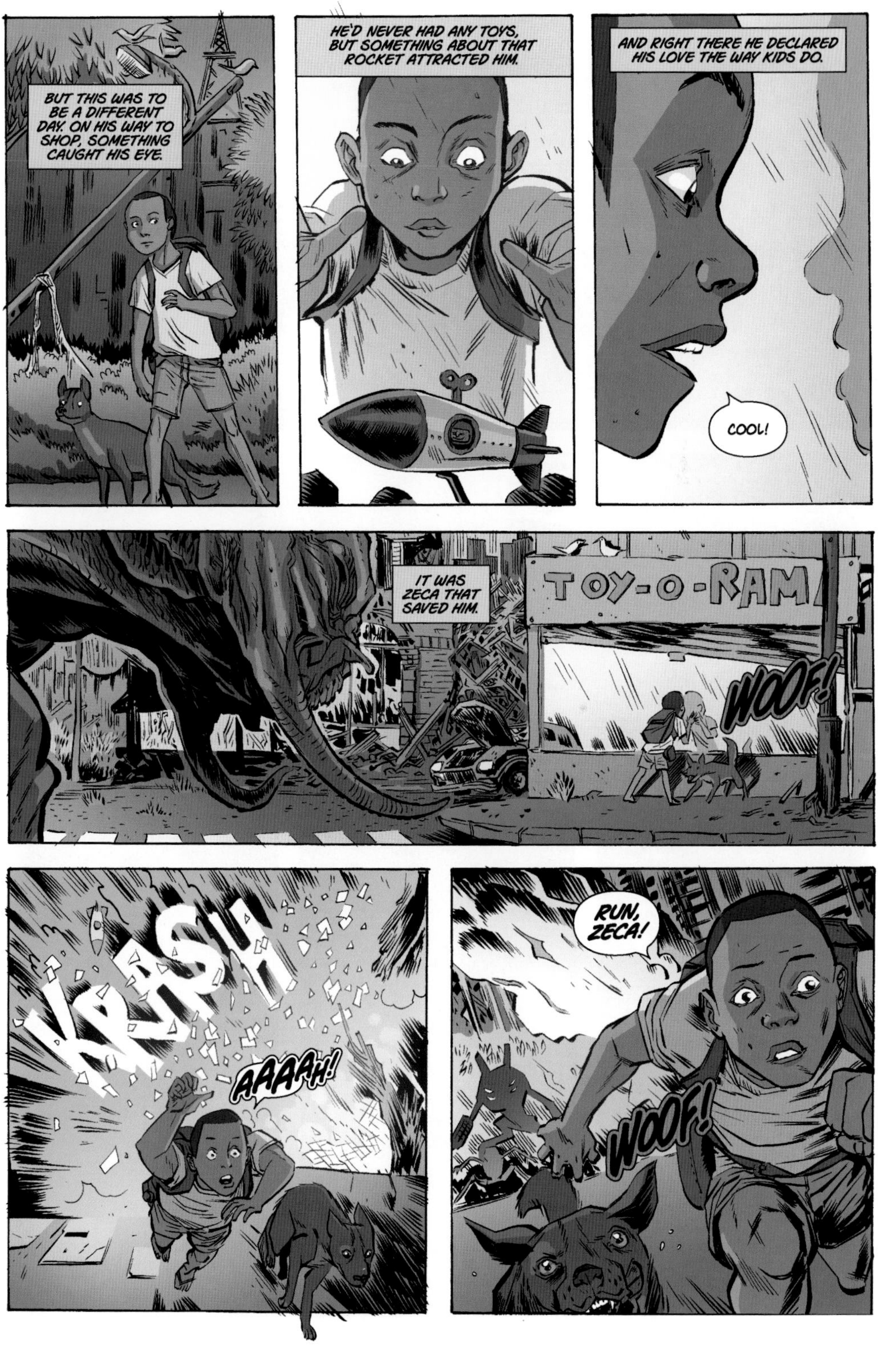
BUT THIS WAS TO BE A DIFFERENT DAY. ON HIS WAY TO SHOP, SOMETHING CAUGHT HIS EYE.
HE'D NEVER HAD ANY TOYS, BUT SOMETHING ABOUT THAT ROCKET ATTRACTED HIM.
AND RIGHT THERE HE DECLARED HIS LOVE THE WAY KIDS DO.
COOL!
IT WAS ZECA THAT SAVED HIM.
TOY-O-RAM
WOOF!
KRASH
AAAAH!
RUN, ZECA!
WOOF!

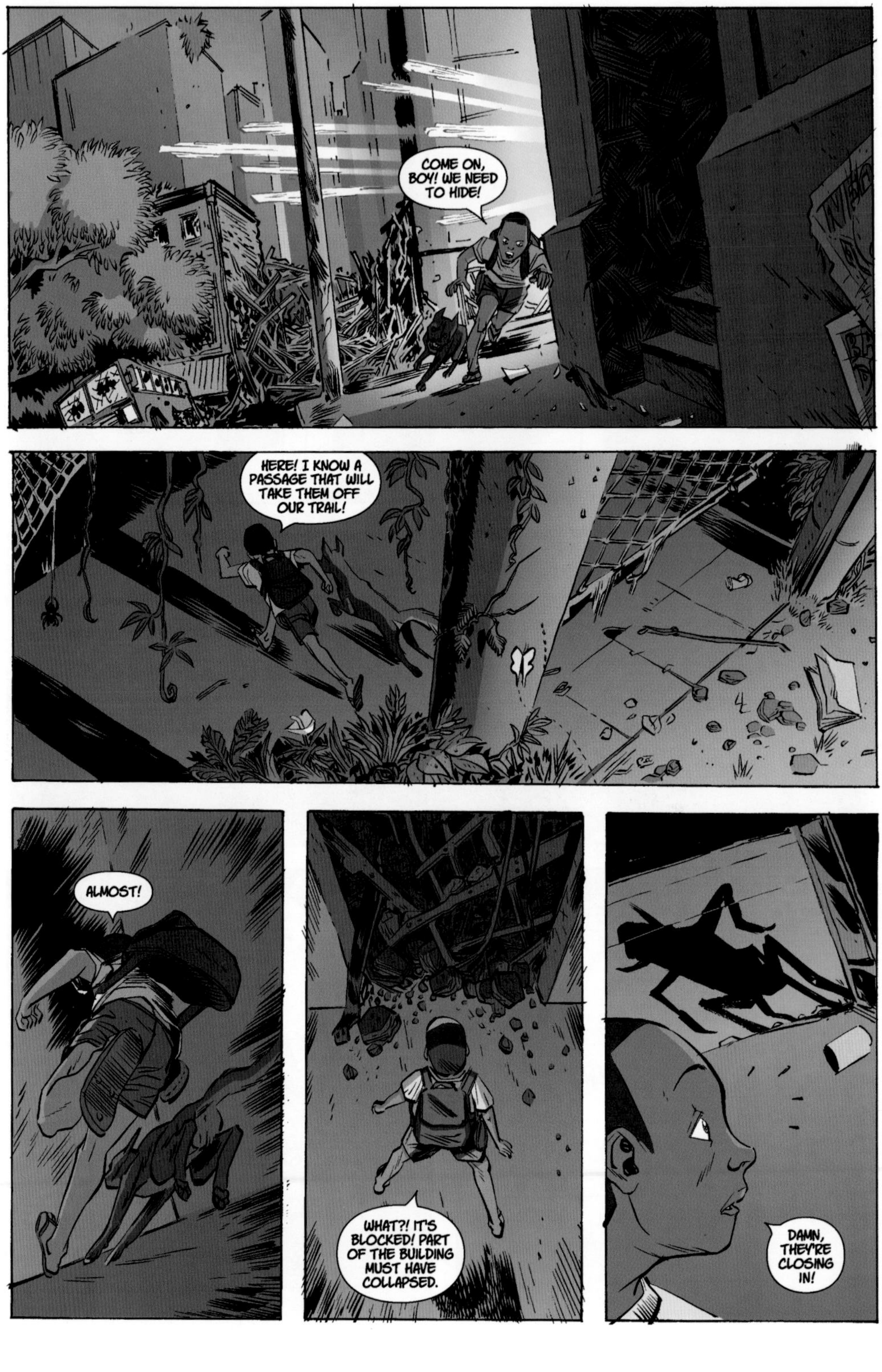

COME ON, BOY! WE NEED TO HIDE!
HERE! I KNOW A PASSAGE THAT WILL TAKE THEM OFF OUR TRAIL!
ALMOST!
WHAT?! IT'S BLOCKED! PART OF THE BUILDING MUST HAVE COLLAPSED.
DAMN, THEY'RE CLOSING IN!

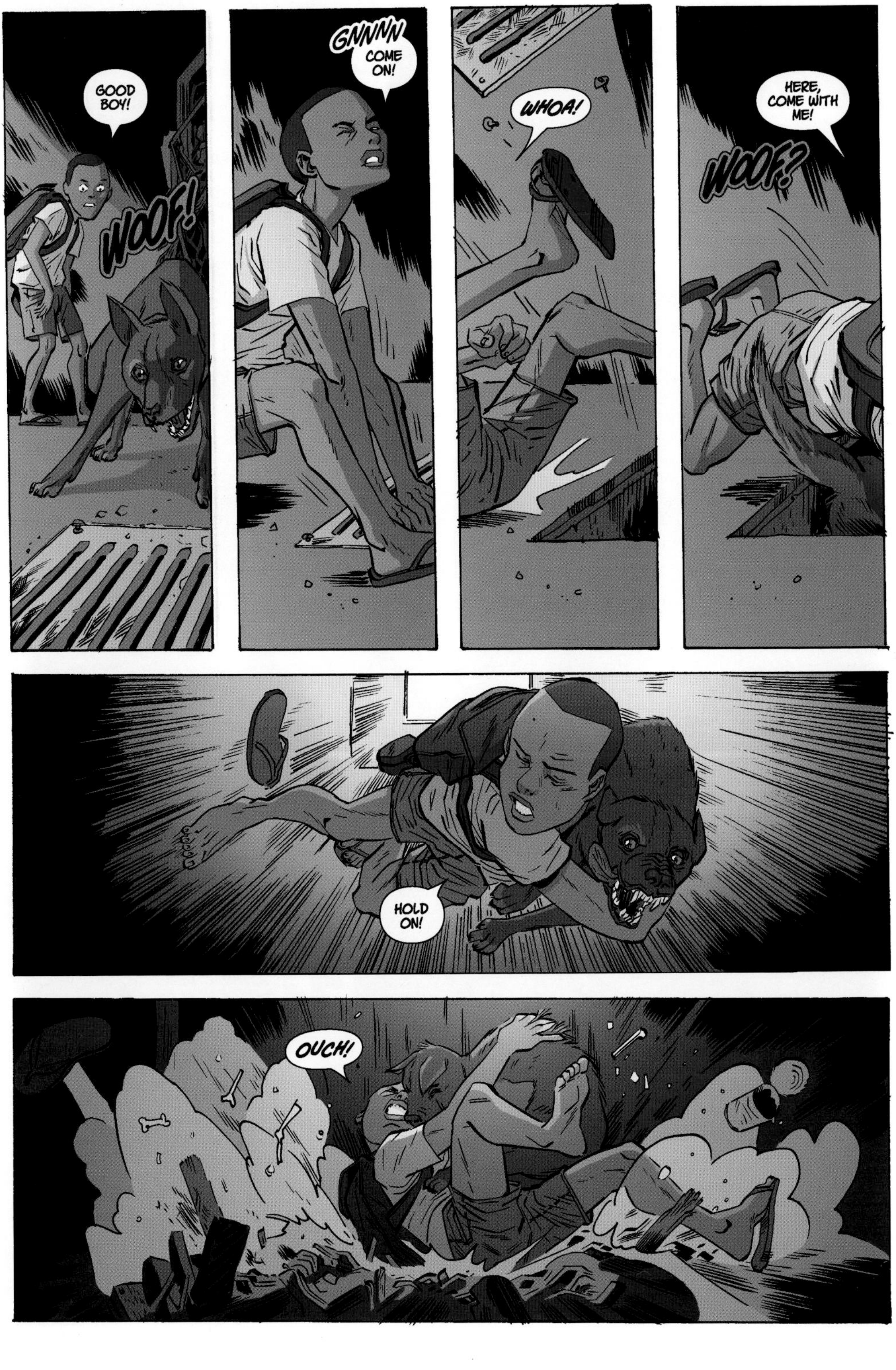
GOOD BOY!
WOOF!
GNNNN
COME ON!
WHOA!
HERE, COME WITH ME!
WOOF?
HOLD ON!
OUCH!

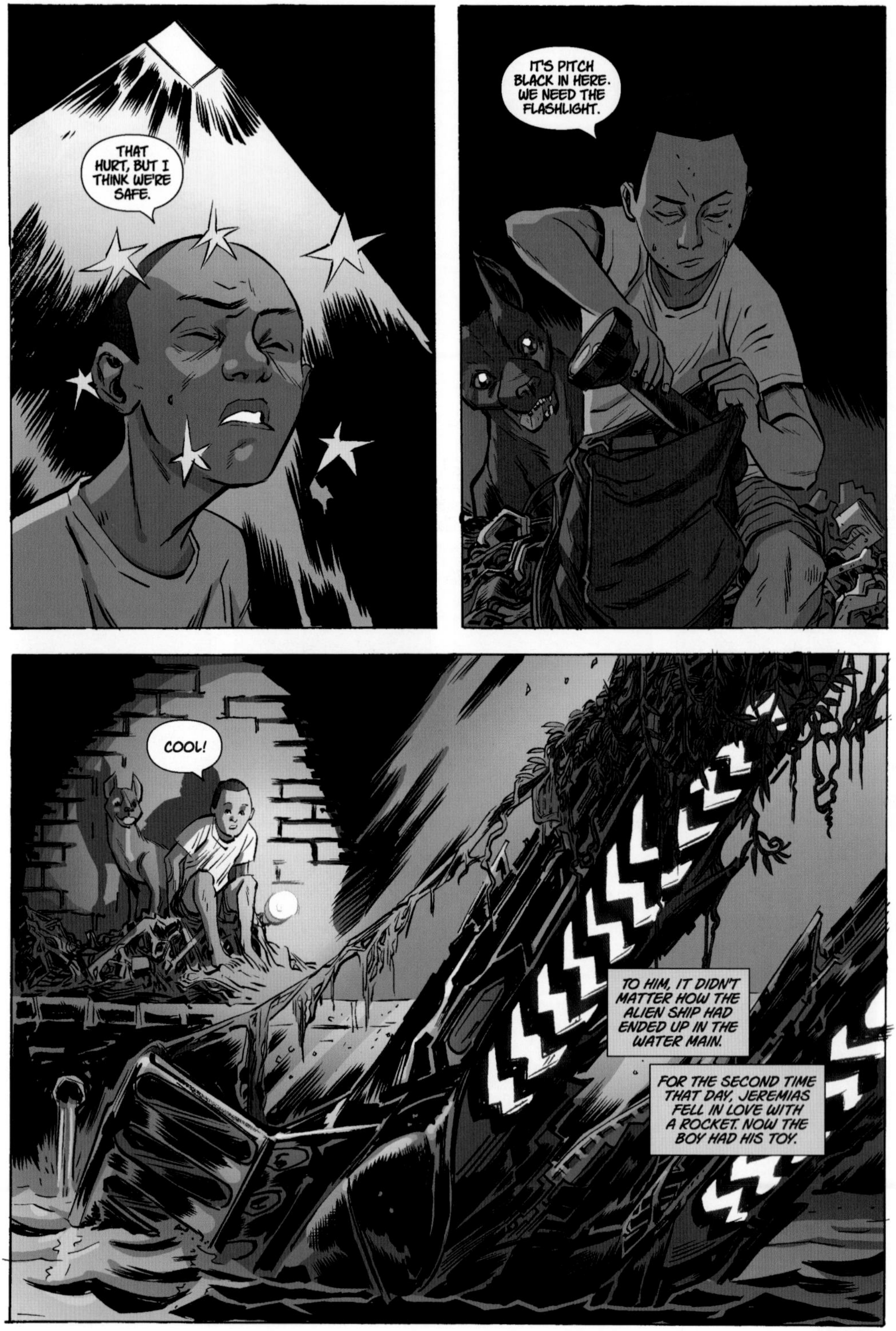
THAT HURT, BUT I THINK WE'RE SAFE.
IT'S PITCH BLACK IN HERE. WE NEED THE FLASHLIGHT.
COOL!
TO HIM, IT DIDN'T MATTER HOW THE ALIEN SHIP HAD ENDED UP IN THE WATER MAIN.
FOR THE SECOND TIME THAT DAY, JEREMIAS FELL IN LOVE WITH A ROCKET. NOW THE BOY HAD HIS TOY.

END

INTERNATIONAL GALLERY

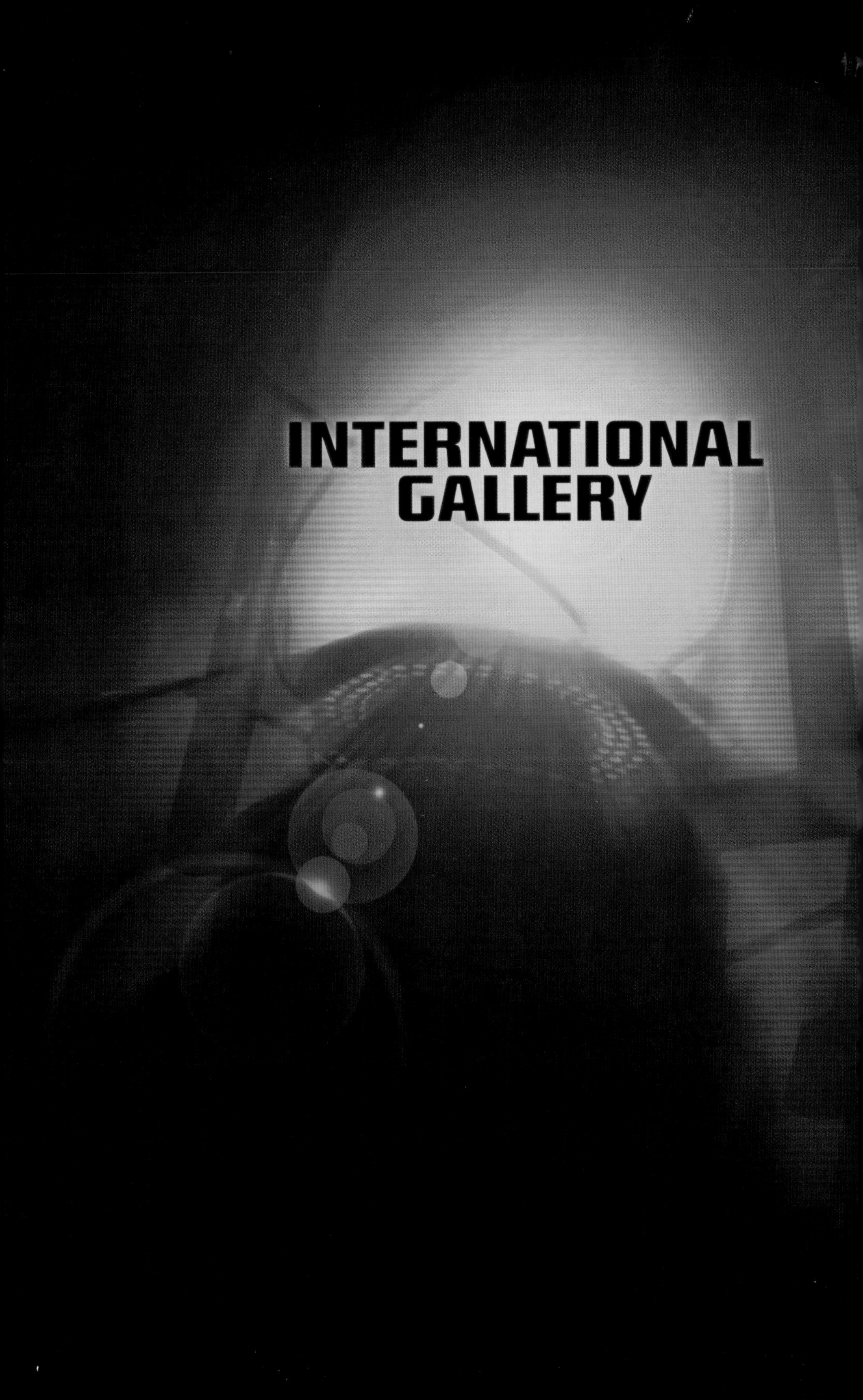

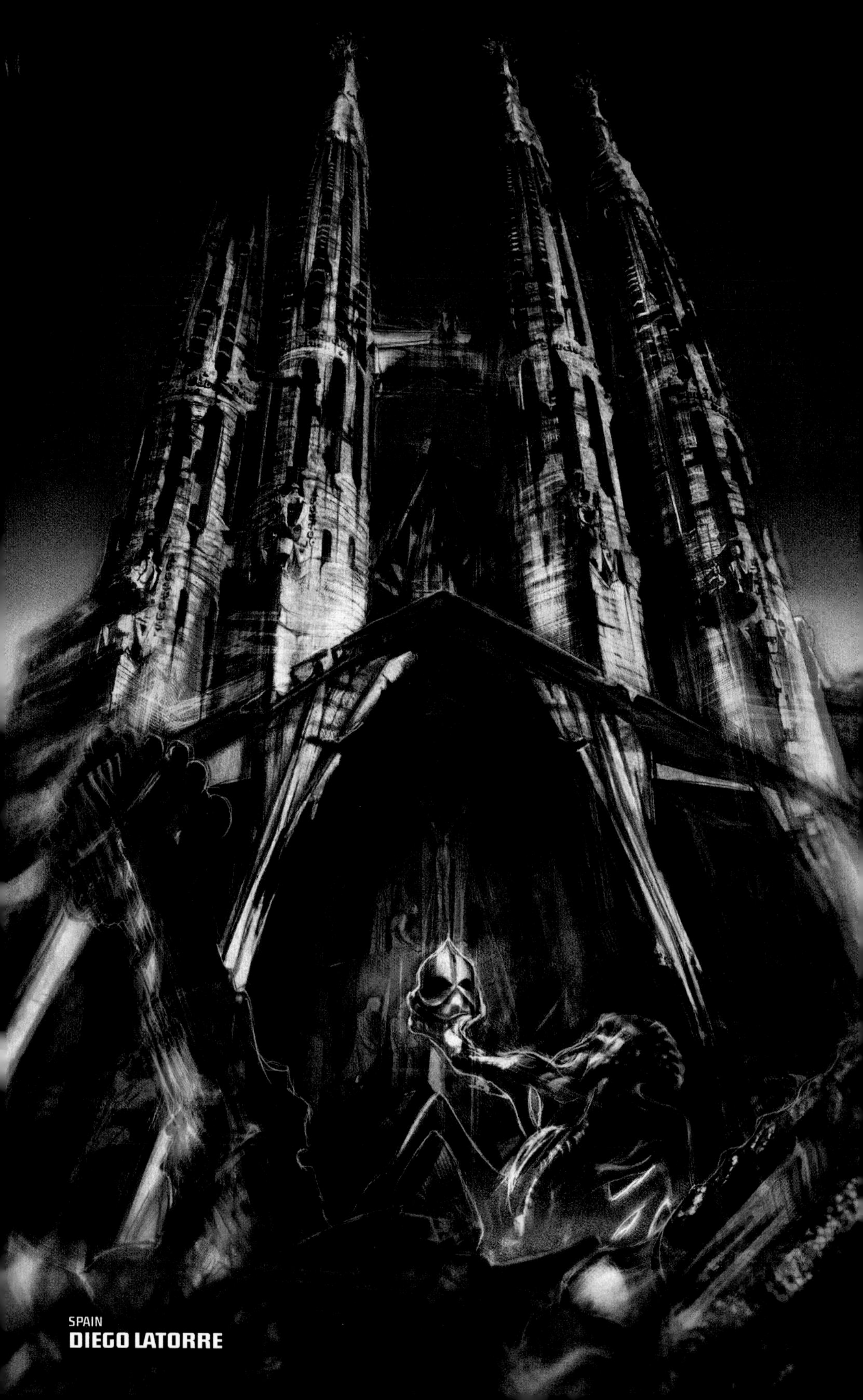

SPAIN
DIEGO LATORRE

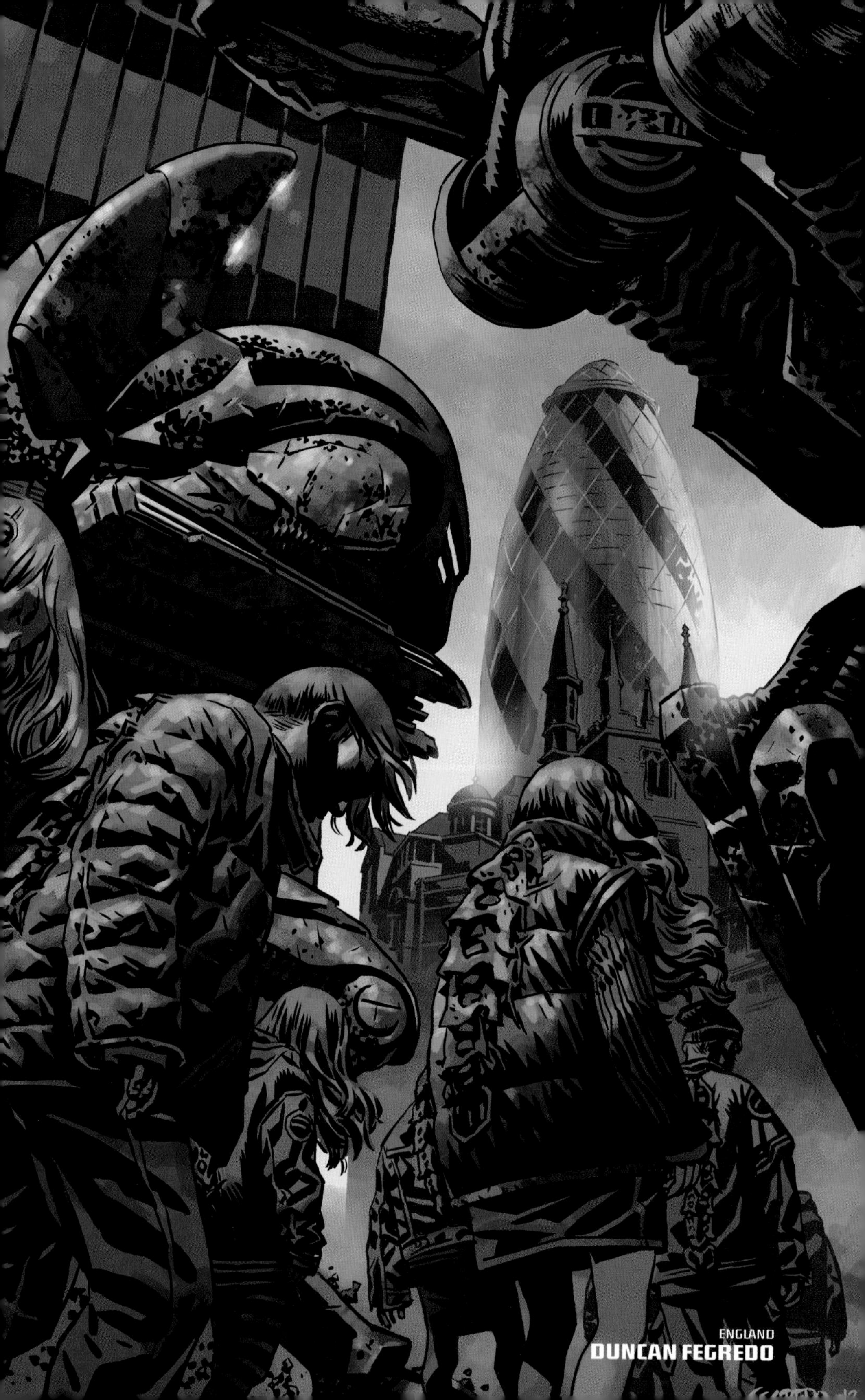

ENGLAND
DUNCAN FEGREDO

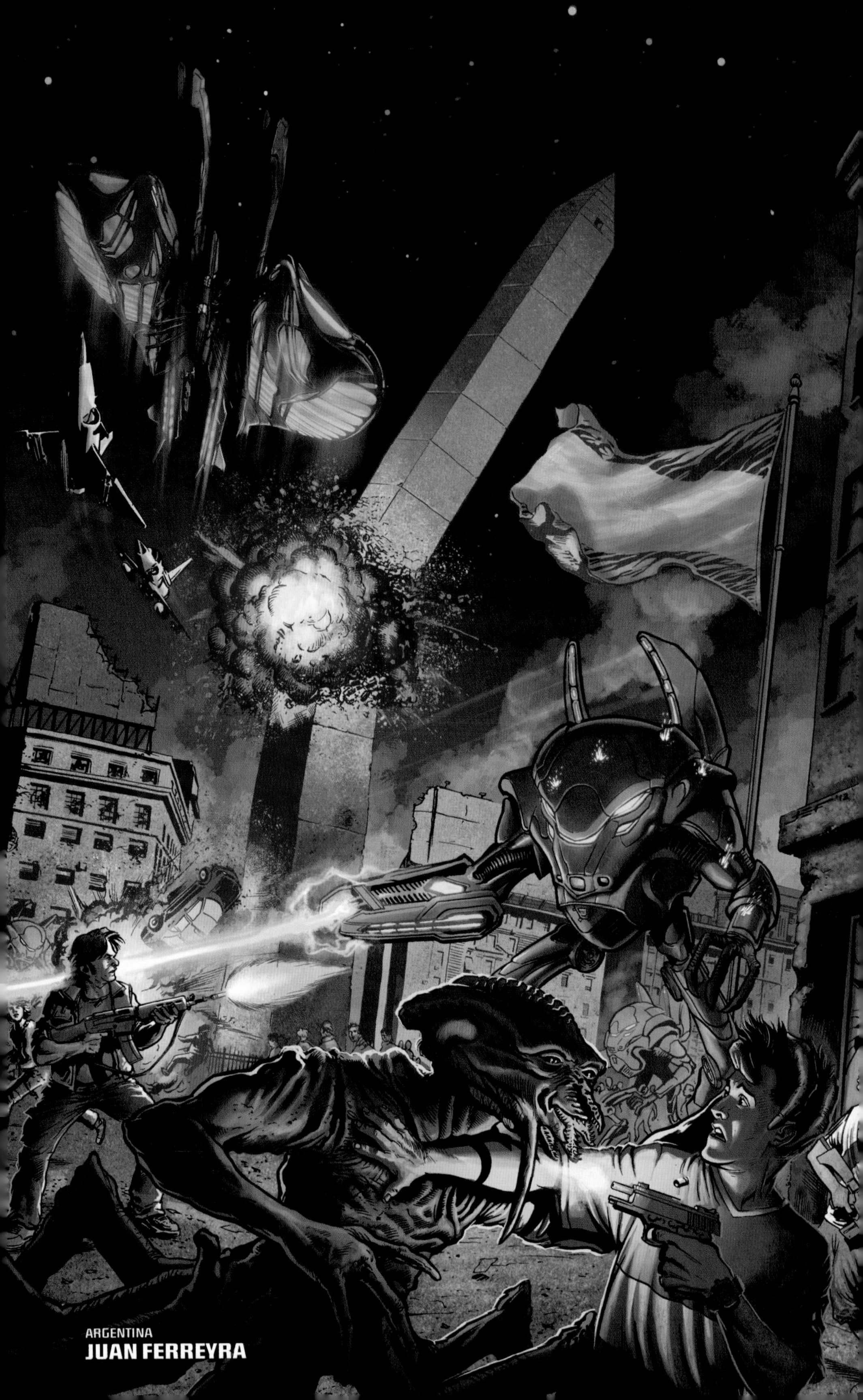

ARGENTINA
JUAN FERREYRA

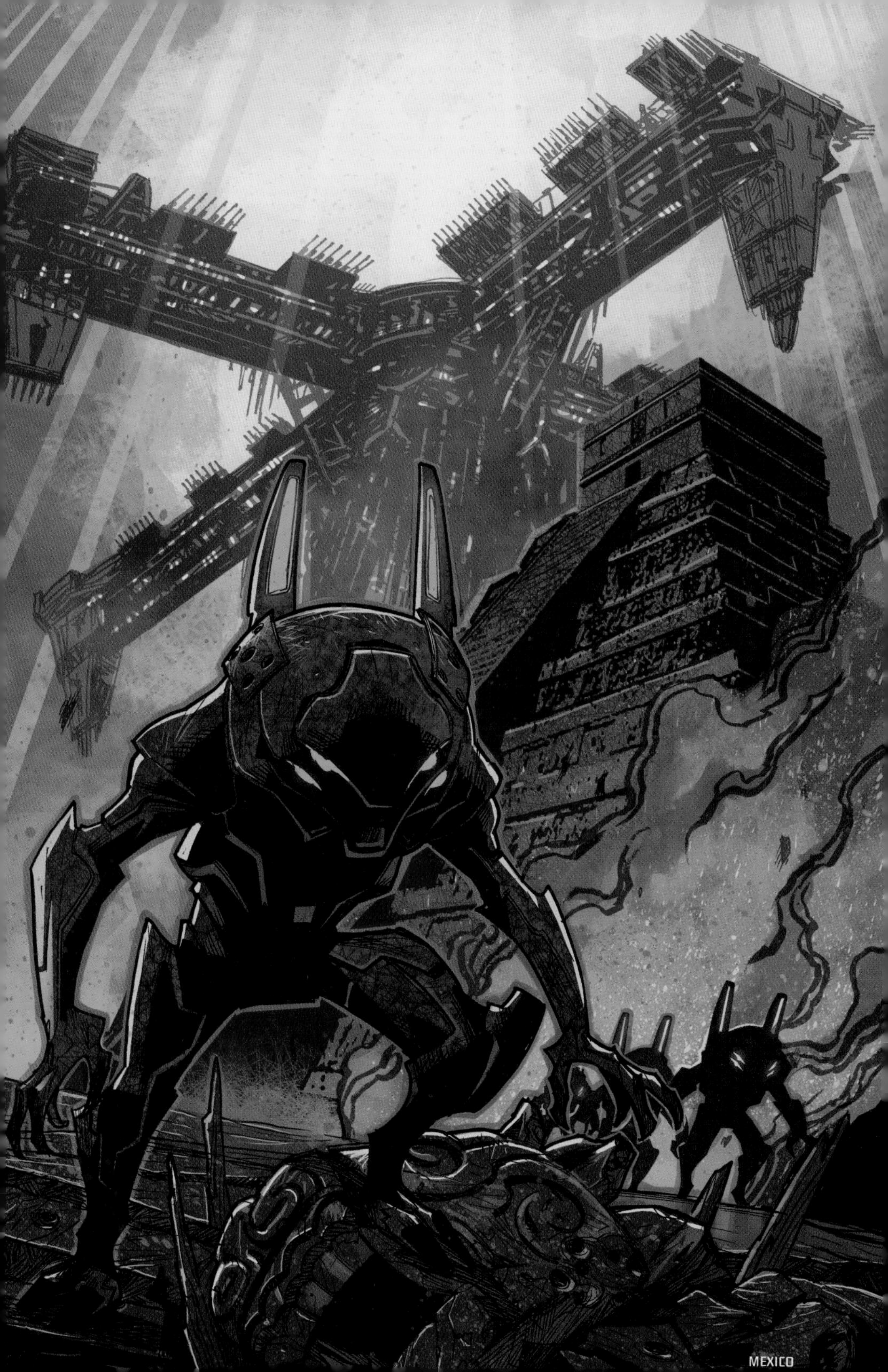
MEXICO

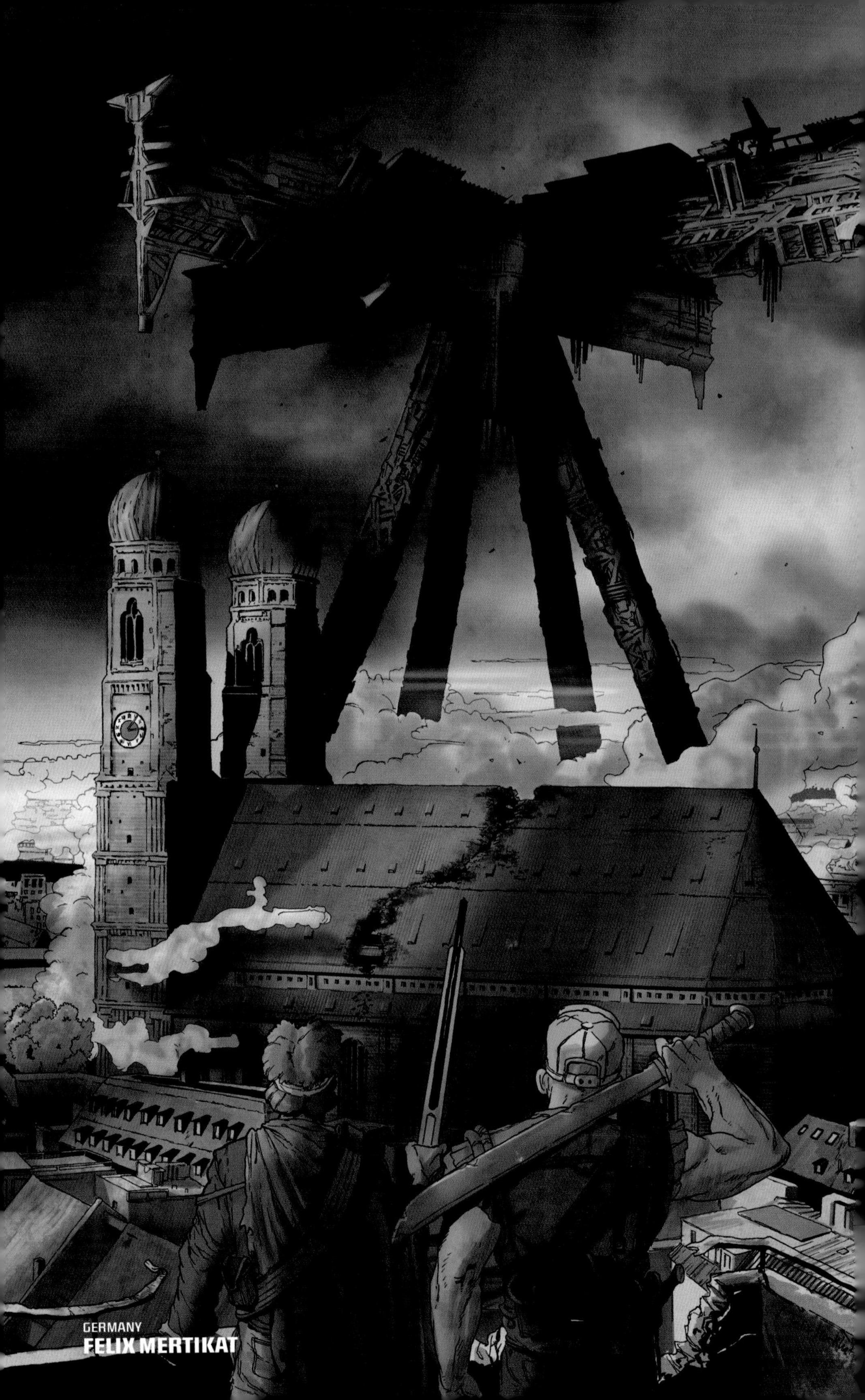

GERMANY
FELIX MERTIKAT

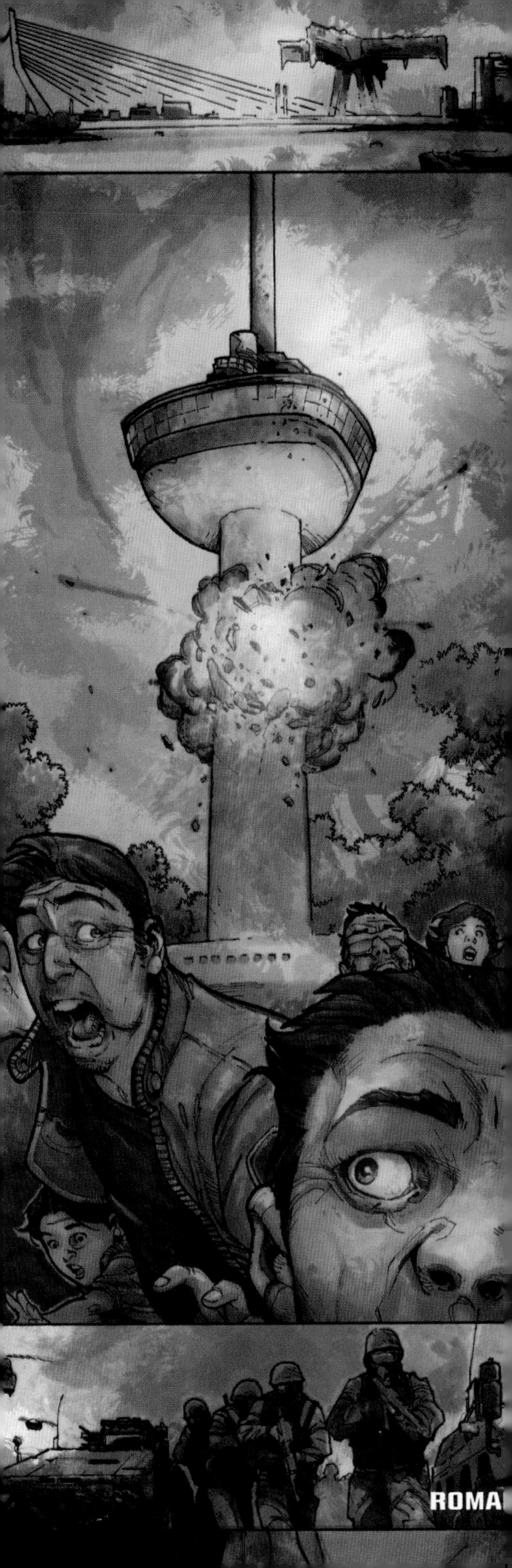

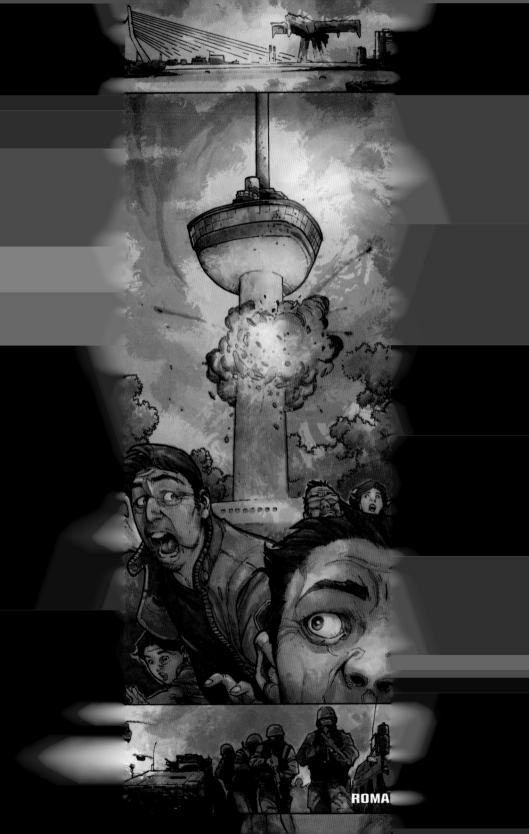

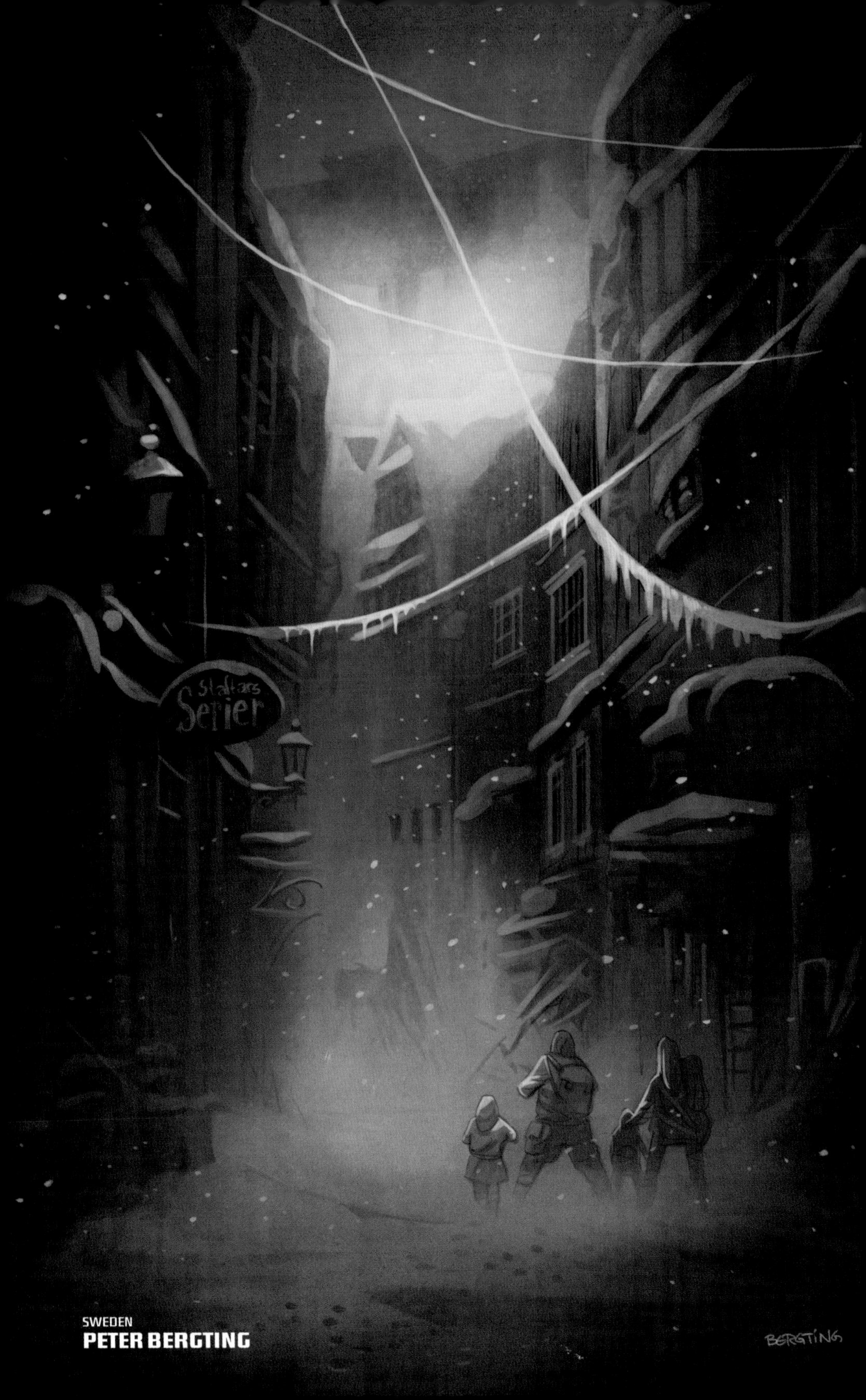
Serier
BERGTING

SWEDEN
PETER BERGTING

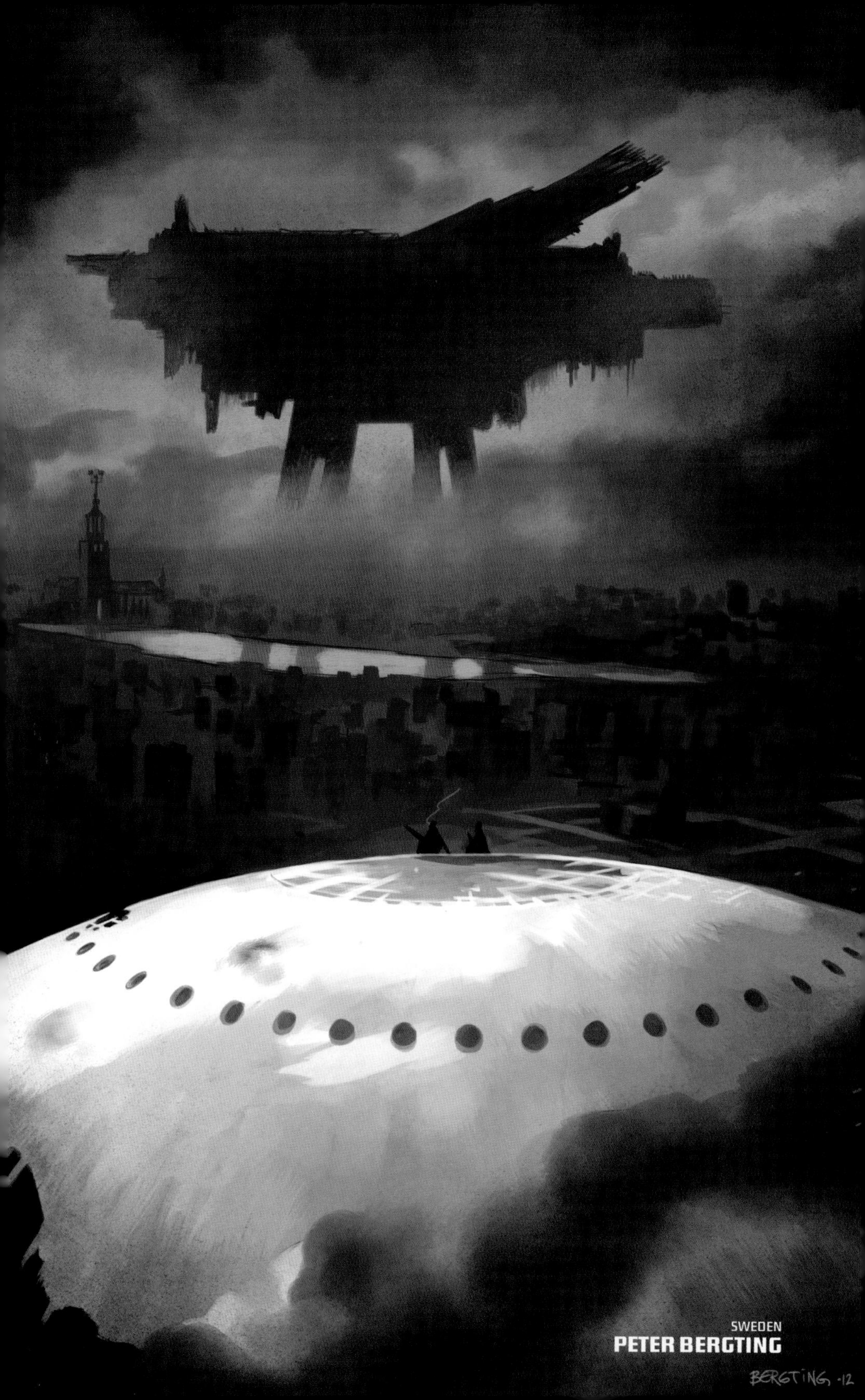
BERGTING -12

SWEDEN
PETER BERGTING

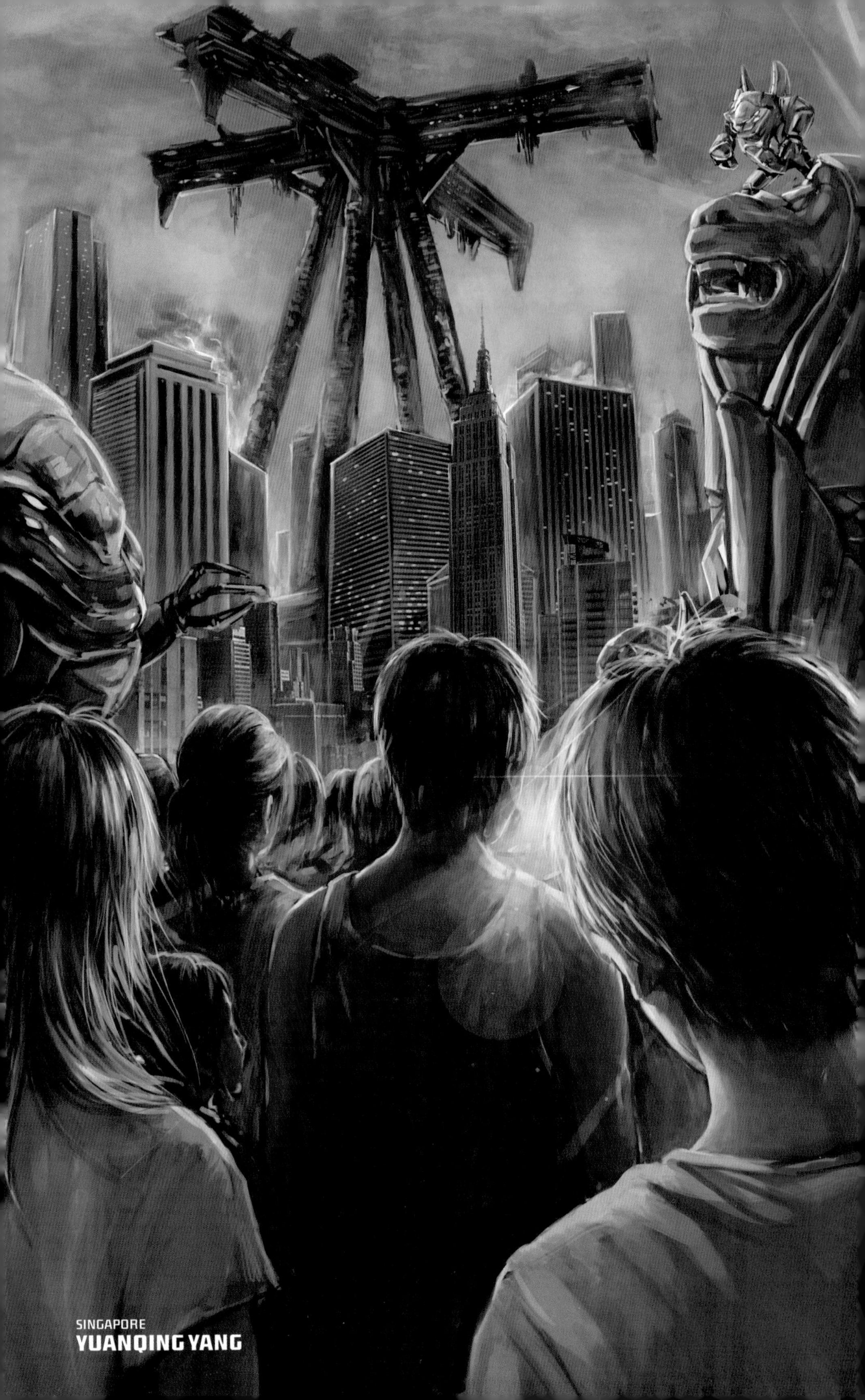

SINGAPORE
YUANQING YANG

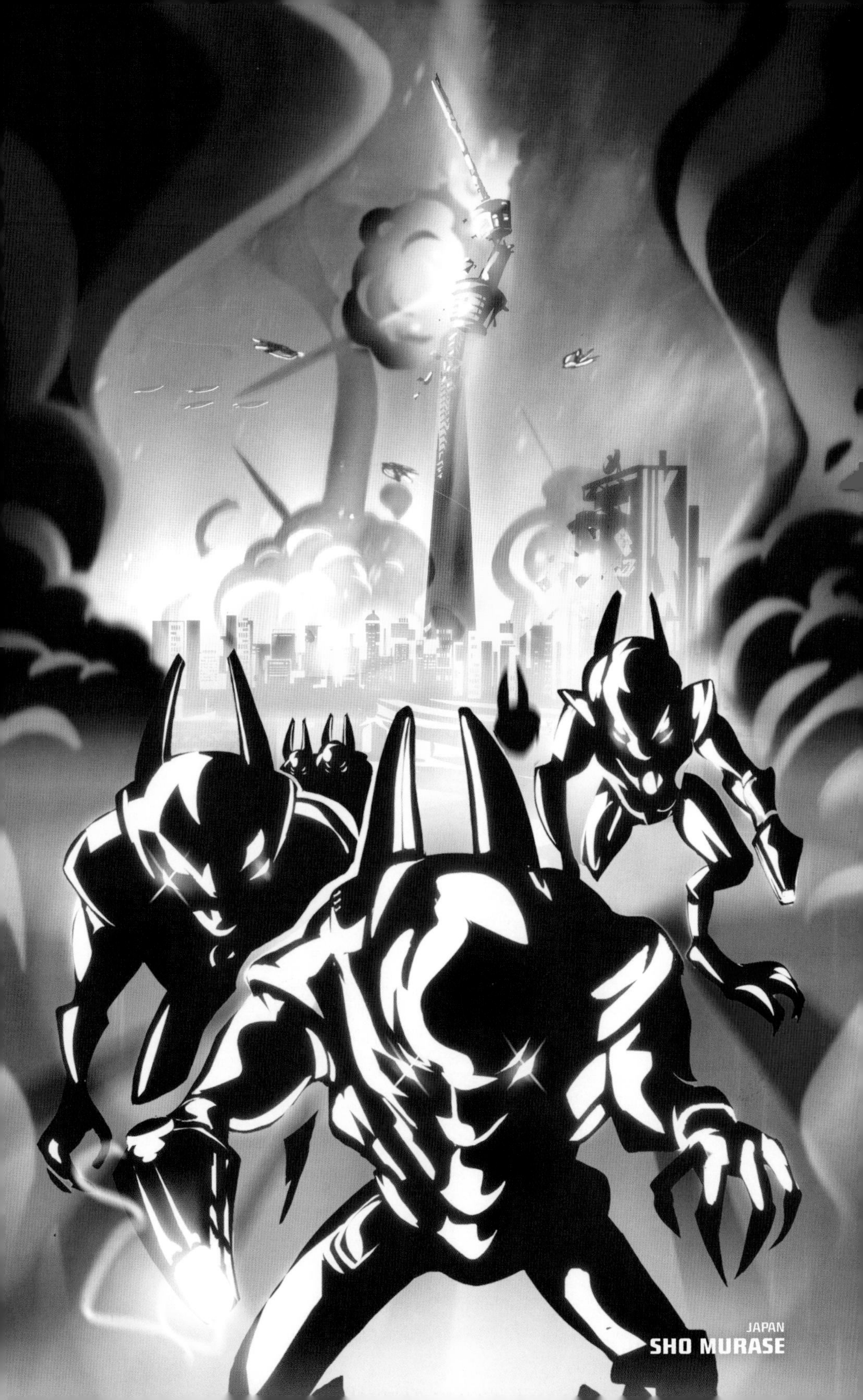

JAPAN
SHO MURASE

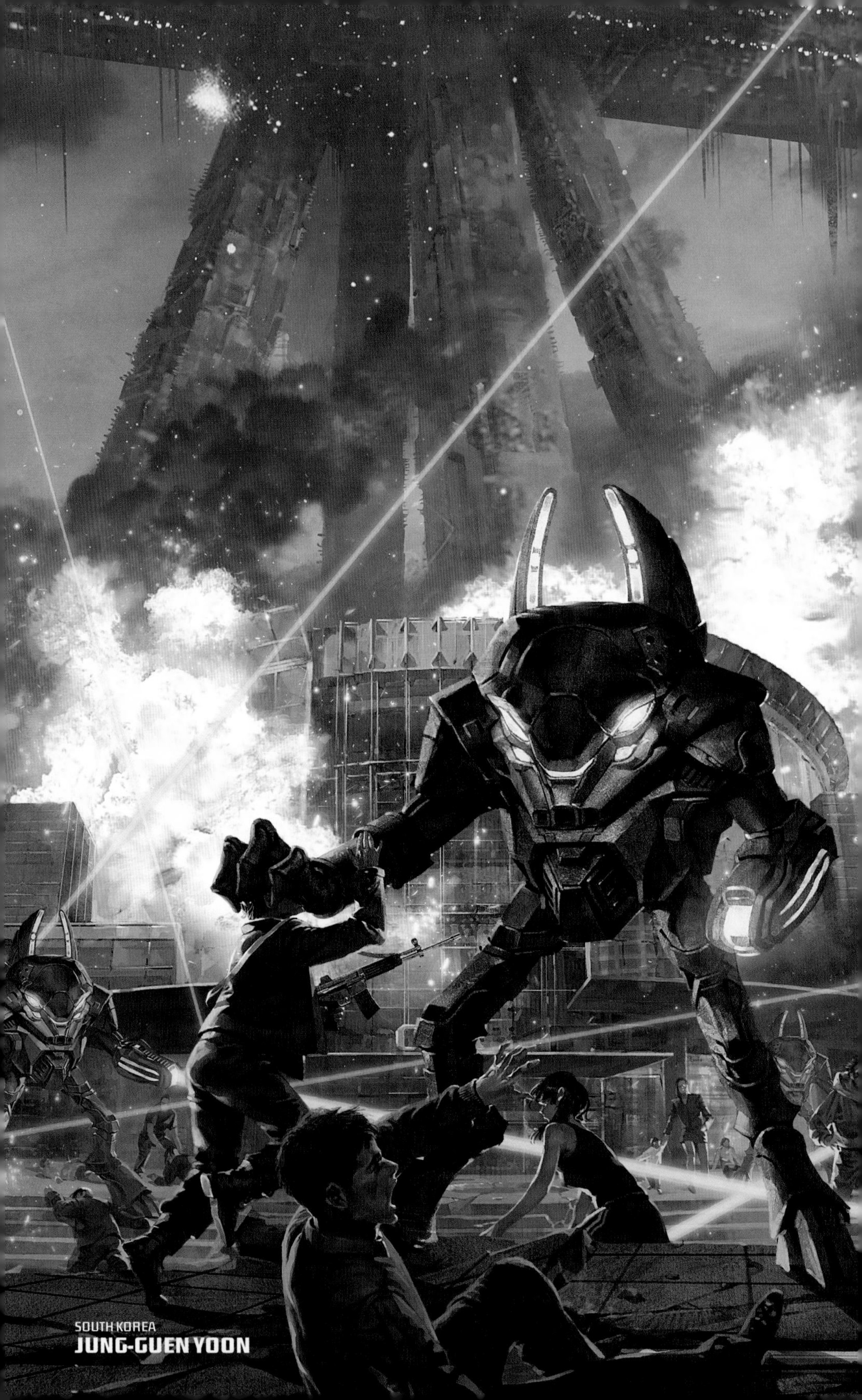

SOUTH KOREA
JUNG-GUEN YOON

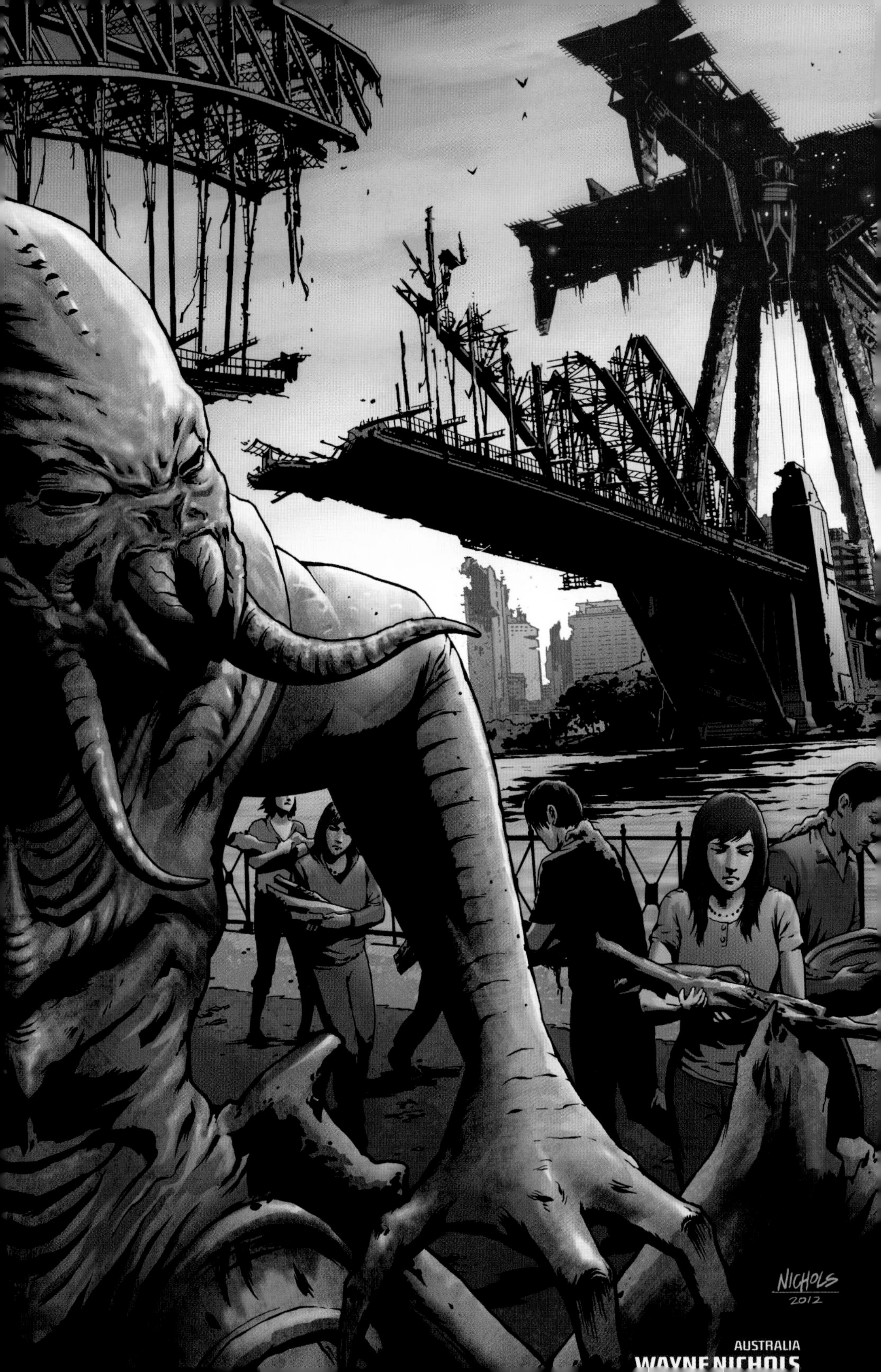
NICHOLS
2012

AUSTRALIA
WAYNE NICHOLS

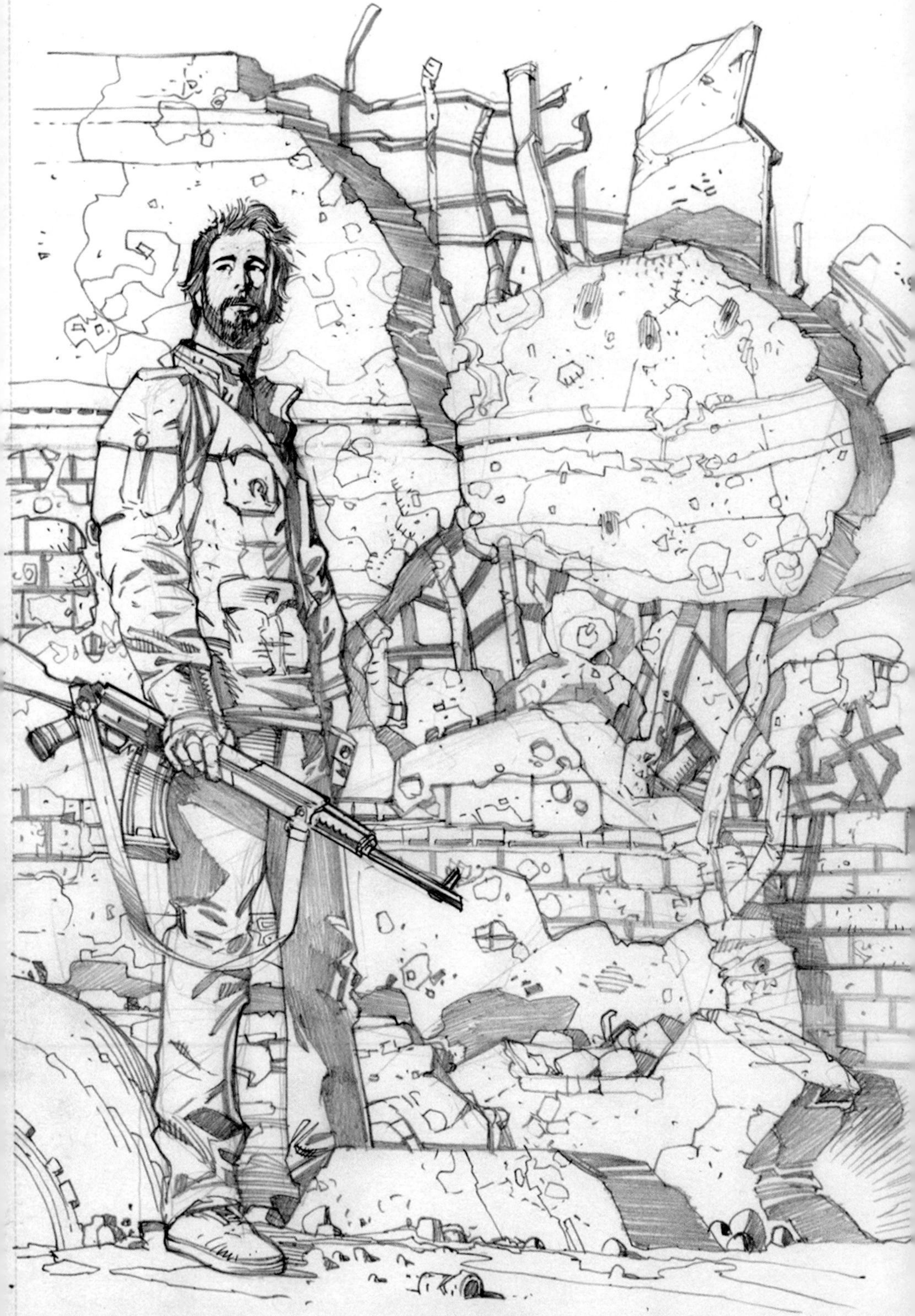

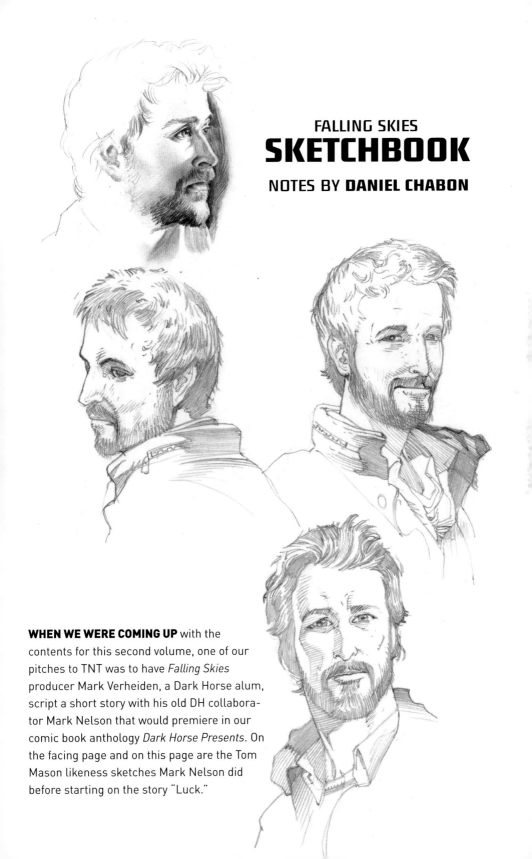

FALLING SKIES

SKETCHBOOK

NOTES BY **DANIEL CHABON**

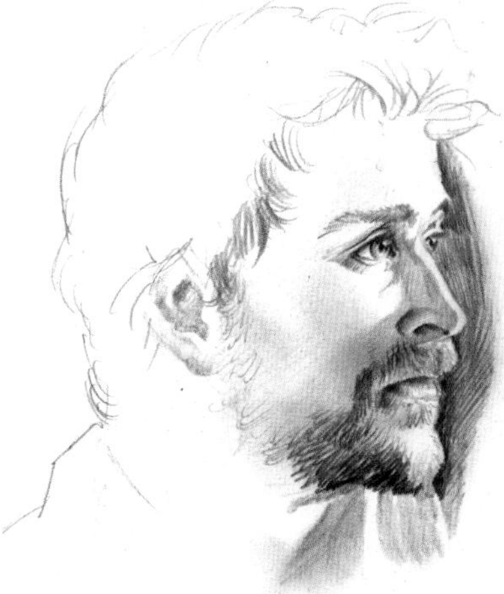

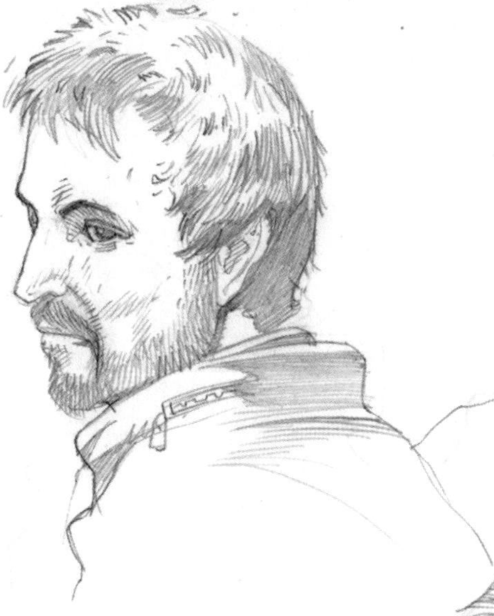

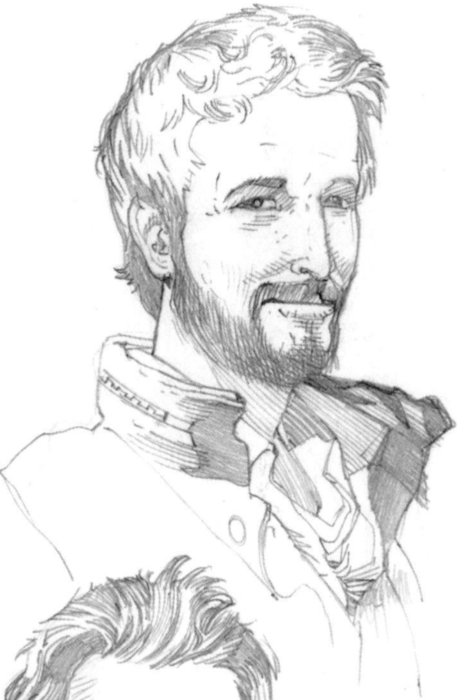

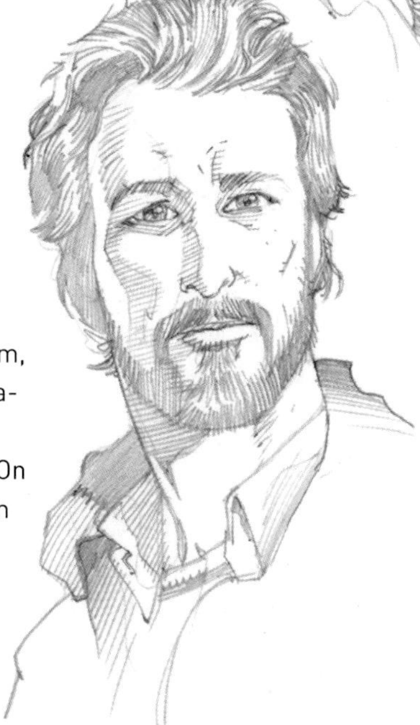

WHEN WE WERE COMING UP with the contents for this second volume, one of our pitches to TNT was to have *Falling Skies* producer Mark Verheiden, a Dark Horse alum, script a short story with his old DH collaborator Mark Nelson that would premiere in our comic book anthology *Dark Horse Presents*. On the facing page and on this page are the Tom Mason likeness sketches Mark Nelson did before starting on the story "Luck."

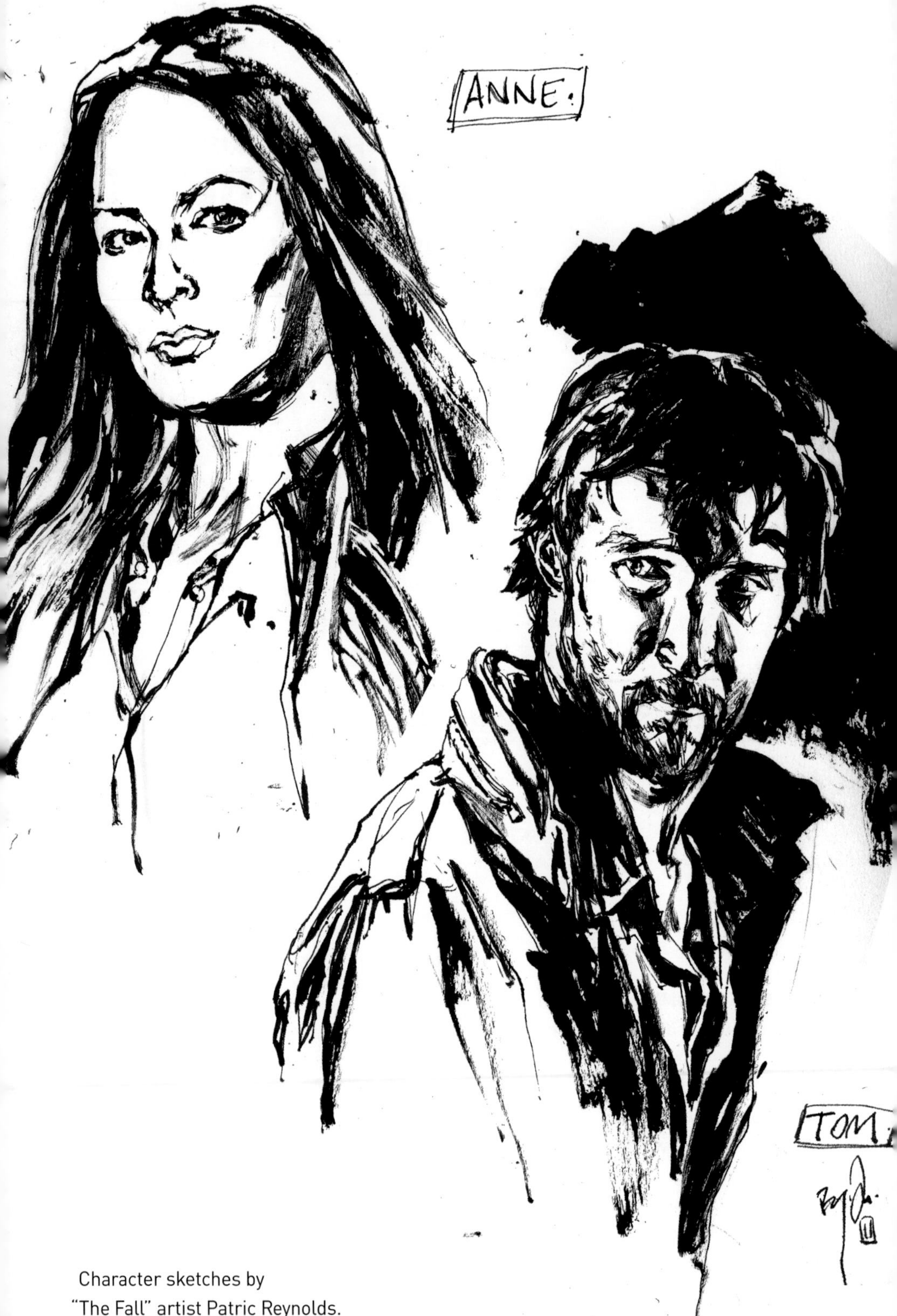
ANNE.
TOM.

Character sketches by
"The Fall" artist Patric Reynolds.

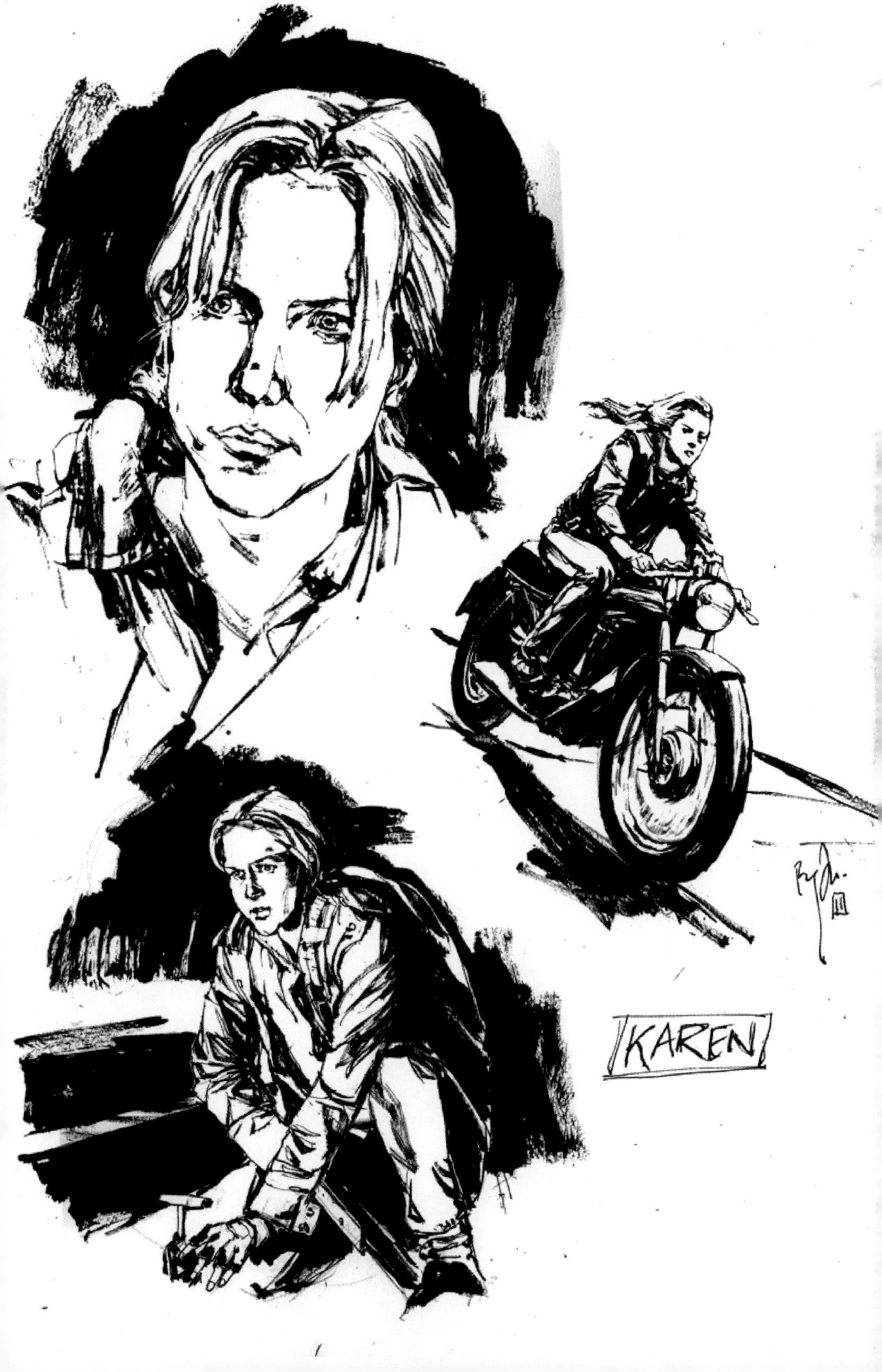
KAREN

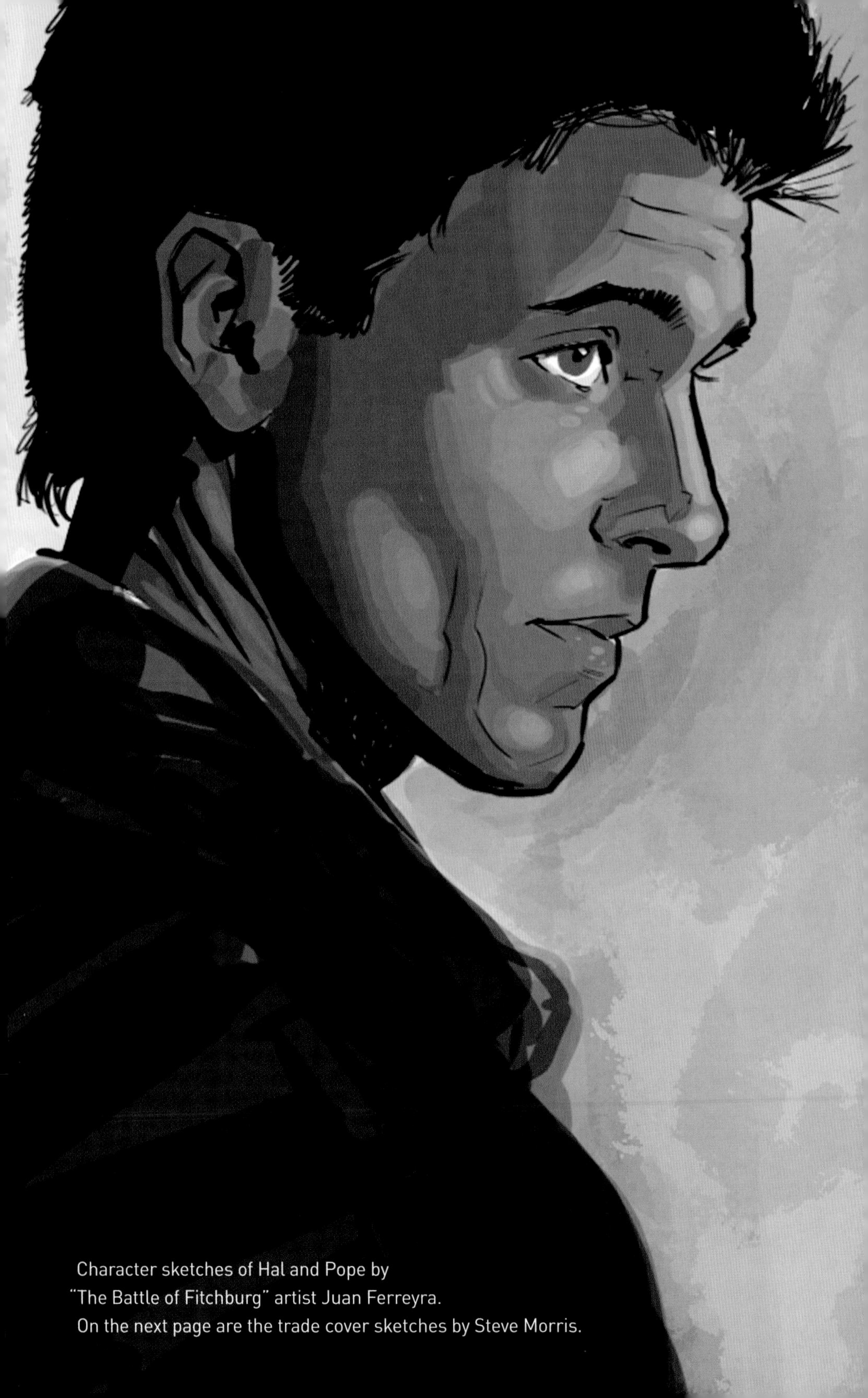

Character sketches of Hal and Pope by
"The Battle of Fitchburg" artist Juan Ferreyra.
On the next page are the trade cover sketches by Steve Morris.

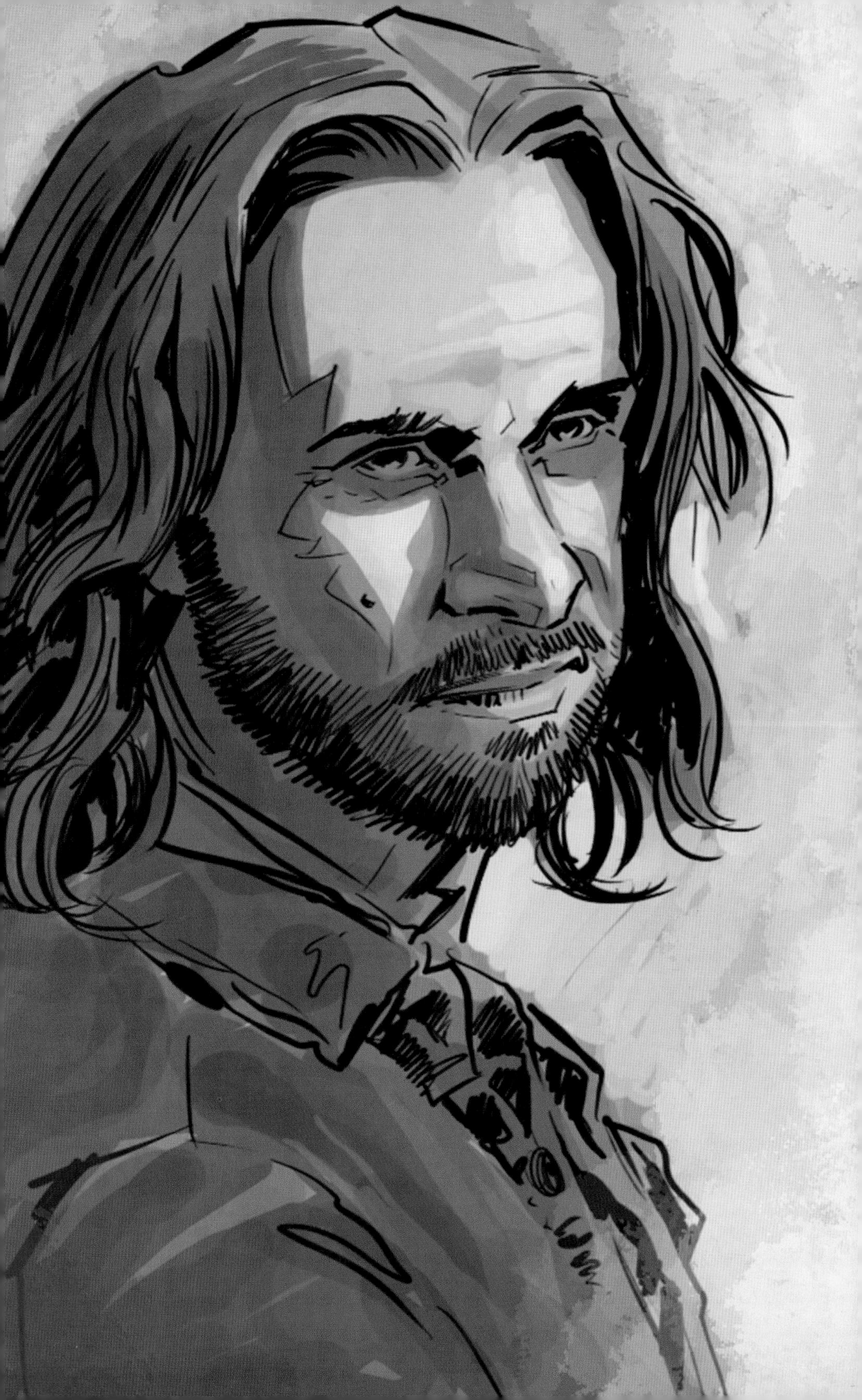

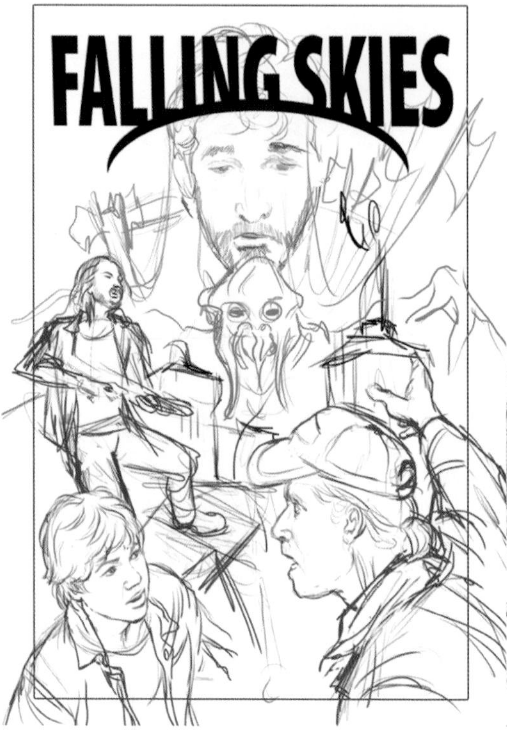
FALLING SKIES
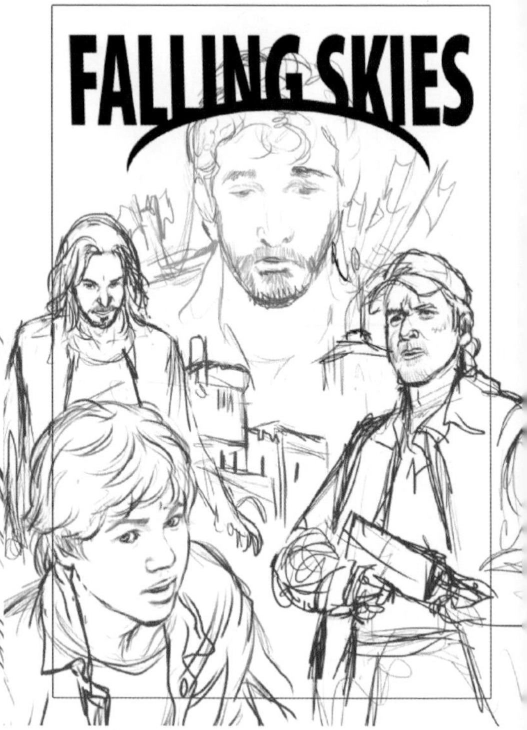
FALLING SKIES
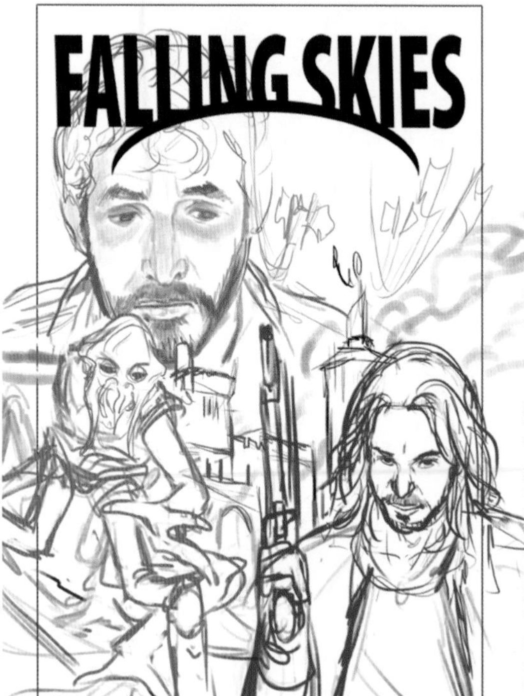
FALLING SKIES
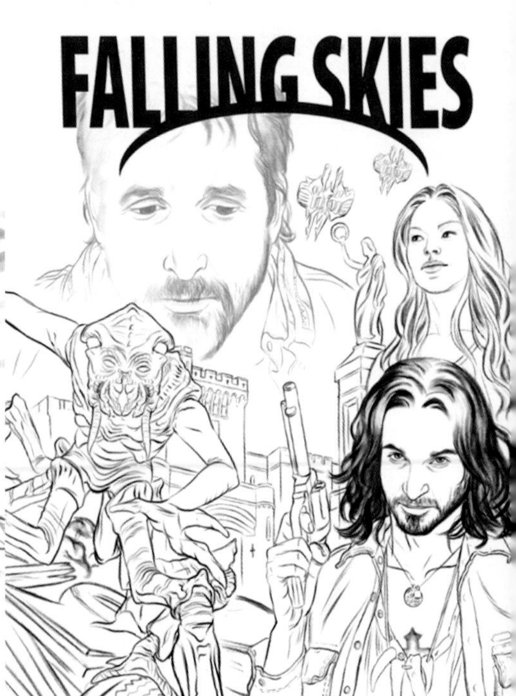
FALLING SKIES

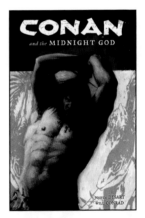

GRAPHIC NOVEL/SCIENCE FICTION/ACTION ADVENTURE

Based on *Falling Skies*
from DreamWorks Television.

Immediately following the events of TNT's *Falling Skies* season 1, the Second Mass gets pinned down by alien forces and sustains heavy losses. With an army of skitters closing in, the resistance group shields themselves in an armory in Fitchburg, ready to finish the battle once and for all.

This collection features art by Juan Ferreyra (*Rex Mundi*), Mark Nelson (*Aliens*), Patric Reynolds (*Serenity*), and Danilo [illegible] (*PopGun*), with pinups by Duncan Fegred[illegible] and more!

DARK HORSE BOOKS | DREAMWORKS TELEVISION | TNT™

ISBN 978-1-61655-014-1
50999>
9 781616 550141

DARKHORSE.COM | FALLINGSKIES.COM | $9.99 US | $10.99 CAN